Librarian's Guide
to Online Searching

Librarian's Guide
to Online Searching

SUZANNE S. BELL

LIBRARIES
UNLIMITED
A Member of the Greenwood Publishing Group
Westport, Connecticut • London

Library of Congress Cataloging-in-Publication Data

Bell, Suzanne S.
    Librarian's guide to online searching / by Suzanne S. Bell.
      p. cm.
    Includes bibliographical references and index.
    ISBN 1–59158–326–8 (pbk : alk. paper)
    1. Database searching.   2. Electronic information resource searching.
I. Title.
    ZA4460B45   2006
    025.5′24–dc22   2006017628

British Library Cataloguing in Publication Data is available.

Library of Congress Catalog Card Number: 2006017628
ISBN: 1–59158–326–8

First published in 2006

Libraries Unlimited, 88 Post Road West, Westport, CT 06881
A Member of the Greenwood Publishing Group, Inc.
www.lu.com

Printed in the United States of America

The paper used in this book complies with the
Permanent Paper Standard issued by the National
Information Standards Organization (Z39.48–1984).

10 9 8 7 6 5 4 3 2 1

Copyright Acknowledgments

The author and publisher gratefully acknowledge permission for use of the
following material:

Chapter 7: MLA International Bibliography. Copyright 1963–2005. The
Modern Language Association of America. All rights reserved. Copyright ©
2004–2005 ProQuest Information and Learning Company. All rights
reserved. Reproduced with the permission of ProQuest Information and
Learning.

Chapter 8: LexisNexis screenshots are reproduced with the permission of
LexisNexis Academic & Library Solutions. Copyright 2005, LexisNexis
Academic & Library Solutions, a division of Reed Elsevier Inc. All Rights
Reserved. LexisNexis and the Knowledge Burst Logo are registered
trademarks of Reed Elsevier Properties, Inc., used with the permission of
LexisNexis.

To my grandfather, Augustus Hunt Shearer, librarian and teacher, and my father, Vern Coventry Bell, inventor and engineer. You may not have understood this book, but you would have appreciated it. Thank you both for the gifts that made it possible.

Contents

vii

Acknowledgments

There are many people who helped make this book possible. In particular, I wish to thank Alan Lupack, who has provided extensive advice, feedback, and mentoring—from project proposal to chapter reviews and comments. Susan Gibbons and Vicki Burns also provided very valuable commentary on the proposal, and have willingly read chapters and provided thoughtful feedback. Nora Dimmock, Stephanie Frontz, Beth Banzer, Helen Anderson, and others have also been eager readers and excellent commentators. I much appreciate Kostya Gurevich's good humor in the face of sudden phone calls requesting explanations of how OCLC works, and Melissa Mead's enthusiasm and assistance with images from Poole's Index. I also want to thank Ron Dow for being very supportive of the project and making my leave of absence possible, as well as my colleagues in the Management Library, who had to cover for me all summer. Sincere thanks go to the great students in the 2005 summer session of LIS 566RE: Digital Information Retrieval, who put up with the book in its "draft" version, and were wonderful at finding typos and letting me know what worked and what didn't. The book is also deeply indebted to the anonymous peer reviewers, who provided extremely helpful advice and suggestions. I don't know who you are, but please know I'm profoundly grateful. Any remaining problems are all my own.

My vision of the book as text supported by (lots) of screen shots would not have been possible without the vendors of these wonderful resources being willing to grant permission to use their material. I am deeply grateful to all the people who made this part of the project possible: Craig Hunt at ABC-CLIO; Duncan Campbell at Chadwyck-Healey; Ed Roche and Scott Bernier at EBSCO; Sherry Sullivan and Deborah Loeding at H.W. Wilson; Gwen Bole and Ryan Runella at LexisNexis; Joyce Rambo and Barbara Lynch at OCLC; Tracy Smith and Kim Landry at Ovid; Ed Yarnell at ProQuest; and Rodney Yancey and Brian McDonough at Thomson Scientific.

In addition, there would have been no book at all without the work of Vivek Sood and the incredible team at Techbooks.com. They pushed production through in record time, dealt with all those screen shots, and provided excellent copyediting. It was amazing and wonderful to do business so quickly and efficiently with a group so far away, and I am intensely grateful for Mr. Sood's attention to the project, his reliable and prompt communications, and his "can do" attitude.

Finally, a very, very special thanks to my husband, a walking Chicago Manual of Style, who gave me a gorgeous new computer to write on, has read every word (sometimes several times), provided excellent editing and advice, never lost his enthusiasm, and kept us fed throughout the project. I couldn't have done it without you, my dear.

Preface

Welcome to the wonderful world of database searching! Roy Tennant's (2003) now famous quote that "only librarians like to search, everyone else likes to find" has perhaps been too frequently repeated—but it's hard not to, because it's *true*. There are certain kinds of minds that enjoy solving puzzles and ferreting out information, and the owners of those minds often find a good talent "fit" in library careers. Librarians do like to search, although generally we aren't born knowing it: it's a realization that emerges later, with experience or in a class. If you are a researcher or a student, in the position of having to search for the information you need, you may also find that there can be some interest and pleasure in the process as well as the product.

If it is true that most people only want to "find," and are perfectly happy with the Google™ model of one simple search box and long lists of results, one might ask "Why should I care about learning more sophisticated search techniques? Why should we still teach a course on database searching?" (or "Why should I buy a book on database searching?") Will there ever be an opportunity to use this information again?

In offering you this book, I wholeheartedly believe those questions can be answered in the affirmative. Yes, learning about more sophisticated search techniques will continue to be helpful, and it will increase your effectiveness in helping others to do research, or your own productivity as a researcher. No matter how simple the initial interface becomes, it still helps to know something about database structure, that is, what is going on "under the hood." This is especially helpful for understanding what is *possible* with any given database: what degree of precision in searching you can expect, and thus what you can expect in terms of results. There will continue to be "Advanced" versions of the interface that will allow experts to do more efficient, targeted, and useful searches. Yes, people will do and are doing more searching on their own: if you are not a librarian and are looking at this book, it will introduce you to resources you may not have been aware of, and help you to be more effective. For librarians and library students, searching is a part of our profession, an area in which we need to be ready to offer our users more skills than they have on their own. Indeed, as users do more searching on their own, the questions they approach librarians with become more difficult. They have taken care of the easy questions—librarians need to be ready for the hard ones. This is still an important part of our skill set.

Most of the techniques and strategies provided in this book are not particularly complex or hard to master, but they need to be stated and learned, because they are not generally how people think. You need to *learn* to parse questions into good search strategies. You need to have really internalized how Boolean logic works to understand that when a search returns only a few results, the tactic to take is to use fewer, broader search terms, not add more, and more specific, terms. One of the most essential techniques sounds like the simplest: to use your eyes and truly analyze what is on the screen. This is something very few people really do, however, so it is also something to learn.

One of the overriding goals in this book is to remain thoroughly grounded in the real world. The examples and exercises involving commercial databases work with ones commonly available at academic and major public libraries. When free Web sites are discussed, they have been carefully chosen for their expected longevity. The emphasis will not be on providing every detail of every database presented, but rather how to look at any interface ("use your eyes"), to use a set of basic concepts to understand what you are seeing ("engage your brain"), and then to use effectively whatever search capabilities are provided. Once you have a basic idea of how databases are put together, and have grasped a collection of concepts and techniques (the "Searcher's Toolkit"), you should be able to plunge into any database that comes along and figure out how it works. In fact, the other main goal for this book is to help you learn to be flexible and adaptable. What more important skill can there be in our rapidly changing world?

This book will expose you to a whole range of databases: "multidisciplinary," social science, medicine, science, bibliographic, humanities, and statistical/numeric. You will learn that even when you don't know anything about a subject, using some good, general principles, you should be able to use an unfamiliar database and do a reasonable search. A discussion of "information seeking behaviors" and how to do an effective reference interview will help with this. Most importantly, you shouldn't be *afraid* of any subject area and declare it off-limits. As all these choices begin to build up, however, the natural question is: How do you know which database to use? Or should you use the Web? We will address these issues as well. Note that while "the Web" will enter into the discussion from time to time, this book does not attempt to teach you to search the Web better. There are already many excellent books on the market to fulfill that purpose. The focus here is on commercial, subscription databases. If you thought searching started and ended with Google, surprise! There's a whole other world waiting for you through the library.

Not only will you learn to search databases, but you'll also learn something about passing your knowledge along: tips and guidance for showing others how to get what they need out of a database. In addition, we'll go over points to consider in evaluating a database, for purposes of writing a review, or, for librarians, as part of collection development. With budgets everywhere as tight as they are, librarians are more frequently finding themselves in the position of having to evaluate and choose among current resources.

If you are a library school instructor, you'll find the chapters after the first three are almost completely freestanding. You can pick and choose, using them in whatever order best suits your needs or teaching style. Exercises and material that can be used as discussion-starters are included with each chapter, and "Recommended Readings" are provided for selected chapters.

We live in the age of the Web, with its incredible capability for change: vendors now change the appearance of their interfaces regularly, and it's crucial to be flexible. This book is intended to help you learn to adapt and change, as well as to give you the tools to understand and use what you're looking at, regardless of what the interfaces happen to look like in the future. I hope the book achieves that goal for you, and in addition, that you'll soon join me in thinking that searching is just great fun.

1

Database Structure for Everyone: Records, Fields, and Indexes

In many library school programs, the database searching course is an upper level, elective course. This means that some of you will have had a chance to take a database course, and will already be familiar with the concepts in this chapter. My goal is to focus on helping you learn and develop strategies to search and interact more effectively with databases rather than getting into the real technology of how databases are built. This chapter provides a very brief and simple introduction to how databases are conceptually put together. In my experience, it's as much as you need to know in order to apply appropriate search techniques and use the database effectively. There's no point in piling on technical detail if it doesn't really further your ultimate goal, which in this case is: searching.

It's always interesting to start with a little history, however. Electronic access to information via the Web is so pervasive that we take it for granted. You have undoubtedly already used databases somewhere in your academic life. But where did these "databases" come from, anyhow? Why are they important? What *is* a database anyway?

Historical Background

Indexing and Abstracting Services

In the Beginning ...

There was hardcopy. Writers wrote, and their works got published in (physical) magazines, journals, newspapers, or conference proceedings.

Fig. 1.1. Index listing and title page (inset) from Poole's *Index to Periodical Literature*. Courtesy of the Department of Rare Books and Special Collections, University of Rochester Libraries.

Months or years afterwards, other writers, researchers, and other alert readers wanted to know what was written on a topic. Wouldn't it be useful if there were a way to find everything that had been published on a topic without having to page through every likely journal/newspaper/etc.? It certainly would, as various publishing interests demonstrated: as early as 1848, the *Poole's Index to Periodical Literature* provided "An alphabetical index to subjects, treated in the reviews, and other periodicals, to which no indexes have been published; prepared for the library of the Brothers in Unity, Yale college." (Figure 1.1).

Not to be caught napping, the *New York Times* started publishing their *Index* in 1851, and in 1896, taking a page from Poole's, the *Cumulative Index to a Selected List of Periodicals* appeared, which soon (1904) became the canonical *Readers' Guide to Periodical Literature*. Thus in the mid-nineteenth century, the hardcopy Index is born: an alphabetical list of words, representing subjects, and under each word a list of articles deemed to be about that subject. The index is typeset, printed, bound, and sold, and all of this effort is done, slowly and laboriously, by humans.

Given the amount of work involved, and the costs of paper, printing, etc., how many subjects do you think an article would have been listed under? Every time the article entry is repeated under another subject it costs the publisher just a little more. Suppose there was an article about a polar expedition, which described the role the sled dogs played, the help provided by the native Inuit, the incompetence on the part of the provisions master, and the fund-raising efforts carried on by the leader's wife back home in England. The publisher really can't afford to list this article in more than one or two places. What will people interested in this topic be most likely to look under? The indexer's career was a continuous series of such difficult choices.

An index, recording that an article exists and where it would be found, was good, but one could go a step further. The addition of a couple of sentences (to give the user an idea of what the article is about) increases the usefulness of the finding tool enormously—although the added information, of course, costs more. But if they thought their customers would pay the higher price, some Index publishers added Abstracts. Thus, "Abstracting and Indexing services" or "A & I." You will see this terminology in the library literature.

The abstracts were all laboriously written by humans. They needed to be skilled, literate humans, and skilled humans are very expensive (even when they're underpaid, they're expensive in commercial terms). Humans are also slow, compared to technology. Paper and publishing are expensive too. Given all this, how many times do you think an entry for an article would be duplicated (appear under multiple subjects) in this situation? The answers are obvious; the point is that the electronic situation we have today is all grounded in a physical reality. Once it was nothing but people and paper.

From Printed Volumes to Databases

Enter the Computer

The very first machines that can really be called "digital computers" were built in the period from 1939 to 1944, culminating in the construction of the ENIAC in 1946 (*Encyclopædia Britannica*, 2005). These were all part of a long progression of invention to speed up the task of mathematical calculations. After that, inventions and improvements came thick and fast: the 1950s and 1960s were an incredibly innovative time in computing, although probably not in a way that the ordinary citizen would have noticed. The first machine to be able to store a database, RCA's Bizmac, was developed in 1952 (Lexikon's History of Computing, 2002). The first instance of an online transaction processing system, using telephone lines to connect remote users to central mainframe computers, was the airline reservation system known as SABRE, set up by IBM for American Airlines in 1964 (Computer History Museum, 2004). Meanwhile, at Lockheed Missile and Space Company, a man named Roger Summit was engaged in projects involving search and retrieval, and management of massive data files. His group's first interactive search and retrieval service was demonstrated to the company in 1965; by 1972 it had developed into a new, commercially viable product: Dialog—the "first publicly available online research service" (Dialog, 2005).

Thus in the 1960s and 1970s, when articles were still being produced on typewriters, indexes and abstracts were still produced in hardcopy, and very disparate industries were developing information technologies for their own specialized purposes, Summit can be credited with having incredible vision. He asked the right questions:

1.   What do people want? Information.

2.   Who produces information, and in what form? The government and commercial publishers, in the form of papers, articles, newspapers, etc.

3.   What if you could put information *about* all that published material into a machine-readable file: a database—something you could search?

Summit also had the vision to see how the technological elements could be used. The database only needs to be made once, at our headquarters, and trained agents (librarians) will then access it over telephone lines with just some simple, basic equipment. We can track usage exactly, and charge accordingly. Think of the advantages!

The advantages of an electronic version of an indexing/abstracting system are really revolutionary. No longer bound by the confines of paper, space, and quite so many expensive skilled personnel:

- Articles could be associated with a greater number of terms describing their content, not just one or two (this still requires some skilled labor).

- Although material has to be re-keyed—typed into the database—this doesn't require subject specialists, just typists (cheap labor).

- Turnaround time is faster: most of your labor force isn't thinking and composing, just typing continuously: the process of adding to the information in the database goes on all the time, making the online product much more current.

- If you choose to only provide your index "online," thus avoiding the time delays and costs of physical publishing, why, you might be able to redirect the funds to expanding your business, offering other indexes (databases) in new subject areas.

As time goes on, this process of "from article to index" gets even faster. When articles are created electronically (e.g., word processing), no "re-keying" is needed to get the information into your database, just software to convert and rearrange the material to fit your database fields. So rather than typists, you need to pay programmers to write the software. And you still need those humans to analyze the content and assign the subject terms.

In the end, the electronic database is not necessarily cheaper to create; it's possible that it actually costs more! Rather, the costs are shifted. But customers will buy it because... *it's so much more powerful and efficient.* It is irresistible. Given a choice between a printed index and an electronic version, most people under the age of 50 won't give the printed volume a second glance. The online database is here to stay.

Database Building Blocks

Fields and Records

Databases, in essence, are made up of fields and records. Fields are like one cell in an Excel spreadsheet: a bit of computer memory dedicated to holding one particular thing, one value (e.g., age) or type of information (letters, numbers, or an image). A set of fields makes up a record. An analogy would be a row in Excel: one row = one record. If you like a good mental image, you can think of it as a whole line of shoeboxes with the lids off, and one thing in each box. Every time you add another record to your database, that's another line of shoeboxes, into which you put the appropriate bit of information into the box assigned to it, e.g., box 1 is always the number of the row, box 2 is always a last name, box 3 is always the first name, etc. Each record—each row of shoeboxes—will have the same number of boxes, but you might not have a piece of information for every box, that is, some fields might be blank. Altogether, all the rows (the records) make up the database.

Think about driver's licenses. They all have an ID number, the owner's name, address, date of birth, eye color, a bad photo, etc. I don't know if this is true in all states, but certainly in New York State all that information resides in a database somewhere. It's easy to imagine the Department of Motor Vehicle's database having fields with names such as: Name, Addr, DOB, Eyes, BadPic, etc. Each record represents a person. The fields in each record represent every bit of information that appears on your license, and probably some that aren't actually printed on the license, too. When you send in the paperwork and the check to renew your license, they look your record up in the database, make any changes you may have indicated in your paperwork (e.g., change the values in your fields), and hit print. Presto, you've gone from being a database entry to being a small card with an unflattering photo.

Decisions, Decisions: Designing the Database

The crucial task in developing a database is deciding what fields the records in your database are going to have, and how big they are going to be, that is, how many characters or numbers they will be able to hold. This "size" represents computer memory allocated, every time a new record is added. (While memory is cheap nowadays, in a huge project, how much memory is allocated is still something to consider.) In the best of all possible worlds, a whole design team including software engineers, subject experts, people from marketing and sales, and potential users, would wrestle with this problem. However, nothing might ever get done in such a large and varied group, so probably a more limited team of software engineers and content experts is the norm. The problem is that the design team had better make good choices initially, because it's very difficult, if not impossible, to make significant (if any) changes to the record structure later.[1] This is good and bad. It means there's a certain inherent stability, or at least pressure on these database products *not* to change too much... but when you wish they *would* fix something, it can take a long time (if ever) for change to happen. You can take a certain amount of comfort, however, in the knowledge that however much the interface to the database—the way it looks—changes, behind the scenes the same types of information (fields), are probably still there.

Fig. 1.2. Database fields.

Fig. 1.3. Database records.

Quick Recap

One full set of fields makes up a record. Every record in the database will have the same set of fields (even if, in some records, some fields are blank). All of the rows (records) together make up the database.

Food for thought

For an article database, you'd probably have a field for the article title, the name of the journal it appeared in... and what else? Think about the other information you would want to capture. Again, the process is something like this:

Define your fields (Figure 1.2):
... that make up records (Figure 1.3) ...
... and form the basis of your database.

Beyond Fields and Records: Field Indexes

Fields and records are the basis, the "data" of a database. What makes a database fast, powerful, and efficient are the *indexes* of the fields. It would be very slow if every time you queried the database, it started at field 1, record 1, and searched sequentially through each field of each record—you might as well go back to hardcopy at that rate.

An index, in the sense we're going to talk about it now, is a list of all the values from a particular field (or multiple fields), with some kind of identifier indicating which record each value came from. This is much like the index at the end of a book that indicates which pages a word appears on. It becomes part of the database, but has a separate existence from the records. An index list can be alphabetized, and in various ways optimized for searching. When arranged as a list of locations for a given word, this list is referred to as an "inverted file." If we continue our very concrete mental image: Picture your rows of shoeboxes lying flat, covering your living room floor. Now imagine copying box 2 from each row, noting on the side of it which row it came from, and stacking those boxes vertically, off to one side. You can arrange that stack anyway you like. Maybe, to return to the driver's license example, that's the field for Last Name. You'd probably want to organize the stack (the index), alphabetically, so if you wanted to find the record for Smith, John, you could zip to the S's in the stack, pull out his box, see that it was marked "record no. 3"—and run over to the third row of shoeboxes. Thus the order of the rows in your database, that is, what order you enter your records, doesn't matter at all. You simply build an index, and search *that* when you want to find something in your database. Or build several indexes: you can make an index of any field you want, although, as always, there are costs and reasons why you might not index every field.[2]

A Very Simple Example

Say we had three articles:

Milky Way's Last Major Merger.

Science News. v. 162 no. 24 p. 376

It's a Dog's Life.

The Economist. December 21, 2002. p. 61

Manhattan Mayhem.

Smithsonian. v. 33 no. 9 p. 44

Let's enhance these just a little by adding a one-line description to each record (so we have a few more words to search on):

Record 1:

Milky Way's Last Major Merger.

Science News. v. 162 no. 24 p. 376.

New clues about galaxy formation indicate early collision affected Milky Way's shape.

Record 2:

It's a Dog's Life.

The Economist. December 21, 2002. p. 61.

From hard labour to a beauty contest, a history of the work and whims of dog breeding.

Record 3:

Manhattan Mayhem.

Smithsonian. v. 33 no. 9 p. 44

Martin Scorsese's realistic portrayal of pre–Civil War strife—*Gangs of New York*—re-creates the brutal street warfare waged between immigrant groups.

My database will have just four fields (Figure 1.4):

1. Record number (4-number places, e.g., my database will never grow to more than 9,999 articles)

2. Article title

3. Journal name

4. Abstract

Fig. 1.4. A very simple database record.

Now we need to index the fields.

The initial list of words from the Article Title field looks like:

Milky

Way's

Last

Major

Merger

It's

a

Dog's

Life

Manhattan

Mayhem

More Database Decisions

There are various things about this list that one might question. What will our indexing program do with those possessives and contractions? Do we want to clog it up with little words like "a"? There are many decisions for database designers to make:

- How will the indexing program handle apostrophes and other punctuation? We take it for granted now that the system will simply preserve it, and users can search for contractions or possessives, but you may still run across systems that insert a space instead of the apostrophe (dog s), or ignore it and treat the letters as a string (ending up with "dogs" for "dog's").

- What will the indexing program do with the "little words?" That is, words such as: a, an, by, for, from, of, the, to, with, etc., which are usually referred to as "stop words." These are words that are so common that the database designers usually decide they don't want to expend time and space to index them. The indexing programs will be programmed with a list of such words, and will "stop" indexing when they hit a word on the list. A more descriptive name would be "skip words," because that is what really happens: the indexing program skips any stop list words, and continues to the next word. Almost all databases employ a stop word list, and it can vary greatly from one vendor to the next.

- Should the system be designed to preserve information about capitalization, or to ignore the case of the words? We are so used to systems that don't distinguish upper and lowercase (so that you don't have to worry how you type in your query), but there are times when you'd really *like* the system to know the difference between, say, AIDS (the disease), and aids (the common noun or verb).

Since this is a modern system, we'll decide to preserve the apostrophes, and that "a" is one of our stop words, so we won't include it in the index. We can then sort the list alphabetically:

Dog's

It's

Last

Life

Major

Manhattan

Mayhem

Merger

Milky

Way's

Can you see the problem here? We have neglected to include an identifier to show which record a word came from. Let's start over again.

Better Field Indexing

Let's make sure our index list includes the record number, and which field the word came from:

0001	Milky	TI
0001	Way's	TI
0001	Last	TI
0001	Major	TI
0001	Merger	TI
0002	It's	TI
0002	Dog's	TI
0002	Life	TI
0003	Manhattan	TI
0003	Mayhem	TI

And one more thing: we can include a number representing the *order* of the word within the field (why might this be useful?) So we get something like this:

0001	Milky	TI	01
0001	Way's	TI	02
0001	Last	TI	03

Now we'll sort again.

0002	Dog's	TI	03
0002	It's	TI	01
0001	Last	TI	03
0002	Life	TI	04
0001	Major	TI	04
0003	Manhattan	TI	01
0003	Mayhem	TI	02
0001	Merger	TI	05
0001	Milky	TI	01
0001	Way's	TI	02

Note how even though we deleted the stop word "a" in "It's a dog's life," the numerical position of "dog's" reflects that there was an intervening word there: its position is recorded as 3, not 2.

Since people might want to search on the name of the publication, it would be good to index that as well. Our index of the Journal Name field:

0002	Economist	JN	02
0001	News	JN	02
0001	Science	JN	01
0001	Science News	JN	01, 02
0003	Smithsonian	JN	01

Note the multiple indexing of "Science News." A technical term for this is "double posting."

To make things even faster and more efficient, after indexing each field, combine the indexes so you only have one list to search:

0002	Dog's	TI	03
0002	Economist	JN	02
0002	It's	TI	01
0001	Last	TI	03
0002	Life	TI	04
0001	Major	TI	04
0003	Manhattan	TI	01
0003	Mayhem	TI	02
0001	Merger	TI	05
0001	Milky	TI	01
0001	News	JN	02
0001	Science	JN	01
0001	Science News	JN	01, 02
0003	Smithsonian	JN	01
0001	Way's	TI	02

We undoubtedly want to index the content of the one-sentence "abstracts," as well. Here is a list of the words in raw form:

new	beauty	Pre-Civil
clues	contest	War
about	a	strife
galaxy	history	*Gangs*
formation	of	*Of*
indicate	the	*New*
early	work	*York*
collision	and	Re-creates
affected	whims	The
Milky	of	brutal
Way's	dog	street
Shape	breeding	warfare
From	Martin	waged
hard	Scorsese's	between
labour	realistic	immigrant
to	portrayal	groups
a	of	

Decisions and cleanup needed on this list of words:

- Stop words—what will they be?
- Hyphenated words—how will they be recorded?
- Proper names—"double post" to include the phrase too?
- Alternate spellings—do we do anything about them or not? (What might you do?)

Luckily, software does almost all of this work for us. You'll probably never see any indexes in their raw state. What we've been going over here is in real life very "under the hood," often proprietary material for the database vendors. You don't need to know *exactly* how any particular database works, you just need to grasp some of the basic principles that govern how databases in general are put together and how they are indexed. Because this determines how you search them, and what you can expect to get out of them.

Quick Recap

A lot of thought goes into the initial database design (what fields to include, what they are called, how much space to allocate for each one), because it is not easily changed later. The information contained in a database's fields can be extracted and used to build an index of terms in the database. Indexes make rapid searching of huge databases possible. Many decisions go into the design of indexes, as well, for example: which fields will be indexed, how contractions and possessives will be handled, which words will be treated as stop words, if and how identification of phrases will be supported.

Examples of Indexes

In the examples that follow, see if you can relate what we've just gone over with the "user's view" of the indexing scheme in these common

Fig. 1.5. The Subject Index in EBSCO's *MasterFILE Select*, several screens into the "self" entries. ©2005, EBSCO Publishing, Inc. All rights reserved.

databases. We'll start with the Subjects index in EBSCO's *MasterFILE Select*, a multidisciplinary database.

The EBSCO *MasterFILE Select* Subject Index

Even in a fairly simple display, there is a lot to look at and look for. In this view of the subject index in EBSCO's *MasterFILE Select* (Figure 1.5), "A" is the area identifying where we are: which database, and which part of the database. You are undoubtedly used to recognizing this without thinking about it, but what is the signal that we are in the "Subjects" function of the database?

The "B" section lets us jump around to any point in the index, that is, to the entries on and around whatever word we put in. Note that the results can be returned in alphabetical, or relevancy ranked order: we're seeing the inverted file at work—there are two ways to stack the shoeboxes.

In "C" the actual subject list is provided. The entries in bold, all-caps are values from the field designated as "subject" in this database. Note how the entries are a mixture of items (books), personal names, and concepts. The initial term entered was "self"; the screen represented here shows the list after paging forward several times, noticing along the way how the entries are sorted. For example, an interesting point to observe here is that the hyphenated terms file *after* all the "self, (space) word" entries. The "View"

Fig. 1.6. The initial Browse Index screen for the ERIC database as provided by First-Search; examples of single-word and phrase indexes that FirstSearch offers for many fields. Screen shots used with permission of OCLC; FirstSearch and WorldCat are registered trademarks of OCLC Online Computer Library Center, Inc.

statements for each entry tell you exactly how many times the term was assigned, and to what type of article (newspaper, periodical, or review). You can begin to tell what is being captured about each article in this database: subject terms assigned to it, and type of publication it appeared in.

FirstSearch Indexes for the ERIC Database

Moving on to another example, the FirstSearch databases provide examples of the use of *separate* indexes for many fields. In the Browse Index interface, as in EBSCO's Subject list above, you have the opportunity to roam around in the indexes, discovering what is there (and thus, what is possible), before committing to a search. There are even multiple indexes for the same fields, as they provide both single word and phrase indexes for many fields, such as author name (Figure 1.6). The icon for accessing the Browse Index screen is part of the FirstSearch Advanced Search interface, discussed in greater detail in Chapter 4. For now, simply observe how it works.

In this case, the "A" area provides three major navigation tabs: you can go Home, change Databases, or go to the Searching interface from this Browse Index interface. The "B" area lets you jump directly to one of three kinds of search. Note that the "where am I?" information also appears nearby, that is, the name of the current database. In the "C" area, the index field being searched is set to "Keyword." In the screens marked "D," the drop down menu has been changed to Author, and Author Phrase.

Fig. 1.7. Results from the single word Descriptors index. Screen shots used with permission of OCLC; FirstSearch and WorldCat are registered trademarks of OCLC Online Computer Library Center, Inc.

Using the descriptors indexes

In Figure 1.7, we've looked up the word "librarians" in the Descriptors index ("A") of a database called ERIC, which is a database that specializes and focuses on education literature. ("Descriptors" are the name FirstSearch has assigned to the field EBSCO calls Subject terms—words that indexers have assigned that capture the essence of an article's content.)

In Figure 1.7 "B," we see the results of this search of the index. Note how the term searched on appears in the *middle* of the list, and is in bold. Why do you think the database designers have chosen to display the results this way? Note the two terms that only have a count of one—you can tell that the indexing process, the harvesting of terms from the field "Descriptor," is done by a machine: it simply picks up whatever is there, typos and all. The "Count" field indicates how many articles in the database have been assigned to each Descriptor. The numbers tell you something about the overall content of the database, and how useful it may prove for whatever question you're working on. In this case, ERIC might not be the best place to look for information about "liberalism" (350 articles, once you add any other terms, will quickly disappear into nothing)—but what do you think of ERIC as a place to look for information about libraries and librarians?

In Figure 1.8, we see the results of a search in the "Descriptors Phrase" index. Again, isn't it interesting to compare, even in an education database, the number of times "open book tests" has been assigned as a Descriptor phrase, as opposed to "online searching" and "online systems."

Fig. 1.8. Results from the multiple word Descriptors Phrase index. Screen shots used with permission of OCLC; FirstSearch and WorldCat are registered trademarks of OCLC Online Computer Library Center, Inc.

Record Structure Reflected in Fields Displayed

Reminder: indexes are built from the fields included in a database record. The fields can be called the record structure, and you can get a sense of how simple, or elaborate, a database's record structure is by studying the fields displayed when viewing a record from the database.

The ERIC database on FirstSearch has quite an elaborate record structure; these database designers were making sure they didn't leave anything out, and that the most complete set of bibliographic information they could assemble would be available to users, as can be seen in a display of a full ERIC record (Figure 1.9).

The ERIC interface designers are trying to convey a great deal of information here. Take some time to study the screen snap, noticing how they've used different fonts and alignments to convey meaning. If you can, go online and observe the colors used. The field names are lined up on the left, followed by colons. The contents of the fields (sometimes complex and hierarchical) appear to the right. Under the gray bar marked "Subject(s)," are listed three types of subjects! There are Major Descriptors, Minor Descriptors, and Identifiers. Some of the fields will probably seem quite mysterious, but think about the purpose of the others, and why the database designers decided to include them. ERIC has been around since the early 1960s, and if invented today, the database designers might have made different choices.

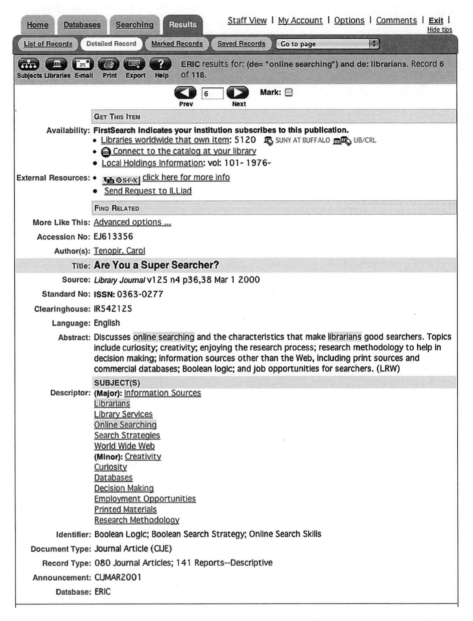

Fig. 1.9. A full record display from the ERIC database. Screen shots used with permission of OCLC; FirstSearch and WorldCat are registered trademarks of OCLC Online Computer Library Center, Inc.

Exercises and Points to Consider

1. What would *your* ideal database record for a journal article look like? Choose any article that interests you, and design a database record for it. What fields will you use? How big will each one be? What will you call them? Sketch out what the overall database

would be like (and why this article would be included), and justify your choices.

2. Why do you think FirstSearch has separate one-word and phrase indexes for the same fields?

3. What is a useful piece of information that is provided when you browse the indexes (in both *MasterFILE* and the FirstSearch databases)? How might this affect your search strategy?

4. Can you do a "field" search with Google™?

5. People generally think of Google as indexing all the words of all the Web pages it visits.[3] In some sense, it offers just one giant index labeled "all the text." Why do you think the commercial database vendors go to so much trouble to provide an elaborate record structure with indexed fields?

6. In the early days of online searching in libraries only librarians performed searches, after a detailed and careful interview with the patron requesting the search. The librarian would plan the search carefully, and then "dial up" to connect to the database, using a password and employing a very terse, arcane set of commands to perform the search. Access fees were charged by the minute, with additional charges for records viewed. Try to picture this, and then compare it to the situation today. How do you think the totally open, "end user" access may have affected databases and their interfaces? Can you think of anything about the current situation that is *not* an improvement?

Notes

1. If you're wondering why it would be so hard to change the record structure, remember to think of these databases as huge things: true, adding a new field to a database of just five records would be trivial. But a database of 500,000 records? How are you possibly going to retrospectively fill in the new field for all the existing records?

2. For one thing, the process of initially building the index can take hours. Although this doesn't mean it can't be done, remember every index will have to be updated, frequently, to reflect any changes in your database. It just adds to the complexity of the whole operation.

3. Or does Google have "stop words," words that it ignores? And does it really index every page all the way to the end? Does it matter?

2

Working with Databases
The Searcher's Toolkit:
Part 1

In my experience, there are a finite number of concepts, techniques, and strategies for searching databases that make all the difference between aimlessly groping around, and efficiently and effectively retrieving useful material. If you spend your whole day searching, then you'll probably discover or develop many more—but for most researchers or reference librarians, the topics in this chapter and the next are most likely all you will ever need. I've dubbed this set of concepts the "Searcher's Toolkit." All of them have applications in searching commercial databases, and some can be used with Web search engines (and once you've grasped these concepts, you'll start to see what's missing in the Web search products, and understand better why searching the Web is—well, the way it is: sometimes perfect, sometimes very frustrating).

Searcher's Toolkit: Part 1

Let us plunge right in with the most fundamental concept of all.

Basic Tool no. 1: Boolean Logic

In fact, this concept is so fundamental that you've probably run into it before, possibly several times through grade school, high school, and college. But do you *really* know what Boolean logic is and how it works? What effects it will have on your searches? Bear with a discussion of it one more time— you may be surprised!

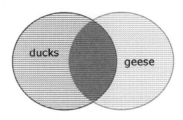

AND

Fig. 2.1. Boolean AND: Ducks
AND Geese.

In the database context, Boolean logic (after a fellow named George Boole (1815–1864))[1] refers to the "logical" (rather than arithmetical) operations on sets. That is, rather than manipulating numbers using symbols for plus, minus, multiply, or divide, Boolean logic controls what happens to sets of things when acted upon by "logical operators." The Boolean operators used in database searching are:

AND

OR

AND NOT (frequently expressed simply as "NOT;" more on this below.)

Venn Diagrams

Arithmetical expressions (2+2) result in some value (4). Boolean expressions result in either a sub- or superset of the original sets—rather than producing a specific value, logical operators have an *effect* on the sets, producing a different output set. The effects of Boolean expressions are traditionally illustrated with drawings called "Venn diagrams." Venn diagrams are always done with circles and shadings as in Figure 2.1, which keeps them nicely abstract. However, feel free to start thinking of the terminology "sets," and these circle illustrations, as "sets of database records" to make the concept more concrete. With just one operator in effect, Venn diagrams are quite simple to draw and to understand what the operator's effect is.

Boolean AND

In Figure 2.1, the circle on the left represents the set of all the database records that include the word "ducks," a few of which also include the word "geese." The circle on the right represents all records that include the word "geese," a few of which also include the word ducks. A search for "ducks AND geese" retrieves only those records that mention *both* terms—represented by the smaller, overlapping section. It is easy to get confused here, because our regular use of the word "and" is additive, it produces more ("two scoops, and sprinkles, and some whipped cream")—but a Boolean AND is very different: an AND operator will always, in practice, return a set that is *smaller* than either of the original sets. Theoretically, the largest set it could return would still only be of equal size to the smaller of the original sets. For example, at one point in time, the ProQuest Research database contained

21,191 records that contained "Bush, George W" in a field called "Person," and 15,216 records containing "Iraq" in a field called "Location." A search on:

Bush, George W in the Person field,

AND

Iraq in the Location field

produced 1,132 records.

Notice how even when the initial sets are quite large, the combined, "ANDed" set is considerably smaller. When one of the initial sets is much smaller than the other, the resulting set is affected even more. In the same database, at the same point in time, there were only 465 records for "Dean, Howard B" as a Person. Combining that with Bush, George W produced a set of only forty-six records.

AND says that *all* criteria must be met for an indicated action to happen (usually retrieval of a record). What the Boolean operators are really doing is evaluating true or false. The computer's thought process goes something like this:

If (ducks) is true (e.g., present in the record)

AND (at the same time, in the same record)

If (geese) is true

Retrieve the record.

So, to reiterate: the number of records meeting multiple conditions is, in practice, always smaller than the set of records meeting just one condition, and usually significantly smaller. The more conditions (criteria, terms) you set, the smaller the number of records retrieved will be: there will be fewer documents about ducks AND geese AND loons than there are about just ducks AND geese. If one of the initial sets is very small, ANDing it with some other term is likely to reduce the results to zero.

Boolean OR

In Figure 2.2, the circle on the left represents all the database records that include the word banana, and the circle on the right represents all the database records that include the word orange. In this case, we don't care what other words they contain, or how much they overlap. Thinking of this as a search, the OR retrieves *all* the bananas records, plus *all* the oranges records (including records mentioning both), for a total of a LOT of records! Again, our common parlance can make this confusing: usually we use the word "or" to mean "either one or the other"—"I'll have the banana *or* the orange." We wouldn't expect to be handed both fruits in response to that statement. But in Boolean logic, OR means "either the one, or the other, or both." Either of the criteria can be met for the computer to retrieve the record:

If (banana) is true (e.g., present in a record)

OR

If (orange) is true (present in a record)

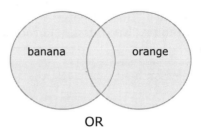

OR

Fig. 2.2. Boolean OR: Banana OR
Orange.

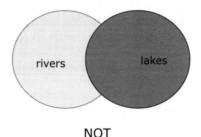

NOT

Fig. 2.3. Boolean NOT: Rivers
NOT Lakes.

Retrieve the record.

Think of it this way: in practice, Boolean OR is (practically) always more.

Boolean NOT

Finally, Figure 2.3 represents the Boolean exclusion operator, which you'll see expressed as "AND NOT" and simply "NOT" with almost equal frequency. For our purposes, they are interchangeable, and this text will generally use just "NOT" to make the operators as distinguishable as possible.[2] If this feels confusing, take comfort that at least the effects of this operator are more in line with our common usage of "not:" rivers NOT lakes retrieves records that include the term rivers, as long as they do NOT also contain the word lakes. Both criteria must be met, in the sense that the first term must be present, and the second term must *not* be present, for a record to be retrieved. The set of records retrieved can be thought of as just the lighter area of the "rivers" circle—anything from the darker "lakes" circle would not be in the results set. Note how the syntax is subtly different (which is further proof that even when a database vendor just uses "NOT," what is really going on is "AND NOT"):

If (rivers) is true (present in a record)

And

If (lakes) is NOT true (not present in the record)

Retrieve the record.

As you would expect, like AND, NOT almost always reduces the number of records retrieved. In general usage, you'll find that you don't often use the NOT operator in commercial databases: the possibility of missing useful records just because they happened to include the "NOTed" out term is too risky. If too many results are coming back, the better strategy is almost always to AND in another term, rather than to NOT out a term.

Quick Recap

The Boolean operators are AND, OR, NOT (also expressed as AND NOT). Adding terms to a search with AND will reduce the number of results, as will NOTing out a term. ORing more terms into a search will increase the number of results. Boolean expressions can be represented graphically with Venn diagrams.

Order of Boolean Operations

A statement using just one Boolean operator—ducks OR geese—is straightforward. But just as you can write arithmetical expressions with several operators (2+2–3*9), you can write Boolean expressions with multiple operators. You will encounter plenty of searches that require more complexity than simply (word) AND (word). Again, just as in the arithmetical statements, the Boolean operators have very specific effects, and the order in which they are processed has a powerful effect on what ends up in the results set. When there is more than one operator in a search statement, they are generally evaluated in this order:

- NOT operations are performed first.
- Then AND operations are evaluated.
- Finally, OR.

This is called the *order of operation*. This is the standard order for processing Boolean operators, but some systems simply evaluate statements left to right, the way you read. The results could be very different, depending on which order is used. Although it's important to be aware of the idea of order of operation, luckily, you don't have to figure out what it is on each system you use. There is a simple way to take control, and bend the order of operation to your will.

The Power of Parentheses

To control the order of operation, many systems allow you group your ANDs, ORs, NOTs with parentheses: (). Just as in arithmetic statements, the use of parentheses is helpful either to just make the order of operation explicit, or to override it. What happens is that the expression in parentheses will be evaluated first, and then the order of operation (standard or left-to-right) will take over.[3] Throwing parentheses into the mix can change the way the system interprets the search dramatically. For example, the statement:

ducks NOT migration OR geese

produces the same result set as:

(ducks NOT migration) OR geese

because in this case, putting the parentheses around the NOT statement (causing it to be executed first) is exactly the same as what happens in the standard order of operation (NOT first, OR last). The set of documents retrieved would be fairly large, and contain records for ducks (as long as those records didn't mention migration), and any records mentioning geese—even records that discuss geese and migration. OR really opens the door to let things back in, in sometimes surprising ways.

Represented as a Venn diagram, the statement (ducks NOT migration) OR geese looks like Figure 2.4.

The results of this search would include all the records except those represented by the visible dark area of the "migration" circle. Note that records about geese that mention migration *would* be included in the results; the NOT only affects the duck records. However:

ducks NOT (migration OR geese)

will produce quite a different result set, much smaller and more focused. These would be records that mention ducks, and only those duck records that don't mention either migration or geese—the lightest area in Figure 2.5. The Venn diagram for this statement is shown in Figure 2.5.

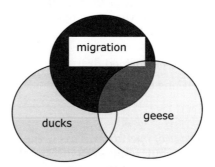

Fig. 2.4. (Ducks NOT Migration) OR Geese.

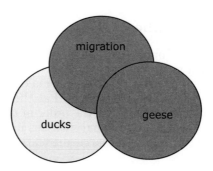

Fig. 2.5. Ducks NOT (Migration OR Geese).

Quick Recap

The standard order of operations for Boolean statements is to evaluate any NOT statements first, followed by AND statements, finally by OR statements. Putting part of the statement in parentheses changes the order of operations because the parenthesized section will be evaluated first.

Basic Tool no. 2: Controlled Vocabulary

The conundrum of online searching is that: "We want to look for concepts, but we are forced to search for words" (Walker and Janes, 1999). Think about it: if you wanted an "overview" of some topic, or a "discussion" of the pros and cons of some action, or especially "one good article on . . ."—how do you express these squishy notions to a digital search engine? Even if you can search the full text, the item you want might not include in its text "this is an overview" or "here is a discussion" and certainly not "here is the latest best article" on topic xyz. So all you can do, in each of these cases, is to search on words that represent the topic. In the world of commercial, subscription databases, there is an additional, powerful option: the provision of "controlled vocabulary," a.k.a. subject headings, a *thesaurus,*[4] *descriptors,*[5] *authority control.*[6] Controlled vocabulary is one of the added extras, one of the contributions of the companies that put together the databases, and one of the reasons they charge a subscription fee to access them. Remember the indexers from Chapter 1? You are paying for a bit of human analysis on each entry in the database. If done well, it is worth the price of admission for the efficiency it provides.

Advantages of Controlled Vocabulary

Why is controlled vocabulary so valuable?

- It saves you from having to come up with, and search for, every possible synonym (or alternate spelling) for a term. For example, if all the articles discussing various kinds of clothing are assigned a subject heading of "clothing," you don't have to worry about looking for all the possible ways clothing might be expressed, for example: dress, raiment, drapery, costume, attire, habiliment, vesture, vestment, garment, garb, apparel, wardrobe, wearing apparel, clothes, designer clothes, outfit, trousseau, suit, togs, day wear, night wear, zoot suit . . .

  - Note: Don't let your synonym neurons atrophy completely, though, because if you try a term in a subject or thesaurus search and get no results, not even a "see" reference—you'll need to think of another term to start with. And, of course, there is no controlled vocabulary on the Web.

- Theoretically the use of controlled vocabulary should make your search more complete: if the indexers at the database company have reliably assigned a subject heading of "waterfowl" *every* time an article mentions geese or goose, duck or ducks, loon or loons, or any other water bird, it should only be necessary to search on that term in order to retrieve everything.

- It can be used to disambiguate words that have several meanings (e.g., mercury—a planet? a car? a god? or a metal?), aiding in the precision of your search results (*precision*, in searching, is an important technical term, rather than just descriptive. See Searching Lexicon 3: Recall versus Precision, below). For author names, "authority control"[7] provides *one* way to look up an author known by more than one name (e.g., Mark Twain/Samuel Clemens).

- It provides a "safe" and helpful entry point into an unfamiliar subject area. Even if you know nothing about the subject, you have the assurance that the terms in the subject list are correct and appropriate. By browsing in the list and getting a sense of the terms (especially if there are "see" or "see also" references), you can often get ideas and develop or refine a search strategy.

Expressing the above points in more formal terms (Walker and Janes, 1999), controlled vocabularies:

- Facilitate the *gathering of like items*
- Help with *comprehensiveness* of results
- Help also with *precision* of results
- Help *broaden understanding* of a topic in an unfamiliar subject area

Basic Tool no. 3: Field Searching

This tool harkens back to the discussion of database structure in Chapter 1: how records in databases consist of a series of fields, each designated to hold a particular value. "Field Searching" simply means the ability to restrict your search to a specific field, for example, to search just the "author" field for a particular value (a name). Most databases offer some kind of default set of fields that get searched, so if you're unsure, or in a hurry, or just getting a sense of what the database might contain, you can always throw a word or phrase into the first available search box and hit search, just like you usually do on the Web. But taking a few moments to determine what fields are available for searching can be very valuable. Field searching will focus your search, and usually make it more efficient. For example, say you wanted to search a database of English literature for works by an author named—English! Just searching on the keyword "English" without limiting to the author field would result in hundreds of irrelevant results, because a great many of the records undoubtedly mention the word in a title or abstract, or English might appear in a "language" field that gets included in a "default fields" search. The database designers spent all that time deciding what fields to have—so definitely exploit this feature if it is available.

Combining Field Searching and Controlled Vocabulary

The combination of field searching with controlled vocabulary is especially effective, e.g., find an appropriate term in the list of subject terms, and then search on it, restricting your search to the "subject terms" field. And, of course, you will often construct searches combining all three of these initial tools, to produce a search such as:

Hanushek → in the → Author field

AND

Economics of Education → in the → Descriptors Phrase field

AND

1990–2000 → in the → Date field

There are more tools for your Searcher's Toolkit waiting in Chapter 3. Before going on, however, there are some terms in what we'll call the Searching Lexicon that, while they may not make you a better searcher, are useful to know because they give you a way to describe or better understand your search results.

Terms in the Searching Lexicon

Searching Lexicon 1—False Drops

A "false drop" is a document that gets retrieved by your search terms—but the terms in the document are not used in the sense you intended, e.g., a search on "employment or jobs or careers" that retrieves articles about Steve Jobs. False drops epitomize the problem of wanting to search concepts but only being able to search words! They are not *wrong* in a technical sense: the words in the records match the words you typed in—they just aren't being used to express the meaning you had in mind. (To make up for the inconvenience, such results are often quite humorous, if not downright bizarre.) When you get what appears to be a completely off the wall result, don't immediately assume the system is defective, or something is wrong. Now you have a term for such a result—it may simply be a false drop.

Controlled vocabulary and field searching can help avoid the false drop problem, although even those tools may not make it go away completely. Systems that search large quantities of full text are especially prone to the false drop problem.

Searching Lexicon 2—Stop Words

Stop words were mentioned in Chapter 1, but are worth revisiting here. Stop words, a.k.a. "noise words," are those little words that most systems (commercial database or Web search) do not index. Typical choices for a stop word list could include: an, by, for, from, of, the, to, with, be, where, how, it, he, my, his, when, there, is, are, so, she, and her. There is no standard list of stop words that all databases adhere to, which is good, in a way, because it allows for the possibility of a database having a relatively short list of stop words, or possibly even none at all. However, it means (if you determine that stop words may be interfering with your search results) that you'll have to dig around in the database's help files and hope that somewhere they have documented their list of stop words. There will be occasions where the words a database or search engine has chosen *not* to index are very important, and you'll need to come up with creative ways to get around the problem. (One of the most famous examples is a search on that famous line, "to be or not to be"—can it be done?)

Searching Lexicon 3—Recall versus Precision

Recall and precision have to do with the number and quality of the results retrieved by your search:

- *Recall* refers to retrieving more results—spreading your net as wide as possible, and probably picking up a number of less relevant results along with the "good" results. High recall means you are unlikely to miss any relevant items.

- *Precision* refers to focusing your search down, retrieving fewer—but more perfectly on-target, relevant—results. High precision means you are unlikely to retrieve very many, if any, irrelevant results (no false drops).

What might be the pros and cons of each?

- With greater recall the chances are better that you won't miss any relevant materials, but you'll invest more time going through your results, reviewing them after the fact to filter out the irrelevant items (in other words, you may wade through an awful lot of junk to find the gems).

- The more precise your search is, the more likely it is that you'll miss some things. There will be items in the database that might well meet your needs, but that your search didn't pick up because your choice of terminology or fields or limits was just a little *too* specific.

Google provides a great example of both ends of the recall-precision spectrum: ultimate *recall* is all the matches to a simple search. Ultimate *precision* is represented by the "I'm feeling lucky" search button, which takes you to just one (theoretically ideal) result.

Should I Aim For Recall or Precision?

Neither one—recall or precision—is intrinsically good or bad. They simply describe an outcome. But recall and precision also provide a useful a way to think about your search, to guide how you go about it: what database or search engine you use, and what search techniques you employ. The outcome desired dictates the search style employed: someone who is testing a choice of Ph.D thesis topic wants to spread the net as wide as possible, to make sure no one has looked at their particular problem before. For that situation, high recall is crucial. Similarly, if you believe you're looking for an obscure topic, but you want absolutely everything and anything that can be found about it—you'll want to try for maximum recall. You might start with a Web search, or in an appropriate database, enter a very simple style of search (no controlled vocabulary, not limited to any specific field). But an undergraduate writing a short paper, or a community hobbyist investigating a new topic, may be perfectly served by a high precision search that identifies a few recent, relevant articles—even though many more related, or equally relevant, articles remain behind in the database. In that case, choose an appropriate database, check for subject terms, perhaps combine two or more with Boolean operators, and use some field searching.

Quick Recap

Now you have three major tools in your search arsenal:

1. The concept of Boolean logic for combining terms: the operators AND, OR, and NOT, and the use of parentheses to affect the order in which the Boolean operators are processed.

2. The concept of controlled vocabulary: terms that the vendor has applied to help you get all the articles on a topic without having to keyword search every variation or synonym, and to disambiguate among various meanings.

3. The concept of field searching: restricting your search to specified fields to make it more precise and efficient.

You also now know that database indexing programs have lists of certain words they do *not* index, known as stop words.

In addition, you have some new language to describe the results of your searches:

- False drops
- Recall
- Precision

Applying the Tools

Let's look at EBSCO's *MasterFILE Select*, a multidisciplinary database, and see how these tools apply there.

MasterFILE Select: Notes and Search Examples

The first challenge with any database is to be able to look at, and interpret what is presented in the interface. We're so used to looking at busy Web pages that we look—but we don't really *see*. To turn yourself into a more efficient and effective searcher, however, it is important to be able to look over an interface, and quickly translate what's there into the tools you are looking for:

- Does it use Boolean operators for combining terms?
- Is it possible to search in specific fields, and if yes, which ones?
- Is there any kind of controlled vocabulary available? (And can you browse it?)

Determining Availability of Search Tools

Many databases offer two search modes: Basic and Advanced. Usually the questions above won't be answered by looking at the Basic search interface—but there should be good information in the Advanced screen. Figure 2.6 shows the Advanced Search interface in *MasterFILE Select*.

Focus on the upper part of the screen for now, as shown in Figure 2.7. What do you see? Are your first three tools available?

Fig. 2.6. Advanced Search Interface in *MasterFILE Select*. ©2005, EBSCO Publishing, Inc. All rights reserved.

Fig. 2.7. Boolean Operators In Search Interface. ©2005, EBSCO Publishing, Inc. All rights reserved.

Check: Boolean operators work here. Take a look at Figure 2.8: do we have the option of restricting our search to certain fields?

Check: there are fields available for searching. The list of fields gives a clue, reinforced by a button in the interface, that there may be some kind of controlled vocabulary available, and that it can be browsed. See the "Subjects" button in the bar across the top?

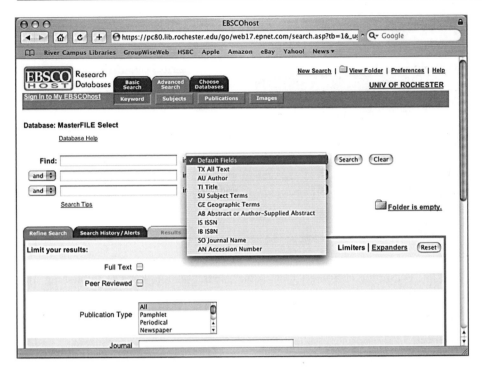

Controlled Vocabulary: The Subjects List

Some databases offer separate lists of the terms that have been in-dexed from various fields (as in the ERIC screen snaps in Chapter 1, there were separate lists of terms for the Descriptors, and the Descriptors Phrase fields). The *MasterFILE Select* Subjects list is an all-in-one affair: it includes terms from many fields, not just "subjects" *per se*. You can use it to identify controlled vocabulary, as well as identify titles of books, poems, companies, places, and people—proper names of all kinds. The *MasterFILE Select* Sub-jects list also provides some nice "value-added" information: each entry in-cludes the number and type of articles available for that heading. Sections of the entries starting at the Subject "mars" demonstrate this well (Fig-ure 2.9a and 2.9b).

The *MasterFILE* Subjects list is useful if you are looking for one thing (person, place, book review, company, etc.), from one sort of publication—for example, academic journal references to Mars (the planet). It makes it very easy to connect directly to the results you intended (minimizing false drops). It does not, however, offer any way to construct a multiple term search, or to view all the articles on a topic, regardless of type of publication.

Multiple Field Searches in MasterFILE

To set up a Boolean search and use specific fields in *MasterFILE Select*, the best approach is to check the Subjects list, determine the correct form of the terms you want to use, then click on Advanced Search and type the terms in yourself, setting the field to be searched to Subject (or Author, etc.). One

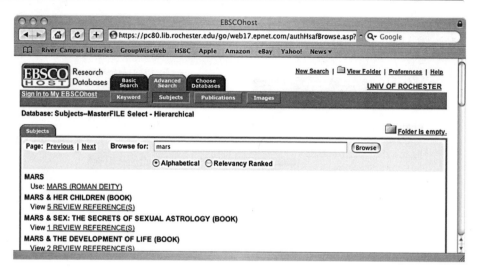

Fig. 2.9a. Beginning of Subject Listing for "Mars." ©2005, EBSCO Publishing, Inc. All rights reserved.

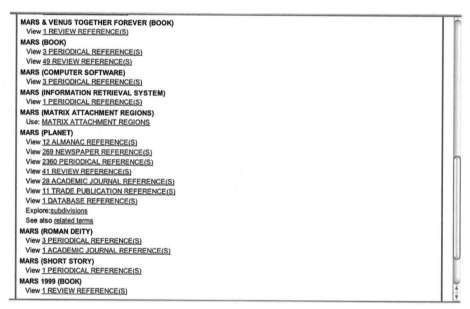

Fig. 2.9b. Further down in the subject listing for "Mars." ©2005, EBSCO Publishing, Inc. All rights reserved.

cautionary note: do not include the parentheses on the terms that have been glossed to distinguish their meaning, e.g., Mars (Planet) has to be entered Mars Planet.

Search Example 1

A patron approaches and says: "I want to find some articles about the Mars lunar lander." Something about this doesn't sound quite right to you, but the patron insists on that terminology.

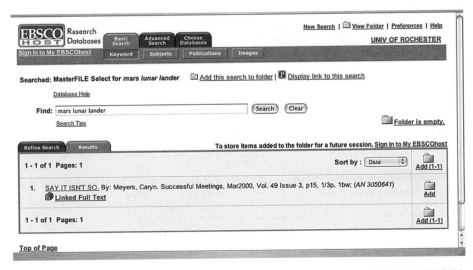

Fig. 2.10. *MasterFILE Select* Basic Search for 'mars lunar lander.' ©2005, EBSCO Publishing, Inc. All rights reserved.

Fig. 2.11. Advanced, subject term search in *MasterFILE Select.* ©2005, EBSCO Publishing, Inc. All rights reserved.

The most simple, literal approach (besides going to the Web) might be to go to *MasterFILE Select*, and in the Basic search, type in: mars lunar lander.

This produces only one result (Figure 2.10)—and a very odd one, at that! (Would you call this a false drop?) You were right to think there was something wrong with the patron's terminology. However, it's always worth taking a look, to figure out why you got something. In this case, one of the subject headings in this odd result is: "space probes." From Figure 2.9 we know there should be lots of entries for the planet Mars. A more effective approach might be to go to the Advanced Search screen, and set up a strategy as pictured in Figure 2.11.

Try this search and see for yourself. (You'll find that the patron was thinking of the Mars Lander or Rover—the "lunar" part was misremembered.)

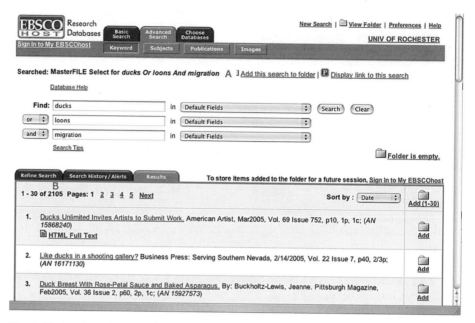

Fig. 2.12. Boolean logic pitfalls in the Advanced Search screen. ©2005, EBSCO Publishing, Inc. All rights reserved.

Boolean Logic: Advanced Search versus Basic Search

As a final note to this chapter, unfortunately we have to reveal that there are no comfortable absolutes in this business. The Advanced Search screen is not always the best answer, as shown in the following two screen snaps. In Figure 2.12, a Boolean search has been set up in the Advanced Search screen. Look carefully at the screen, and notice A, how it interpreted the search, and B, how many results it returned.

What the searcher *meant* was (ducks or loons) and migration, that is, anything about the migration of ducks or loons. If the searcher thought to type "ducks or loons" all into the first search field, and then AND in "migration," the search would work. But the interface structure doesn't lead you to think of doing this, so the results are full of false drops.

In the Basic screen, however, it's a snap to do it right, using those powerful parentheses (Figure 2.13).

This is a point to keep in mind. "Basic" doesn't necessarily need to mean simplistic. Since you are now a master of Boolean operators and parentheses, it can be *easier* to do some searches in the Basic mode. (There are even ways to indicate what field to search in the Basic mode, but that can wait.) For quick iterations of a search, testing various terms and combinations, the Basic search box is very useful.

Exercises and Points to Consider

1. Consider these statements:

    ducks OR geese NOT migration

    (ducks OR geese) NOT migration

(ducks AND geese) OR loons

ducks AND (geese OR loons)

(ducks OR geese) AND migration

(ducks OR geese) NOT migration

(ducks OR (geese NOT migration)) AND lakes

2. Try drawing Venn diagrams for the paired statements to see how (or if) they differ. Then try describing in words what the content of the documents retrieved by these statements would be. Test out the statements in *MasterFILE Select's* Basic search mode.

3. Pick three terms relating to a subject that interests you, and explore searching them in various ways in *MasterFILE Select.* Try a number of Boolean combinations in Basic search mode, try setting up similar searches in Advanced mode, and see if your terms appear in the Subjects list.

4. In describing the benefits of controlled vocabulary, you will have noticed a consistent use of terms such as *should,* as in "use of subject headings *should* ensure that you retrieve everything on a given topic," rather than the more certain term "will." What do you think might prevent controlled vocabulary from being a perfect retrieval panacea?

5. If you had part of a citation, and were trying to find the rest of the information (a "known item" search), what type of search would you probably try first—one that had high recall, or high precision? Based on your answer, what type of resource (commercial database or Web search), and techniques would you use? What if your first approach didn't work?

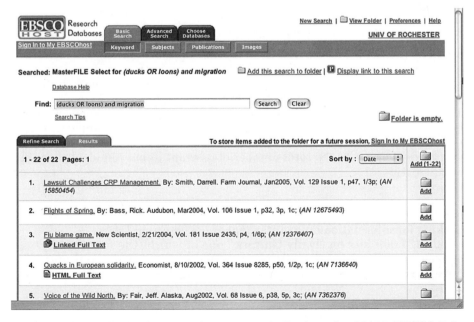

Fig. 2.13. Successful Boolean search statement in Basic mode. ©2005, EBSCO Publishing, Inc. All rights reserved.

Sidebar 2.1. Analyzing Recall versus Precision

Say there are N relevant items "out there." You have a search engine that retrieves items based on a query. We can make a chart that describes the efficacy of the search, in terms of the four possible types of results (Table 2.1). You can think of actual numbers being substituted for all the types of results.

True positives are search results that indeed are relevant items. You can clearly count these.

False negatives are failures of the search: relevant items that are out there but are not retrieved. If you know there are N relevant items altogether, then this number is N—(true positives). This is called a "Type II" error in statistical hypothesis testing (the test wrongly reports that a true hypothesis is false).

False positives are search results that are useless and irrelevant. You can count these since you're looking at them. This is called a "Type I" error in statistical hypothesis testing (the test wrongly reports that a false hypothesis is true).

True negatives are all those items not found that indeed you don't care about because they are irrelevant. There are presumably a great many of these unless something is really off in the system. We don't usually use this number.

Considering the NUMBERS of these types of results, we can define:

Recall: the number of relevant items found divided by the number of relevant items out there (N):

recall = (true positives)/((true positives) + (false negatives)) = (true positives)/N.

Precision: the number of relevant items found divided by the number of items found (relevant and irrelevant):

precision = (true positives)/((true positives) + (false positives)).

One error measure is the number of false results divided by the number of relevant items out there (N):

error rate = ((false positives) + (false negatives))/((true positives) + (false negatives))

= ((false positives) + (false negatives))/N.

So if you have good recall (near 1) you don't wind up with lots of missed but relevant items. But your results could be diluted by lots of false positives, or items that are wrongly retrieved as being relevant when they are not.

If you have good precision, on the other hand, you can be more sure your results are actually relevant, but you might be missing a lot of other relevant items in your search (you could have a large number of false negatives). Error rate is just the proportion of both types of errors to the total number of relevant items you ideally would like to retrieve.

Self Test

You're looking for information on a guitar maker called David Daily.

Google finds 131,000 hits on "Daily Guitars," one of which (the first, luckily) is relevant. You have reason to know that there are actually two relevant Web sites out there. What are the recall, precision, and error rate for this search?

Google finds 4,110 hits on "hog farm waste runoff problems," of which 570 are relevant. The authoritative document you are consulting says there are "several thousand" relevant items on the Web. What are reasonable ranges for the values of recall, precision, and error rate for this search?

Sidebar Table 2.1. Retrieval versus relevancy chart.

	Retrieved Items	
Actual Items	Relevant	Irrelevant
Relevant	True positives	False negatives
Irrelevant	False positives	True negatives

Notes

1. Boole was a British mathematician and philosopher. "As the inventor of Boolean algebra, the basis of all modern computer arithmetic, Boole is regarded as one of the founders of the field of computer science." This and more details about George Boole are available from the online *Wikipedia*, the free encyclopedia, http://en.wikipedia.org/wiki/George_Boole (accessed February 26, 2005).

2. Strictly speaking, in mathematical logic terms NOT and AND NOT are different. NOT is a unary operator, that is, it can take just one argument: NOT argyle, for example, if you were offered a world of socks and were willing to take anything but argyle. AND NOT is a binary operator, that is, it takes two arguments: pie AND NOT banana cream—you must provide a first set, and then a second set you wish to exclude. Databases and Web search engines, even when they express the operator as "NOT," mean AND NOT. This is subtly conveyed in the advanced search interfaces of databases: the "AND OR NOT" options don't start until *after* the first text input field.

3. You can have multiple levels of parenthetical expressions, a syntax known as *"nesting"* or nested statements, in which case the most deeply nested statement will be evaluated first, followed by the parenthetical expression around it, etc. You may very seldom, if ever, need to construct a nested statement, but it's interesting to know you can.

4. Thesaurus, plural thesauri. The formal term for controlled vocabulary. Specific to the database discipline, a thesaurus may also describe relationships between the terms, and provide pointers to the best terms to use.

5. Certain databases use the term descriptors for subject headings.

6. Most often associated with library catalogs, authority control refers to a system of controlled vocabulary specifically for author names.

7. With thanks to the *ARTFL Project: Roget's Thesaurus, 1911*, http://machaut. uchicago.edu/cgi-bin/ROGET.sh.old?word=clothing (Accessed February 26, 2005).

3

The Searcher's Toolkit: Part 2

The "tools" covered in Chapter 2, Boolean operators, controlled vocabulary, and field searching, are the most fundamental. The tools we'll add here are further refinements: additional search functions; a simple search strategy that can be used in any situation, which will enable you to execute ever more sophisticated searches; and finally a list of "mental tools." The intent is always to enable you to get the information you're after more efficiently and effectively.

Searcher's Toolkit: Part 2

Basic Tool no. 4: Proximity Searching

In addition to allowing you to specify that your search results must include certain terms (Boolean AND: ducks AND geese AND loons), most of the subscription database systems also allow you to set up an even more sophisticated search, in which you set a rule for the relationship between those terms. That is, you can state how close to each other, and sometimes in what order, they must appear in the text to qualify for retrieval. This is known as "proximity" searching.

Proximity searching allows you to specify that termA appears within so many words of termB. For example, if you were trying to discover names of consulting firms that work with the food and beverage industry, it's quite possible that such a thing would only be mentioned as an aside—neither concept would be enough to merit a subject heading. Searching "consulting AND (food OR beverage)" would probably result in a large number of false drops, because the words could occur in the documents but have nothing to do with each other, e.g., consulting could show up in the first paragraph and food or beverage in the last paragraph, in a totally different context. The only way you're going to have any chance of getting something meaningful is if the terms are somewhat close to each other: at least within the same paragraph, and, even better, within the same sentence, within five to ten words of each other. And there's nothing to prevent you from combining the two approaches: termA within five words of (termB or termC).

When your search topic falls below the radar of subject headings (controlled vocabulary), and you have some text to work with (at least an abstract, if not full text) proximity searching is a wonderful way to get greater precision in your results. You will still get false drops, but not nearly as many as you would using only Boolean operators.

Proximity Searching Strategy

In setting up a proximity search, start by trying to envision how the writer might have expressed what you're looking for: in this case, it might be phrases such as "...consultants to the consumer packaged goods, personal care, and food and beverage industries..." or "...a leading food industry consultant..." or "...has chosen ABC, a Boston consulting firm, for their new beverage marketing campaign..." This helps you decide whether to set the proximity number lower (4 or 5), or higher (8 or 10). In this case it would be good to set it higher, because it's possible the writer might have listed a number of industries, as in the first phrase example. Obviously, this presupposes that you are fairly familiar with the literature of the topic at hand. What if you aren't? In that case, simply experiment: start with a proximity of five words, and (as described in "pearl growing," below) learn from the results, increasing or decreasing the proximity number as seems appropriate.[1] There's no rule that you have to get it exactly right the first time!

Proximity Operators

Like a Boolean search, a proximity search is expressed with special operators. Unfortunately, unlike the universal and easily recognized AND, OR, NOT (AND NOT) used for Boolean expressions, proximity operators vary from system to system, so it's harder to produce a nice neat list to memorize. Even the syntax—the operators—can be mysterious looking, using simply N (for "near") or W (for "within"), and a number to indicate the number of possible intervening words. Some systems, such as EBSCO, even offer two flavors of proximity operator: one for specifying just proximity, the other for dictating both proximity and word order (termA must occur within so many words, and *before* termB). Let's look at some examples.

Proximity Search Examples

ProQuest

ProQuest uses the syntax "W/<number>" for proximity[2] (the command letter does not need to be capitalized):

homeless w/4 teenagers

In response to this search, the ProQuest system will return records where the word "homeless" appears within four words of "teenagers," regardless of word order. All of the following phrases would meet the search criteria:

...teenagers who have been homeless for more than...

...From Homelessness to College, One Teenager's Journey

...those involving teenagers, prostitutes, and the homeless...

...even teenagers who are not homeless...

...has been homeless ever since he was a teenager...

EBSCO

EBSCO's syntax looks similar, but the effects are slightly different. EBSCO has two proximity operators: N and W (note there is no slash between the operator and the number). They are used as follows:

Near

teenagers N5 homeless

That is, "teenagers" must appear from zero to five words away from "homeless" in the text for a document to be retrieved. The terms can be in any order—teenagers first, or homeless first.

Within

homeless W3 teenagers

Meaning, "homeless" must appear within three words of "teenagers," *in that order* (homeless first), to be retrieved. Note how this contrasts with ProQuest's W operator, which does not specify word order. These subtle variations are the norm, so be prepared to be flexible, and to take a quick glance at each database's Help file for guidance.

Factiva

In another variation on this theme, in *Factiva* you spell out "near" and append a number, such as near5, to set the parameters for your proximity search. If you were looking for information about gourmet or specialty pickles, you'd probably be interested in an article that mentions "...the specialty market now extends to pickles, teas..." The search:

specialty near5 pickles

would pick up this article. The pickle reference is so casual that the subject headings for the whole article give no clue that it might mention pickles. (And trust me: if you are trying to find information about the specialty pickle market without spending a fortune for a market research report, you'll take any reference, no matter how casual.)

Factiva also provides a conceptual rather than numerically bound operator with "same" to specify "in the same paragraph." For example, "Merck same research" will retrieve articles in which Merck and research occur in the same paragraph, in any order.

Determining Proximity Operators

Unlike Boolean operators, proximity operators usually don't appear as drop-down menu choices in the database interface. While the use of N or near, and W or within, is fairly standard, the way they are interpreted, and the use (or not) of additional characters such as a slash mark, make each database just a bit different. Given that there are several subtle variations that might be used, it's best not to just guess. To find out whether a database provides proximity searching and the syntax to use, you'll need to explore files such as Help or Examples.

Importance of Proximity Searching in Full Text Databases

Proximity, while requiring a bit more effort to discover, is becoming an ever more valuable function as vendors strive to provide more and more searchable full text. A database that is just an electronic version of an index simply doesn't offer that many words to search on. The text fields (author, title, journal name, and abstract) aren't that big, so the use of Boolean operators in that situation is just fine (using proximity in such a situation might well reduce your results to zero, in fact). Matches on termA AND termB in the limited realm of index fields are likely to be relevant because the terms are, in a sense, by definition "close" to each other. In a full text situation you could certainly still restrict your search to just subject headings (if they are available), or a field such as title, and use Boolean operators—but by searching the full text you have the opportunity to get at more deeply buried aspects of an article, to tweeze out nuances and secondary topics that cannot possibly be covered by a few, necessarily broad, subject headings. The more searchable full text a database has, the more important the ability to do proximity searching becomes, as it is the only useful way to really mine all that text for everything it has to offer.

Really Close Proximity: Phrase Searching

Searching on exact phrases can be extremely important in some cases, and the inability of some databases to do this (easily) can really inhibit how effectively you can search. In the commercial database world, the way you indicate to the system "this is a phrase search" can vary considerably.

EBSCO databases, *Factiva*, and the *Web of Science*® perform phrase searches without quotation marks or indicators of any kind: their search functions assume multiple word entries in the search box should be searched as a phrase. FirstSearch and ProQuest databases work like the Web search engines: enclose the terms to be searched as a phrase in double quotes. (ProQuest and LexisNexis will actually treat two-word queries as a phrase by default.) The proximity syntax used by Gale's Infotrac databases for phrase searching is somewhat awkward: spring w1 break.

Uses for Phrase Searching

Phrase searching is useful any time you're searching for things such as the name of a place or an organization (especially if the name is made up of common words), a multiword concept or topic (latch key children, gourmet pickles, missile defense shield), or—especially on the Web—for tracking down more complete information from incomplete fragments. Problems such as the rest of the lyrics, or indeed the real title, of a song whose only line you can remember is "is the moon out tonight?" can be quickly resolved and put in context (and possibly bar bets won) by plunking the quote-bound phrase into Google. In a more academic scenario, say you have a bad or incomplete reference to a thesis or a journal article. If available to you, head for a database such as Dissertation Abstracts, or an appropriate subject database, and try a partial phrase from the title, or the author's name and a word from the title, depending on what information you (seem) to have.[3] (If that doesn't work, try only the most distinct words as a title field search, and if that doesn't work, go to the Web. You may not find the actual item, but you at least you may find a more accurate, complete reference to it from someone else's bibliography.)

Proximity and phrase searching are useful for reducing and focusing your results; they tend to increase the precision of the search. The next tool takes us back the other way, providing a way to broaden the search net (to increase recall).

Basic Tool no. 5: Truncation

"Truncation" is an efficient way of extending your search to pick up many variations on a word without having to (a) think of all the possible variants or (b) input them with endless "OR"s. Truncation allows you to search on a word stem and retrieve any word beginning with those letters, e.g.,

harmon*

to retrieve harmony, harmonious, harmonica . . .

In another database, the syntax and results for the truncation function might be:

employ$

to retrieve employ, employs, employee, employment, employer, employed . . .

Note that when the stem (the letters being truncated) is a word in its own right, that word will be included in the search results. Truncation generally means the word stem, and any number of characters following, from zero on up.

Using Truncation

Truncation is a tool that is equally useful in field searching and in full text searches in commercial databases. In a field search, for example, truncation is a wonderfully efficient way to pick up several related subject headings at once (searching poet* to pick up poet, poetics, poetry), or variations on author names (with and without a middle initial, for instance, or even with or without a first name being spelled out: Adams, J!). In a full text search, obviously, truncation greatly increases the number of documents that will be eligible for retrieval. When you are fishing around for a concept or topic that you think might be rather rare, and that isn't expressed with any set phrases or words, the combination of truncation and a proximity search can be invaluable. The earlier example of trying to identify any articles mentioning companies that act as consultants to the food and beverage industry is a prime candidate for this technique:

Consultan* near10 (food or beverage*)

to retrieve consultant, consultants, or consultancy, within a ten-word radius of food or beverage or beverages.

Table 3.1. Truncation and wildcard symbols used by various vendors.

Vendor	Truncation Symbol	Wildcard Symbol(s)	Other
EBSCO	*	?	
Endeavor (OPAC)	?	N/A	
OCLC FirstSearch	*	#, ?[a]	+[b]
Gale (InfoTrac)	*	?	![c]
LexisNexis	!	*	
ProQuest	*	?	
Web of Science	*	?	

[a] "#" replaces one character only; ? replaces zero to nine characters; ? used with a number, e.g., ? 2 would replace exactly two characters.
[b] "+" finds plural forms using "s" or "es" only.
[c] "!" replaces zero or one character only, either within or at the end of a word.

Common Truncation Symbols

Truncation symbols vary somewhat from database to database, but the ones most frequently used are:

- ' * '
- ' ! '
- ' ? '

Factiva uses the symbol "$," which is more unusual, but always strikes me as appropriate for this resource from the financially focused Dow Jones company.

Determining Truncation Symbols

As is the case with the other tools in this chapter, there is likely to be nothing in the initial search interface to indicate whether truncation is supported, and if so, what symbol to use. There are databases that don't offer a true truncation function, but simply search on a limited set of variants (e.g., plural forms) automatically. Some information is supplied in Table 3.1, but if the database in question is not listed, or to check the most current usage (it could change), look for links to "Help" or "Examples" to determine how the database at hand handles truncation.

Wildcards

Closely related to truncation are "wildcard" symbols, in the sense that a symbol is used in place of letters. Where truncation symbols represent any number of characters, wildcards are used to substitute for characters on a one-to-one basis. Be prepared for confusion: the symbols used for wildcards are the same as those used for truncation, but with the effect changing depending on the vendor. That is, one vendor may use "!" for truncation, and "*" for a wildcard, while another exactly reverses those two meanings. For example, ProQuest and LexisNexis use "*" as their wildcard (one-to-one replacement) symbol. In EBSCO and the *Web of Science*, "*" is used as the truncation symbol (any number of characters, at the end of a word), and "?" is used as the wildcard symbol, replacing interior characters on a one-to-one basis.

Using Wildcards

Wildcards are probably most frequently used to replace just one letter, for example:

wom*n

retrieves woman, women, womyn. Multiple wildcards can be used to substitute for an equal number of characters, e.g.,

manufactur**

will retrieve manufacture, manufactured, or manufactures, but not manufacturing.

A search situation in which single wildcarding is really helpful is for picking up U.S.–U.K. alternate spellings, e.g.,

labo!r to get either labor or labour
surpri!e to get either surprise or surprize

If you were searching a database that included British publications, and you wanted to be sure you picked up relevant material from them, this use of wildcarding could be very important.

Table of Symbols by Vendor

Some information on common truncation and wildcard symbols used by different Vendors is supplied in Table 3.1, but you are always encouraged to consult the database's Help file for the most up-to-date information on what functionalities the database supports, and the appropriate symbols to use.

This probably strikes you as a fairly esoteric capability, and in general it's likely you won't need to use such functionality very often. In real life, you're much more likely to stick a truncation symbol on the end of "manufactur" and be done with it. But knowledge is power!

Sidebar 3.1. Department of Confusing Things

In everyday speech the term "wildcard" is often used to mean "truncation," e.g., you'll hear the symbol used at the end of a word to retrieve multiple endings expressed as a "wildcard." I'm quite guilty of this myself: when working with a student who has never heard of "truncation," the easiest course of action is to call the odd thing being demonstrated a "wildcard," because almost everyone immediately grasps the sense of that notion. If you are getting serious enough about searching that you're looking at the Help files, however, it's good to know the technical terms used in the business, and to understand that different symbols can have different effects (one replaces only one character, while another is used to replace any number of characters).

Quick Recap

Proximity searching allows you to search for documents containing terms within a given number of words of each other. Proximity searching is particularly valuable for searching full text. Phrase searching is available in commercial databases, and can be very important for retrieving accurate results. Truncation refers to the use of a symbol to substitute for 0–N characters at the *end* of a word. Wildcards are symbols used to substitute on a one-to-one basis for characters *within* a word. Proximity and phrase searches tend to narrow and focus results, truncation and wildcards help increase the potential set of results. To determine the symbols or syntax to use, in all cases consult the database's Help or Examples files.

Basic Tool no. 6: Limits to Constrain Your Search

Limits or Limiters are preset options in the search interface that can be used to further define your search. They are described here as "preset options" to distinguish them from the words or subject terms that you have to come up with and type in. Limits make use of fields in the database record that are used to store attributes of the record rather than conceptual content: you could say limit fields are about the article, not what the article is about. Limiters usually appear as check boxes or drop-down menus. Typical Limit choices include:

- Scholarly ("peer reviewed")
- Publication or article type (book, conference proceeding, review, editorial, etc.)
- Language
- Full text (e.g., in a database that offers some records with full text and some without, this limit will constrain the search to retrieve only matching records offering full text).[4]
- Date

The Date Limit

The Date limit is a bit of an anomaly. In the context of a known citation, you would consider it a "content" field: the date would be part of the unique information identifying that citation (Joe Blogg's 1996 article is not Joe Blogg's 1998 article). However, if you are searching for material published before or after a certain date, or in a particular date range, the date information becomes an attribute used to limit your search results. The way the date option is displayed in the search interface is frequently hybrid as well, offering both a drop-down of preset choices, as well as fields for specifying a specific date (or date range).

One Last Search Tool: Case Sensitivity

This last capability doesn't even merit a "Basic Tool no.," but any discussion of searching should at least mention the issue of case sensitivity. Think of case sensitivity, e.g., the ability to distinguish upper from lower case, as the toothpick in the Swiss army knife, tiny but needed once in a great while. How does the database handle case recognition, if at all? You'll have to troll the database's Help files to find the answer in each case, and the results will vary widely. ProQuest does not support case sensitivity, while LexisNexis offers three special commands for case sensitive searching.

Uses for Case Sensitive Searching

There are certain situations in which the ability to search for the capitalized version is crucial; otherwise you'll get an incredible number of false drops. Acronyms that are the same as common words are a prime example. At one time searching for "AIDS" caused all sorts of problems, but now that the term is so prevalent, and indexers have added it to their lists of subject terms, you are much less likely to get false drops. There was a situation once that required searching a full text database, which did not recognize case, for the acronym MIT. What came back in the results was a lot of baseball mitts, believe it or not! A similar problem could arise in searching for the "Research in Motion" company, which is usually referred to by its acronym, RIM.

Sometimes you can go to the database's subject list and get the term you want from there. But in some cases the term you are searching for may not be a major theme in the article, and not represented in the subject headings (or the subject indexing may not be very good). In that case you'll be in the situation of needing to search the full text, with all its potential pitfalls.

Basic Tool no. 7: "Pearl Growing"—A Useful Search Strategy

This charming expression[5] refers to the process of doing a very simple search first, with the intent of achieving high recall, and then examining the results to find appropriate subject headings, or discover further terms to search on, from the most on-target hits. You then add one or more of these terms to your search strategy to produce a more precise list of results. This is very useful when you are venturing into a new database or unfamiliar subject matter, or when you simply don't have the time or inclination to do formal preparatory work by hunting around in the subject indexes.

A Search Example Using Pearl Growing

For example, let us say you're an engineer, and tired of your straight engineering job. A colleague suggests you look into jobs in engineering sales. Whenever you're working with someone doing this sort of "career exploration"—What is the work like? How is the pay? Are there openings, or is it a stagnant market?—a good first thing to check is the *Occupational Outlook Handbook* (OOH).[6] If you had come to see me, we'd start there. At the OOH, a keyword search for "engineering sales" produces just one result, for Public Relations Specialists. Huh? Browsing the index under E doesn't help either. A search on just "sales" finally does it, and we find that such people are referred to as "sales engineers." This is useful. Let's move on to a database and try for some articles about sales engineers.

Going to a database of business articles, ProQuest's *ABI/Inform*, we can start by seeing if, by chance, "sales engineer" is a subject term. It's not. So then we can try the quick and dirty approach: simply searching "sales engineers" in the citation and abstract, hoping to pearl grow from the results. We can prescreen the results a bit by choosing the "Scholarly journals, including peer reviewed" limit. Among the results is an article titled "Control and Autonomy among Knowledge Workers In Sales: An Employee Perspective." Despite the "Knowledge Workers" in the title, the abstract is full of the phrase "sales engineers." This looks useful! From the subject headings: *Employee Attitude, Control Sales, Studies*, and *Human Resource Management*, we decide that *Sales* could be useful, or *Employee Attitude*. Examining some of the other results, we notice that "Salespeople" is also a subject term. We go back to the search interface, and try:

Employee attitude—in Subject

AND

Sales engineers—in Citation or Abstract

Another variation we can try is:

Sales OR Salespeople—in Subject

AND

Sales engineers—in Citation or Abstract

The ProQuest system also automatically provides helpful, usually insightful search suggestions in the results interface, in this case:

Engineers and Personal profiles (both terms will be searched as subjects).
Engineers and Organizational behavior (both terms will be searched as subjects).

To reiterate, the strategy in pearl growing is to start with a fairly simple, broad search, examine the most likely results, and learn to refine or improve the search based on subject headings or other terminology used in the "on target" results. This technique is really only useful in the structured, subject-headings-world of commercial databases. On the Web, you may encounter links in search results saying "More like this," which are trying to do the same thing. How well they do it, and what they are basing the similarity on, are open questions.

Quick Recap

Limits are preset options built into a search interface that enable you to search by document attributes such as language, article or document type, peer reviewed, and date. The ability to distinguish upper from lower case in a search term is sometimes important, but is not offered by all databases. Pearl growing refers to a strategy of starting with a very simple keyword search, examining the results, and discovering useful subject headings or additional terms to search on from the most on-target records.

Your Mental Toolkit

Understanding and being able to use concepts such as Boolean logic, controlled vocabulary, proximity searching, and limits will definitely go a long way towards making you a more effective searcher. In addition, there are certain mental attitudes that will help you a great deal as well. There are, of course, some aspects of mind or personality that you either have or you don't: general curiosity, interest and enjoyment in puzzles, and an ability to think "out of the box," that is, to make connections or have ideas (light bulb moments) *beyond* the research request as explicitly stated. But there are three "mental tools" you don't have to be born with; rather, you can make a conscious effort to develop them. These are tools to employ in any search, and which may be just as important in your success as a searcher as your knowledge of search functions.

The mental toolkit:

- A healthy skepticism: do not trust anything someone tells you that "they remember," or even anything that is printed in a bibliography.

- *Willingness to let go*: someone may offer a great deal of information, but if the results keep coming up zero, or wrong, *let go*: drop pieces of information, one at a time.

- Maintain mental clarity and patience: be systematic about your searching, don't just thrash around rapidly trying this and that. It may seem longer to stop and think and try one change at a time, but in the end it will save time.

To add emphasis to the second point: one of the biggest pitfalls in searching is not being willing to *not* look for a part of the information provided. In general: be flexible, not fixated.

Summary and Advice

And that's your toolkit. You now have some concepts, some tools that you'll use over and over, in various combinations, and some attitudinal tools to use as well. My advice on how to employ this information to the best advantage is fairly simple:

1. Master the concepts.

2. Do not attempt to memorize exactly which databases offer which capabilities. Instead...

3. Train your eyes!

Learn to scan an interface quickly. Look for "Help" or "Search Guides." (And actually read them, although be prepared: sometimes the "Help" is not updated as quickly as changes are made to the database.) You now know *what* to look for,[7] so just look for it. Nothing on that screen should be "noise" or ignored. This is the most important thing you can do: LOOK with your trained eyes. Why? Because:

Things can change at any time—and they will change!

Especially now that database vendors have moved their products to the Web, their interfaces have become more fluid. They are more stable than most Web pages, but still, the lure and the ability to change things so easily is hard to resist. Indeed, by the time you see this book, the interfaces shown in the figures here may have already changed anywhere from a little to a lot. You need to be flexible, and able to relearn continually as the interface designers move things around and change their terminology. Let me assure you that you will get good at it, but you need to be alert, and ready for change ("oh, now that tab is orange and they've changed the name Advanced Search to More Options. Same thing. OK."). I cannot emphasize this enough:

USE YOUR EYES—They are the best tool you have.[8]

Exercises and Points to Consider

1. Consider again this search: homeless W/4 teenagers, which produced this result:

   ...has been homeless ever since he was a teenager...

Count the words between homeless and teenager. Why would the article containing this phrase be retrieved by this search?

2. What do you think would be the best way to search for a personal name, especially if you wanted any article that made any mention of the person? Would you use a phrase or proximity search? What are the pros and cons of each method?

3. Consider again this search: Consultan* near10 (food or beverage*). How might you alter this slightly to make even more documents eligible for retrieval? What might be the pros and cons of doing that?

4. Going back to ProQuest's suggestions when we did the "sales engineers" search:

Engineers and Personal profiles (searched as Subjects).
Engineers and Organizational behavior (searched as Subjects).

What would be an elegant way to accomplish both of these searches at once?

5. One major vendor whose syntax wasn't addressed in this chapter was Wilson. Go to a Wilson database, and see if you can find out: does it support proximity searching, and what is the syntax, if so? Phrase searching? What about truncation, and wildcards? Does Wilson distinguish between upper and lowercase?

Suggested Reading

Tenopir, Carol. "Are You a Super Searcher?" *Library Journal* (March 1, 2000): 36, 38.

Notes

1. When dealing with a totally unfamiliar subject area, it's also very useful do a Google search, just to get a sense of how people write about the topic.

2. ProQuest also simply treats three-word queries as proximity searches by default, that is, if you entered: total homeless teenagers—ProQuest would automatically search for those three terms in proximity to each other. Phrases such as "...the total number of homeless teenagers..." and "...teenagers who are homeless are not included in the total..." would be retrieved.

3. Reference Desk Rule no. 1: citations almost always have a mistake in them somewhere.

4. Beware, though, that if the database is enabled with a technology for linking to full text in other databases to which the library subscribes, turning on the full text limit may eliminate potentially useful results.

5. Why "pearl growing"? Well, you throw out a small bit (one or two words, say), a seed. Then from all the results, you add layers, the way a pearl adds layers of nacre around a grain of sand. I guess you could call it onion growing but it doesn't sound quite so nice! To be honest, this is one of my favorite and most frequently used techniques.

6. Available on the Web at http://www.bls.gov/oco/.

7. Just in case you had a momentary mental lapse, "what to look for" is: Boolean operators, proximity operators, fields you can search, controlled vocabulary you can use, truncation and wildcard symbols, and limits you can set.

8. Well, they need to be connected to your brain, of course . . .

4
Social Science Databases

Introduction to Subject Databases

Before plunging directly into the nuts and bolts of the following databases, let's pause for a moment to think about the whole idea of subject-specific databases. The following statement may fall into the "duh" category, but sometimes it's good to start with the absolute basics: a subject specific database is a searchable, electronic resource devoted to a particular topic. It focuses on a subject area by only including the journals, books, conferences, or other published materials in that discipline. Naturally, there are journals that are useful and interesting to more than one subject area, and you will discover that some journals are indexed in several different databases. But in general, if you are doing research that falls into an identifiable subject area, working with the appropriate subject databases is the most efficient, effective way to pursue that research. Why is a subject database better than a Web search in this case? A Web search is just that: it will find *Web pages* and various other media that are freely available on the Web, but it is not an organized, structured index of commercially published material. A Web search is by definition "all subjects"—it's anything the search engine's indexing program has picked up. A Web search may well find someone's paper, if they have put it on the Web, or a reference to a paper within another paper that someone put on their Web site. But it is *not* a complete, orderly scan of all the appropriate journals and other published materials in a subject area. That kind of organized, thorough, ongoing effort implies an organization, staff, and money, and is not something anyone is going to give away for free. They are each very powerful in their way, but subject databases and Web search engines are very different animals.

How do you know what databases there are for your subject? Go to the Web site of any major university, find the university library page, and look for links such as "databases," "electronic resources," "subject guides," or "resources by subject." Almost all institutions of higher education at the university (and certainly many at the college level now as well) will have so many of these databases that they will offer a list of them "by subject." Simply roving the alphabetical list, you will probably be amazed at the number and variety of different databases that are out there.

The number and variety of databases on the market is remarkable. But who knew? Even though they are different kinds of things, why don't at least some of these databases have the name recognition of Google? Is it simply the difference between free and fee? Access to the subject databases is all by subscription, but you certainly get value for money. Yet compared to Web search engines, subject databases are almost unknown among the general public, and this is a shame, because they are so good at what they do.

This chapter will look at three databases that support research in the social sciences. There are many more, of course, but these three will make us look at three different interfaces, and are each significant in their own way.

Library Literature & Information Science

Background and Coverage

Since many readers of this book will probably be librarians or library school students, it seems only right to start with the original database of librarianship: H.W. Wilson's *Library Literature & Information Science*. Started as a print index in 1921, *Library Literature* has been available online for many years, first through Dialog, and since the movement of databases to the Web, via Wilson's own WilsonWeb. A full-text version has been available since 2000. The WilsonWeb database provides indexing for materials back to the early 1980s, and full text dating from 1997. While there are two other library science specific databases (LISA—*Library & Information Science Abstracts*, and ISTA—*Information Science & Technology Abstracts*), and other databases that index some library journals, *Library Literature* still stands out for "its high-quality indexing, full text, complete coverage of the journals that are indexed, and participation of an advisory committee for journal title selection (Tenopir, 2003)." In addition to journal and review articles, *Library Literature* has records for books, book chapters, conference proceedings, library school theses, and pamphlets. Coverage is international.

Notes and Search Examples

Advanced Search Interface

Let's take a look at the Advanced Search interface (Figure 4.1). What are all the parts and what do they do?

- Tan section at top: access to other databases
- Buttons on left: access other search modes, indexes, thesaurus, and output functions
- Central search area (white): text input fields, Boolean operators, limit options, and a Sort function

Fig. 4.1. *Library Literature* Advanced Search interface. Reproduced with permission from the H.W. Wilson Company.

- Note the "as" drop-downs—all the fields this database uses
- Bottom blue bar: contextual function buttons. Keep your eye on this bar; it's easy to overlook, and often a crucial function (such as "Back") is located here. (In some cases using the browser's Back button can lead to problems; the database would really prefer you use its Back button.)

Library Literature Thesaurus

One of the great strengths of the *Library Literature* database is its Thesaurus; a hierarchical guide to the subject headings of this database, in a sense, the language of librarianship. For example, we might go to the Thesaurus and look up OPAC (Figure 4.2), the acronym for Online Public Access Catalog. Since "OPAC" is one of the "Used for" terms, the Thesaurus system automatically takes you to the subject heading "Online Catalogs," as shown in Figure 4.3.

"Online Catalogs" is the term the Thesaurus designers have decided will be the subject heading assigned to all articles on this topic, no matter how it is referred to in the article itself. The "Used for" terms represent many possible variants that people might look up (as we just did), and guides them to the one subject heading they need to search on and retrieve all the material on this topic. As noted before in discussing controlled vocabulary: otherwise we might have to think of all these variations and search them all. A good set of subject headings, consistently applied, makes searching so efficient.

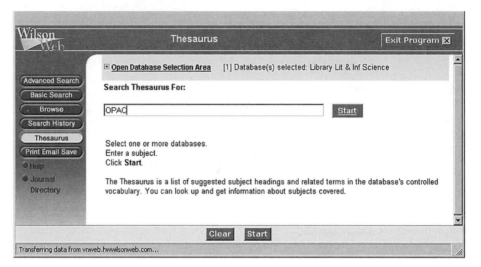

Fig. 4.2. *Library Literature* Thesaurus interface. Reproduced with permission from the H.W. Wilson Company.

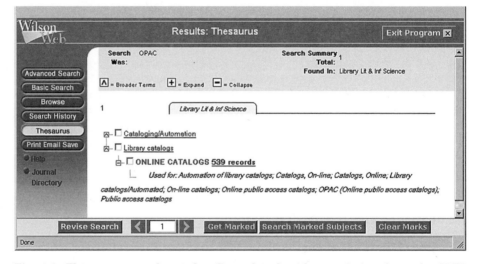

Fig. 4.3. Thesaurus search results. Reproduced with permission from the H.W. Wilson Company.

Sidebar 4.1. Analyzing Disparities in Subject Heading Results in Library Literature

A small *caveat emptor* regarding the *Library Literature* Thesaurus: while it guides you to the appropriate term or phrase to use, it may not be exactly equivalent (in terms of number of records) to entering the term or phrase, and searching it as a subject via the search interface. Consider the following.

If you look up "information seeking" in the Thesaurus, you are presented with the heading Information Needs, and told that it is "Used for" Information-seeking behavior, among other terms. As of April 2005, the Thesaurus states there are 360 records associated with Information Needs. (If you click that 360 record link, your search results will show 442 records. That discrepancy was small enough that I decided to ignore it.) However, if you go back to the Advanced Search interface, and enter the search:

Information Needs as: Subject(s)

The system returns 1674 records! This discrepancy is too large to ignore. What can account for it?

Checking the "Browse" index begins to show why: if you Browse Information Needs as a Subject, you discover that, indeed, "Information Needs" just by itself is associated with 360 records. However, the subject heading Information Needs has a plethora of additional subheadings, both of locations (e.g., Information needs/Australia) and of topics (e.g., Information needs/Case studies). By searching the heading via the Advanced Search interface, it is picking up the phrase wherever it appears in a subject heading, that is, with any subheading (/term or phrase), or even possibly embedded in some other subject heading. The syntax reflected in the "Current Search" statement at the top of the screen indicates that something different is going on in each case: searched as a subject heading unto itself (by searching directly from the Thesaurus or the Browse index), the syntax is:

(<yesno>("~/Information needs/~" <IN> SU))

Searched against the Subject(s) field in the Advanced Search screen, the syntax is much simpler:

(Information Needs) <in> SU

There is nothing wrong with any of this, *per se*. It is only that because the Thesaurus does not give any indication of all the possible subheadings, you might either: (a) miss a great many useful articles searching just from the Thesaurus, or (b) be quite surprised by greater number of results when searching the (apparently) same term by typing it into the search interface.

In sum, just a cautionary note that while the Thesaurus is very useful, and can really help you sort out the best term(s) to use—it doesn't hurt to also Browse the subject index, or use what you find in the Thesaurus and enter it yourself in the search interface. It might make an important difference.

Search Example 1

We'd like to find articles on how library school curriculum is changing in response to advances in information technology (IT).

Identifying Terms Using the Thesaurus

Since we know this database is already focused on libraries and librarians, we might start by typing:

changing curriculum

into the Thesaurus.

Figure 4.4 demonstrates another great feature of this Thesaurus system: if the word or phrase you type in does not exactly match a subject heading or "used for" term, rather than leaving you high and dry with a "not found" message, it offers suggestions. The suggestions are usually quite

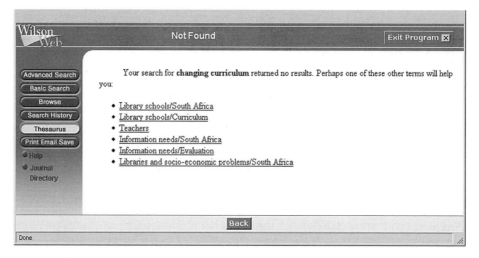

Fig. 4.4. Thesaurus "Not Found" suggestions. Reproduced with permission from the H.W. Wilson Company.

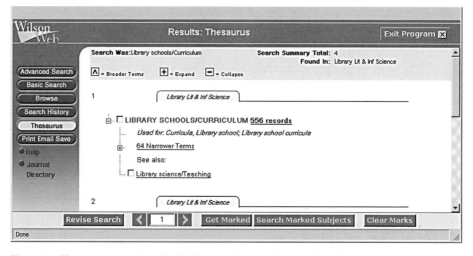

Fig. 4.5. Thesaurus results for "Library Schools/Curriculum." Reproduced with permission from the H.W. Wilson Company.

useful, and often rather interesting (you wonder what's going on in the "suggestion algorithm" to produce the results). Obviously the most appropriate suggestion here is the second one: Library schools/Curriculum. Clicking that brings us to the next screen (Figure 4.5), where there are both useful and frustrating features.

In Figure 4.5 we are in the Thesaurus at Library Schools/Curriculum. It's useful to know there are 556 records that have been assigned this heading, and that there are sixty-four (!) "narrower" terms we might want to explore, as well as a related term ("See also"). If you scroll down, you will see there is also the additional, even more specific, subject heading of "Library Schools/Curriculum/Syllabi." At this point things get slightly awkward.

Fig. 4.6. Advanced Search Strategy using Thesaurus entries and keyword. Reproduced with permission from the H.W. Wilson Company.

Thesaurus Limitations

You can click the checkboxes of the headings in red, or of any of the sixty-four narrower terms, and then click the "Get Marked" (which will add the headings to a continuing list) or "Search Marked Subjects" buttons at the bottom of the screen. However, clicking multiple checkboxes has the result of ORing the multiple entries together. There is no way to opt for an AND effect, nor is there any way to AND in a keyword. We encountered a similar problem with the *MasterFILE Select* Subject list: you can quickly pick something from the list, but there is no easy way to combine, in an AND sense, more than one concept. Also, as with *MasterFILE*, there is no easy way to integrate a Thesaurus search with the Advanced Search. So we'll learn all we can from the Thesaurus, and then use that knowledge in the Advanced Search screen by typing in what we now know are good subject terms, and adding a keyword to focus our search, as shown in Figure 4.6.

(Trust me, the results are quite good.)

Browsing Library Literature Indexes

The Browse button is your way to see the raw contents of the *Library Literature* index lists (cf. the index browsing in FirstSearch in Figures 1.4 and 1.5 in Chapter 1). It is a strictly alphabetical, "left-anchored" list—you only get terms *beginning* with whatever word you put in. If the term you entered doesn't exactly match anything in the index list you chose, the message "your term would have been here" appears in the appropriate alphabetical spot.

Browse is a quick way to check the spelling of an author's name, to see if a term is a Subject, to find out if a particular journal is indexed by *Library Literature*, or to check the content of any of a number of other indexed fields.

Fig. 4.7. Browsing the Document Type index. Reproduced with permission from the H.W. Wilson Company.

For some of the fields, it would be useful if you could simply see what all the valid entries are: document type, for example. In that case, putting in any term, and letting the index come up with its "your term would have been here" message, in the list of other valid entries, can be quite useful (Figure 4.7).

Browse Exercises

Try looking up "librarians in film" as a Subject in Browse. Use your eyes! Look at the other entries in the list. Even if you don't hit exactly the right wording with what you typed in, often the subject heading you need will be nearby. Now compare the results of looking up "interlibrary loan" by Browsing the Subject Index, and as a term in the Thesaurus.

Search Example 2

You want to find some information on chat services as part of reference. You start by looking up "reference chat" in the Thesaurus. It suggests:

Reference Services/Automation, among other things (Figure 4.8)—it's quite smart, this suggestion screen.

Reference services/Automation is a good term, but if you follow the link, you'll see there is a daunting number of articles associated with it. And as noted previously, there's no way to select this term from the Thesaurus, then AND in a free text term to focus the results to only articles about "chat" services. We'll use what we've discovered here and set up the Advanced Search ourselves.

Fig. 4.8. Thesaurus suggestions for "Reference Chat." Reproduced with permission from the H.W. Wilson Company.

Copy and paste (to save typing) the "Reference Services/Automation" heading into the Advanced search screen (search as: Subject), plus let's use another term we saw suggested: in the next field, OR in "Instant messaging" as a Subject. Then AND in "chat" as a Keyword. Voila! An excellent collection of articles on a timely topic.

Working with Results: Mark and Output

Marking Selected Results

No matter how good your search skills are, there are bound to be items in your results that are not as useful as the others. The database vendors understand this, and therefore will generally offer a "marking" functionality, usually with checkboxes. You click the checkboxes of all the entries in your results list that you want to output from the database. Typical output options are to print or save, and many database vendors offer an e-mail (send records and/or full text to yourself) option as well.

Output Options

Wilson offers the options of: "Print Email Save." The "Print Email Save" screen (Figure 4.9) is nicely laid out so you can choose to display only the information pertaining to the function you are going to use:
Note in particular:

- You can include your "Search History."
- On the Print screen, the "Estimate" number of printed pages function is very useful.
- You can send just "Marked Records" or all records or a range of records.

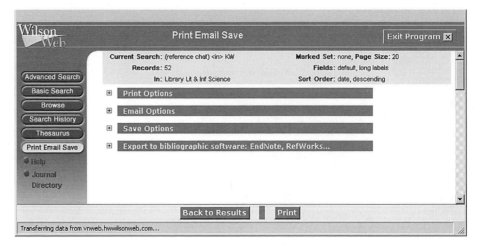

Fig. 4.9. "Print EMail Save" output interface. Reproduced with permission from the H.W. Wilson Company.

- Mail to: allows you to send to multiple addresses using a semicolon in-between, like this: me@mine.edu; you@yours.edu.
- You get to fill in the "Mail subject" (this is important especially if you are sending results to someone else, because a system-supplied subject and the unfamiliar sender e-mail address will tend to make such messages look like spam, and cause your recipient to delete it without looking at it).

Quick Recap

H. W. Wilson's *Library Literature & Information Science* is the oldest and longest running index devoted to this field. *Library Literature* indexes journal articles, books, book chapters, conference proceedings, library school theses, and pamphlets. Materials are mainly in English, but coverage is international, and a number of other languages are represented. The *Library Literature* Thesaurus is custom-built for this database, and is an important tool for discovering subject headings and relationships between headings. The Browse button provides access to the contents of many fields, arranged as alphabetical lists. Browse is useful for seeing all the possible subheadings that have been applied to a Subject Heading, and for discovering all the possible values for a field, such as language. The Advanced Search interface provides a number of useful limits. Note that navigation buttons such as Back and Revise Search, and function buttons such as Search Marked Subjects and the Full/Brief record display toggle, are located at the *bottom* of the screen.

ERIC via Firstsearch

Background and Coverage

ERIC, the Education Resources Information Center, is another database with a long history of excellence, which has recently gone through some significant changes. ERIC was a "born digital" effort: in 1966, the

Department of Education established 16 "clearinghouses," each with its own educational subject specialty, to "gather, index, and input bibliographic information" (Tenopir, 2004) for journal articles as well as documents known as "grey literature." Grey literature is material that has not been commercially published, but has scholarly value: papers presented at conferences, progress reports, working papers, technical reports, lab notebooks, student papers, curriculum guides, and so forth. One of the great contributions of the ERIC database was the amount of effort put in to gathering, evaluating, indexing, inputting, and making available (via a microfiche program) a vast amount of otherwise unpublished and inaccessible, but valuable, grey literature. At over 1 million records, the ERIC database is now the largest, and foremost, subject resource for education.

But what the government creates, the government can change. Starting with the Education Sciences Reform Act of 2002, the ERIC effort began to change. In December of 2003, the sixteen clearinghouses were closed, "as part of an effort to revamp, streamline, and centralize" the system (Viadero, 2004). The Education Department's goals were laudable: one centralized, easy-to-use resource, with more full-text. What followed, however, was a period of interregnum: the database and the materials already indexed continued to be available, but no new material was being added, even though production continued apace. The issue of this ever-mounting backlog troubled many in the Education community. Thankfully, it appears that the loading of new materials has resumed, and further agreements with previous and new suppliers of material are in process (Institute of Education Services, 2005), ensuring the continued viability of this important resource.

Luckily, even when there were sixteen clearinghouses offering various services in support of their educational topic area, there was still only one ERIC *database* to which they all contributed records. A variety of vendors contract with the Department of Education to obtain the ERIC data, and each vendor then offers the database via their own search interface. (In addition to these choices, the Education Department also provides free access to ERIC via their own Web site.) We'll take a look at the "flavor" provided by OCLC's FirstSearch system. We've already had a preliminary introduction to this search interface in Chapter 1.

Notes and Search Examples

Advanced Search Interface

Functions and Fields

Take a look at Figure 4.10. What do we have here? You'll find many of the same functions as in the WilsonWeb interface, but arranged differently: here everything is arranged in horizontal bands rather than having a separate set of navigation buttons on the left side. Starting from the top, we have tabs for major locations: Home, Databases (to change to another First-Search database), Searching, and Resource Sharing. Since we are in Search mode, the next band offers buttons relating to searching, either to change the type of search (Basic, Advanced, or Expert), or to review what you've tried so far in the current session: your Search History. Next band: two useful buttons, Subjects and Help, as well as News, and a reminder of which database you are currently using. The Subjects button is your access to the ERIC Thesaurus, which we will return to later. This brings us to the main area, devoted to setting up your search and applying limits. The very first drop-down menu, however, is yet another chance to switch databases: you'll

Fig. 4.10. ERIC via FirstSearch: Advanced Search interface. Screen shots used with permission of OCLC; FirstSearch and WorldCat are registered trademarks of OCLC Online Computer Library Center, Inc.

find this is a common theme in the interfaces of vendors that supply many databases. But here we are in familiar territory! Search boxes, the opportunity to restrict the search to a particular field, Boolean operators, and limit capabilities. The icons at the end of the text input field selector drop-downs are the equivalent of WilsonWeb's "Browse" button: your access to the lists of terms in the database's many indexes (see the black, lozenge-shaped buttons with white up-down indicators). These indexes were first introduced in Chapter 1, Figure 1.3; as noted there, FirstSearch has separate indexes for single words and for phrases.

Limits

In addition to the three most common types of limits (year, language, and document type), FirstSearch offers some very useful "availability" limits, such as the library at your own institution. The FirstSearch databases have a bit of an inside track here, because they are OCLC products. Libraries around the world contribute their catalog records to OCLC, which then, among many other uses, produces from these records the largest union catalog in the world (we'll meet this as a database called *WorldCat* in Chapter 6). They have been able to integrate the information from the catalog records with their article databases, and thus provide a limit based on what they know of your library's (or any "contributing" library's) holdings. It's quite a nice reuse of already existing information.

Ranking

Finally, you can "rank" your results, if you wish, by relevance or by date. Relevance is mainly applicable if you are only doing keyword searches. Making use of subject headings and field searching should ensure that your results are "relevant." The default, "No ranking," will display the results in the order in which they were added to the database, which is not quite the same as a strictly chronological list.

Search Example 1

The search example we'll use for our tour of the ERIC database is to find material on teaching deaf students.

As noted previously, FirstSearch uses the label "Descriptors" for its subject heading fields. There are two sets of subject fields for each record: major and minor. ERIC records are so carefully analyzed that they are assigned both Major and Minor Descriptors, that is, subject headings for both the primary and secondary topics in the article or document. Since we know that we want material that is focused on deaf students, it suggests we look for a term in the "Major Descriptors" field, so we might go straight to checking the index of terms in the Major Descriptors field. By clicking one of the black, "up-down" indicator icons (that follow each field drop-down menu in the Advanced screen), we can get into and Browse the Major Descriptors index for "deaf" (Figure 4.11).

But here is a dilemma—the index includes both "deaf" and "deafness." Which is more appropriate, or doesn't it matter? If there are two terms, it suggests that it might well matter. The answer can be found in the ERIC Thesaurus, which is accessed via the "Subjects" icon. (In Figure 4.10, the Subjects icon is located immediately below the "Basic Search" link.)

ERIC Thesaurus

Just as in the *Library Literature* Thesaurus, the system behind the Subjects icon lists all the subject headings used in this database, and displays them in hierarchical, thematic groups. (The field indexes that you can "Browse" are a straight alphabetical list.) Notes are provided to disambiguate meanings, if necessary. Working with this Thesaurus, the indexers then assign the headings as either Major or Minor aspects of each document.

We discover that deaf is really the first half of "deaf blind," if we go into Subjects and type in "deaf," as in Figure 4.12. If we "Expand" that term, we find that "deafness" is a related subject (Figure 4.13).

Department of Confusing Things

If you click on "Deafness" in the Thesaurus screen (Figure 4.13), First-Search will run a search and retrieve *all* the records that have Deafness as either a major or minor descriptor. If you then click on the "Searching"

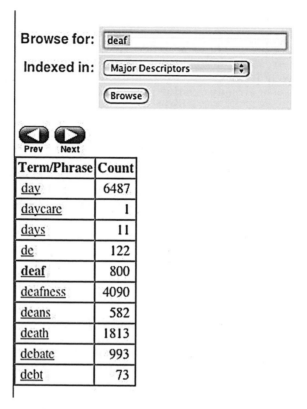

Fig. 4.11. Browsing the Major Descriptors index for "Deaf." Screen shots used with permission of OCLC; FirstSearch and WorldCat are registered trademarks of OCLC Online Computer Library Center, Inc.

Fig. 4.12. Checking the ERIC Thesaurus (Subjects) for "Deaf." Screen shots used with permission of OCLC; FirstSearch and WorldCat are registered trademarks of OCLC Online Computer Library Center, Inc.

Expanded Subject Heading

- Click on the subject heading link to search **ERIC** for that subject heading or click the Expand text link to get more information on that subject.

Fig. 4.13. Expanded ERIC Thesaurus (subject heading) for "Deaf." Screen shots used with permission of OCLC; FirstSearch and WorldCat are registered trademarks of OCLC Online Computer Library Center, Inc.

tab, you'll find that FirstSearch has very helpfully recorded that search, by retaining Deafness in the first search box...and has set the search field for that box to "Subject Phrase." Oh no! Does this mean there are Major Descriptors (single or phrase), and Minor Descriptors (single or phrase), *and* Subjects? I'm afraid it does. Setting the field to Subject (for a single word) or Subject Phrase will search the term or phrase as either a major or minor descriptor. It's really very useful...but it could be confusing.

Back to the Major Descriptors Index

Let's not get too wrapped around the axle about this. We'll stick with the plan, and search deafness as a Major Descriptor. The other concept we were after was about teachers who work with deaf students. Let's browse for the single term "teacher" in the Major Descriptors *phrase* index, to see all the possible phrases that begin with the word teacher (Figure 4.14).

If you keep browsing forward, there are more and more entries beginning with "teacher" (you can certainly tell this is the "education" database!)—and there could be several of these that might be good. Using a truncation symbol, we can pick up any and all of the possibilities.

Final Strategy and Results

Figure 4.15 shows the strategy we decided to use for this search. There are 196 citations in the results list, and they appear to be right on target, as indicated by the initial entries showing in Figure 4.16.

Note the eighth item in the list: it differs from the rest in a couple of ways. Rather than "Source" and the name of a journal, it has "Access ERIC" and a FullText link, and its "Accession No." begins with "ED." This is an example of an *ERIC Document*, one of those pieces of grey literature mentioned in the Background and Coverage section for this database.

Fig. 4.14. Searching a single term in a phrase index. Screen shots used with permission of OCLC; FirstSearch and WorldCat are registered trademarks of OCLC Online Computer Library Center, Inc.

Fig. 4.15. Search strategy for teaching of deaf students. Screen shots used with permission of OCLC; FirstSearch and WorldCat are registered trademarks of OCLC Online Computer Library Center, Inc.

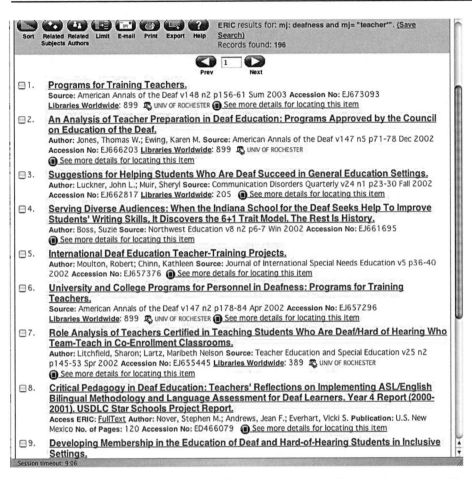

Fig. 4.16. Deafness and Teacher* descriptor search results. Screen shots used with permission of OCLC; FirstSearch and WorldCat are registered trademarks of OCLC Online Computer Library Center, Inc.

Search Example 2

Keywords and Pearl Growing Strategy

In Search Example 1 we used a very structured approach, and carefully checked the indexes and Thesaurus entries before deciding on our search terms and setting up the strategy. Compare that example with the following much less structured approach. We could simply search:

Teaching the deaf—as Keywords

This search results in a great many more records (over 1,000). Looking over the titles visible in Figure 4.17, while some of the results are "on-target," others probably aren't—while our search *recall* has gone up, the *precision* of our search has gone down.

For example, the ideal record that came up first before is now ninth in the list (Figure 4.17). However, what should you immediately do upon seeing that "ideal" record? Take a look at it to find out what subject headings it has,

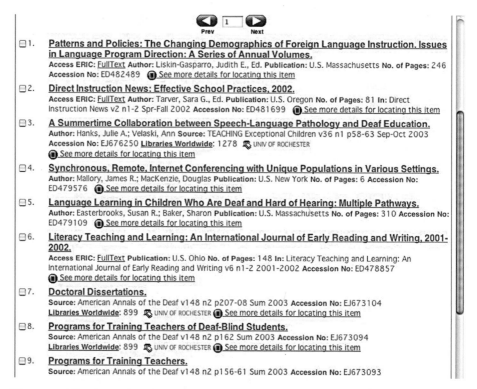

Fig. 4.17. "Teaching the Deaf" keyword search results. Screen shots used with permission of OCLC; FirstSearch and WorldCat are registered trademarks of OCLC Online Computer Library Center, Inc.

and try working one or more back into your strategy, to refine the search, e.g., to "Pearl Grow." The subjects (Major and Minor Descriptors) for record 9 are shown in Figure 4.18.

Ah! Teacher Education Programs—that looks like the perfect heading. However, be aware that while it's very tempting to click on that linked subject heading, if you do—you'll get *all* the records with the heading Teacher Education Programs, but the context of your current search (the "deafness" part) will be left behind. To use this information, you'll need to return to the Searching interface, and type in the phrase (or copy and paste from this page). The revised search might look like Figure 4.19. This search strategy will net you far fewer (but very focused) records.

More Strategy Alternatives

To increase the number of results, you might loosen things up by making deafness a Subject (i.e., either a Major or Minor Descriptor), or just a keyword. You probably have the impression at this point that searching by subject headings is the only way to go, but adhering to only that strategy was not exactly my intention. It *is* an excellent way to increase precision, but it's not the one and only answer. (There is no "one and only" answer!) Always stay flexible. You never know when the indexer might have been having a

SUBJECT(S)

Descriptor: **(Major):** <u>Academic Degrees</u>
<u>Deafness</u>
<u>Hearing Impairments</u>
<u>Institutional Characteristics</u>
<u>Special Programs</u>
<u>Teacher Education Programs</u>
(Minor): <u>College Students</u>
<u>Postsecondary Education</u>
<u>Special Schools</u>
<u>State Programs</u>

Fig. 4.18. Subject headings in record 9. Screen shots used with permission of OCLC; FirstSearch and WorldCat are registered trademarks of OCLC Online Computer Library Center, Inc.

Fig. 4.19. Search example 2 revised by "Pearl Growing." Screen shots used with permission of OCLC; FirstSearch and WorldCat are registered trademarks of OCLC Online Computer Library Center, Inc.

bad day, and didn't assign the best headings, so that the ideal record is only retrievable by keyword. It never hurts to try several strategies.

Expert Search Interface

So far we've stayed with the Advanced Search interface. For those of you who really like to get under the hood and tinker, uninhibited by the constraints of drop-down menus, you can really get into it in the Expert search screen (the mysterious field codes are all provided in the "Indexed in" drop-down menu).

Fig. 4.20. Search strategy in Expert Search interface. Screen shots used with permission of OCLC; FirstSearch and WorldCat are registered trademarks of OCLC Online Computer Library Center, Inc.

Search Example 3

Figure 4.20 shows a search for materials that were assigned the subject heading Adult Students or Nontraditional Students, and in which "college" appears as a Major Descriptor.

This search produces a large number of results. You could arbitrarily limit the results to the past N number of years (which is perfectly valid), or you could, as usual, play with the search: instead of college as a keyword, add "college attendance" as a Minor Descriptor. That might reduce the results a bit too much. Any Minor Descriptor beginning with the word college could potentially be useful, which we could accomplish with the syntax: Mn=college*.

Working with Results: Mark, Functions, and Output

Mark

As you can see in Figures 4.16 and 4.17, each record in your results list has a checkbox associated with it, so you can mark the records you wish to output.

Results Screen Functions

There are a number of functions available in the Results list display, as indicated by the icon bar shown in Figure 4.21.

Sort

Sort is what you would expect: you can sort your results in various ways. Note that the Sort function will not appear for results sets of over 500 records.

Fig. 4.21. Functions available in the Results List display. Screen shots used with permission of OCLC; FirstSearch and World-Cat are registered trademarks of OCLC Online Computer Library Center, Inc.

Related Subjects

Be somewhat wary of the "Related Subjects" option: all of the subjects you check are "ORed" together, which might not be the effect you were after. On the other hand, you could make that work to your advantage: you could mark a number of subjects, search them, and then click back on the Searching tab from the results list. At that point you could AND in a new term (ERIC will have transferred the search syntax for the string of ORed terms into the first search field), and focus your search back down.

Related Authors

Related authors will show a list of all the authors represented in the current results list. The ones at the top of the list are those with the most articles, thus, are the names that may be important to you as you continue your research.

Limit

Limit provides the opportunity to add limits to your search without having to return to the main search screen.

E-mail, Print, Export, and Help

E-mail and print are the usual useful output options. Export is a feature that not all databases offer: it is a way to download citations directly into applications such as EndNote or RefWorks, or to produce a text file that can be imported into Reference Manager or ProCite. All of these applications are used for creating correctly formatted footnotes, endnotes, and bibliographies. And if you're in doubt about anything—there's the Help!

Quick Recap

ERIC, the Education Resources Information Center, is produced by the U.S. Department of Education. It is the premier database for Education, and dates back to 1966. ERIC indexes journal articles as well as "grey literature"—scholarly works that have not been commercially published. The ERIC database is offered by many different vendors, as well as being freely available at the Education Department's Web site. ERIC via First-Search offers many searchable fields, and browsable single word and phrase indexes. The indexes are accessed via an icon following each text input field in the advanced interface. The hierarchy of ERIC subject headings (the ERIC Thesaurus) can be browsed via the "Subjects" icon in the upper left area of the interface. Note that the field name for subject headings in First-Search is "Descriptors." The advanced search interface offers year, language, and document type limits, as well as an "availability" limit ("my library" or another specific library) that is unique to FirstSearch databases. (Made possible because the vendor, OCLC, also offers the WorldCat database of library holdings records.)

PsycINFO® from Ovid

Background and Coverage

PsycINFO is the online version of the American Psychological Association's venerable *Psychological Abstracts*, a print abstracting and indexing service dating from 1927. *PsycINFO* is probably the largest, and most well-known, index of the literature of psychology and the behavioral sciences. In addition to journal articles, document types indexed in the database include books and book chapters, dissertations, and electronic collections. The American Psychological Association (APA) draws on international sources, with journals in more than twenty-five languages, and English language books and book chapters from all over the world ("OCLC" 1998). The Thesaurus terms (subject headings) used to index entries in the *PsycINFO* database are developed and applied by APA indexers.

One of the truly remarkable features of *PsycINFO* is the range of time it covers. *PsycINFO* has abstracts of books and journal articles dating from as early as 1806, although most journals are from the 1880s to the present and the majority of books are from 1987 to the present. The database is updated weekly, and the latest updated week is reflected in the search interface (see Figure 4.22). As noted in the Ovid Technologies, Inc. (2005) "Field Guide" for this database, "over 80,000 references are added annually" via the weekly updates.

Like ERIC, the *PsycINFO* online database is available from quite a few different vendors. Depending on which vendor and what backfile option your institution has chosen to subscribe to, you may have access to the complete file in one database, or the file may be divided in various ways, and you may have access to all or only to the most recent file.

Extensive Set of Search Fields

Another aspect of the *PsycINFO* database that sets it in a class by itself is the amazing array of search fields the database developers decided to build in to the record structure. If you thought ERIC had a lot of fields ... take a look at the following list.

Some of the fields listed are recent and very topical additions, which deserve a few extra words of explanation:

- Cited references (the article's bibliography)
- Supplemental material (a field that notes that there is material in the online full text that is not in the printed full text)

Abstract	Format Covered	Publication Month/Season
Accession Number	Heading Word	Publication Type
Age Group	ISBN	Publisher Information
Author	ISSN Electronic	Publisher Location
Book Series Title	ISSN Print	Publisher URL
Cited Reference	Institution	Reprint Year
Cited Reference author	Intended Audience	Reviewed Item
Cited Reference Author Word	Issue/Part	Source
Cited Reference DOI	Journal Name	Special Issue Title
Cited Reference Date	Journal URL	Subject Headings
Cited Reference Publisher	Journal Word	Supplemental Material
Cited Reference Source	Key Concepts	Table of Contents
Cited Reference Title	Language	Tests & Measures
Classification Code	Location	Title
Classification Code Word	Notes	Translated Book Series Title
Conference Information	Original Title	Translated Parent Book Title
Corporate/Institutional Author	Pagination	UMI Dissertation Order Number
Correspondence Address	Parent Book Author	URL
Digital Object Identifier (DOI)	Parent Book Institutional Author	Update Code
Form/Content Type	Parent Book Title	Volume
Format Availability	Population Group	Year of Publication

- DOI, Journal URL, Publisher URL (all fields to help users link to full text if their library holdings do not allow direct access)
- Tests & Measures (a new field listing tests used in the study, plus an indicator if the test is actually printed in the article)

Lastly, the latest addition to the record structure is a "Peer review" field, to indicate for users that a journal is peer reviewed.

Why Look at Ovid's *PsycINFO*

We're going to take a look at *PsycINFO* as offered by the database vendor Ovid. The Ovid interface differs from the previous two we've seen so far in a couple of interesting, and to me, quite useful ways:

- It has a built-in "map to subject heading" feature that tries to offer you the best subject heading choices based on what you type in.
- It encourages you to build your search one concept at a time, which turns out to be very handy because when you have all the conceptual pieces, it is then very easy to experiment with putting them together in different combinations.

Fig. 4.22. *PsycINFO* Advanced Search interface. *PsycINFO* screen shots are reprinted with permission of the American Psychological Association, publisher of the *PsycINFO* database, all rights reserved. OVID interface © 2005 Ovid Technologies Inc.

Notes and Search Examples

What do you notice about the interface shown in Figure 4.22? The first thing that strikes me, after looking at the Wilson and FirstSearch advanced search screens, is how much simpler this appears. There is just as much power here, but the initial impression is perhaps less daunting.

Advanced Search Interface

Let's work through the areas of the Advanced interface, from top to bottom. The topmost area contains the usual database identification information, to make it very clear what database (and dates) you are searching. As with the other vendors that offer many databases, you are provided with a link to change to another Ovid-provided database. This is also where you can access any saved searches or "alerting" searches you have set up.

Next is the Search History table, which will become very important as you work in this database. As mentioned above, you'll build your search one step at a time, with the results of each step recorded in the "Search History" display. These individual "search elements" can then be combined in various ways, as we will see.

Then we have the search interface region. There is only one text entry field, and the "Map Term to Subject Heading" option is turned on by default. The keyword or phrase search mode is also a default, but if you want to search for an author's name, the title of a work, or for a particular journal (to see if it is indexed in this database, for example), the buttons above the search box provide easy access to those other search modes. In addition, the More Fields icon takes you to a screen where you restrict your search to a particular field by clicking its checkbox. (This is quite different from the drop-down menu approach.) The Search Tools icon provides direct search access to the supporting materials, such as the Thesaurus and scope notes (definitions of subject headings), which govern the content of *PsycINFO*.

The Limits area is clearly set off below the search section. The standard limits you might want to invoke are ready and waiting (more detailed limits are available, via the "More Limits" icon). Note that a standard limit in this subject area is "Human" (to rule out articles about tests or studies on animals).

Here is what the Ovid interface is like to use.

Search Example 1

We'd like to search the psychological literature for material on the effect of Peer Pressure on Self-Esteem.

We'll start by typing into the search box:
peer pressure

and pressing return. This brings up the "Mapping Display" screen, shown in Figure 4.23.

The Mapping Display

Because the "Map Term to Subject Heading" feature was turned on, the system automatically tries to match, or "map" what you type in against its Thesaurus, the hierarchical list of subject headings for *PsycINFO*. The results can be quite fascinating, because even in the case of an exact match (as we have here: Peer Pressure is a subject heading), the system also offers all the other headings that have a Thesaurus relationship to this heading, that is, they are broader, narrower, or "related." The immense amount of thought the Thesaurus designers put into their product can make your searching life so much easier, suggesting relationships and lines of thought that might not have occurred to you.

Each heading has two options: Auto-Explode (if you scroll down, the interface explains that this will pick up the heading and any narrower headings, ones indented below it in the hierarchy), and Focus. Focus is equivalent to FirstSearch's "Major Descriptors," it means that the indexers decided the heading was a main aspect, or "focus," of the article. Only a few of the subject headings assigned to an article will be designated as a "Focus," so you may want to use it sparingly in the initial phases of your search.

For the current search, we'll leave "Auto-Explode" on, but won't check "Focus"—we'll leave it a little more open. Clicking the "continue" button returns us to the main search page, which now displays our search history, the interface to start another search, and the beginning of our results list, as shown in Figure 4.24.

Fig. 4.23. *PsycINFO* Mapping Display for Peer Pressure. *PsycINFO* screen shots are reprinted with permission of the American Psychological Association, publisher of the *PsycINFO* database, all rights reserved. OVID interface © 2005 Ovid Technologies Inc.

Building the search

Now to add the second concept of our search, by typing:

self-esteem

into the search box. Again, this maps exactly to a subject heading.

As shown in Figure 4.25, this time we'll click the "Focus" box, because we really want the main theme of these articles to be about self-esteem. There should be over 10,000 results for this search.

Combining Search History Sets

Now we will combine the results of these two searches. We could use the "Combine Searches" icon, but here's an insider's shortcut—you can simply type:

1 and 2

into the search box, as shown in Figure 4.26. (Or whatever numbers correspond to the searches in your "search history" that you wish to combine.)

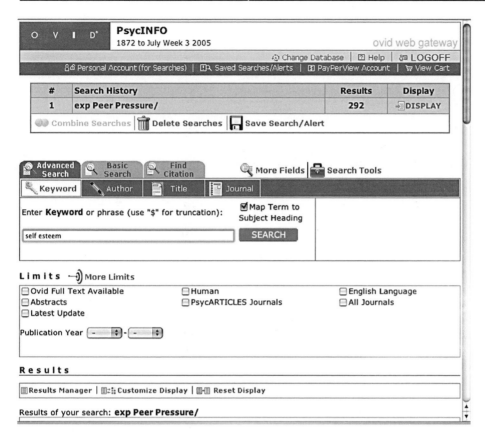

Fig. 4.24. Return to main page: Search History, Next Search, and Results. *PsycINFO* screen shots are reprinted with permission of the American Psychological Association, publisher of the *PsycINFO* database, all rights reserved. OVID interface © 2005 Ovid Technologies Inc.

You can use any of the Boolean operators, and parentheses for making nested statements, to combine Search History set numbers. Each variation will, of course, produce a set of results that differs to a greater or lesser extent. If you have built up a series of searches, this is a very fast and easy way to experiment with them, to arrive at an "optimal" set of results.

Results

Presto: our combined sets result in ten articles, as indicated at the very top of Figure 4.27. The result list begins further down on the same screen (allowing us to see the search history, search interface, and results all on the same page). If the first result is any indication, all ten may be perfect, but ten isn't a lot. How might we get more?

Search Example 1 Redone

Getting More with OR

Let's do this search again. We'll type "peer pressure" into the search box again. This time in the Mapping Display, let's select some more terms in addition to Peer Pressure. Note the "Combine selections with" drop-down

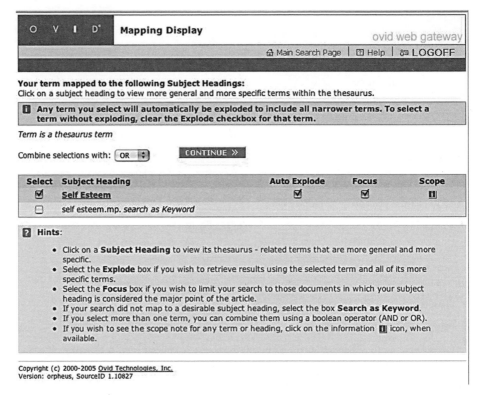

Fig. 4.25. Mapping display for "Self-Esteem." *PsycINFO* screen shots are reprinted with permission of the American Psychological Association, publisher of the *PsycINFO* database, all rights reserved. OVID interface © 2005 Ovid Technologies Inc.

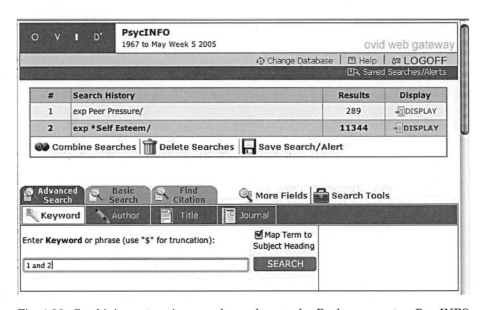

Fig. 4.26. Combining sets using search numbers and a Boolean operator. *PsycINFO* screen shots are reprinted with permission of the American Psychological Association, publisher of the *PsycINFO* database, all rights reserved. OVID interface © 2005 Ovid Technologies Inc.

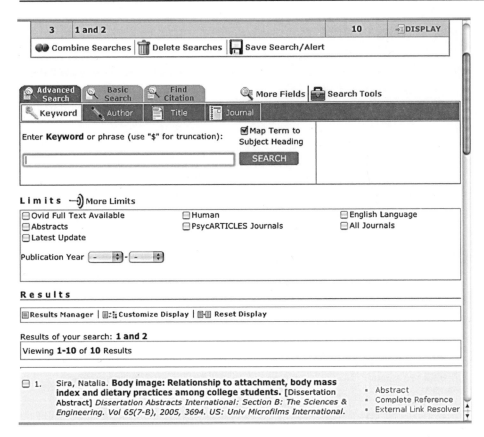

Fig. 4.27. Result of combining sets 1 and 2: ten articles. *PsycINFO* screen shots are reprinted with permission of the American Psychological Association, publisher of the *PsycINFO* database, all rights reserved. OVID interface © 2005 Ovid Technologies Inc.

at the top of the page. It's set to: OR, which is what we want. After picking several headings and ORing them together, yes, the number of results is enormous (search set 4 in Figure 4.28).

Don't panic.

Combining from the Search History

There were LOTS of hits for self-esteem when we searched it before, so let's re-use that search, and combine it with our new set of "peer" topics (here is the beauty of quickly and easily reusing previous sets). Simply type the numbers of the sets you want to combine into the search box, in this case: 2 and 4.

Applying Limits

OK, 724 records is still a lot. Still, don't panic. Let's make use of some of those limits that are so easily provided in the interface: English Language, and Publication Year. If a list of 348 results still seems daunting, try another limit: to Full Text. Simply select the Limits you want to use, and click the "Search" button. It feels odd, because there is nothing in the input field

Fig. 4.28. Result of selecting several subject headings related to Peer Pressure. *PsycINFO* screen shots are reprinted with permission of the American Psychological Association, publisher of the *PsycINFO* database, all rights reserved. OVID interface © 2005 Ovid Technologies Inc.

next to the "Search" button, but the system understands you are applying limits.

Ahhh—19. Now that's a manageable set of results (Figure 4.29).

More Search History Advantages

The Ovid "piece-by-piece" approach to searching is also helpful if you decide to change direction as you're working. If you get a new idea, you simply start that new thread, and then experiment with combining it with previous searches. You can delete searches if you're really sure they aren't useful (see the trash can icon below the Search History), but you can also just keep adding new ones. Although the interface will default to showing you only the four or five most recent searches, note the small "Expand" tab on the upper right of the Search History table.

Figure 4.30 shows an example of adding a new search (for material about advertising), and seeing the results of combining it with previous searches. We find that the new search set 8 does not intersect with search

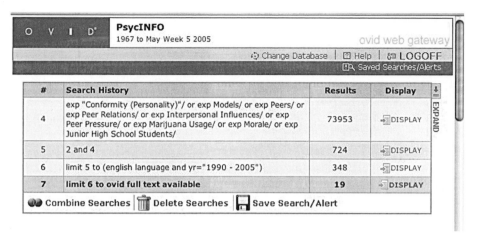

Fig. 4.29. Applying limits to reduce numbers of results. *PsycINFO* screen shots are reprinted with permission of the American Psychological Association, publisher of the *PsycINFO* database, all rights reserved. OVID interface © 2005 Ovid Technologies Inc.

#	Search History	Results	Display	
1	exp Peer Pressure/	289	DISPLAY	
2	exp *Self Esteem/	11344	DISPLAY	C O N T R A C T
3	1 and 2	10	DISPLAY	
4	exp "Conformity (Personality)"/ or exp Models/ or exp Peers/ or exp Peer Relations/ or exp Interpersonal Influences/ or exp Peer Pressure/ or exp Marijuana Usage/ or exp Morale/ or exp Junior High School Students/	73953	DISPLAY	
5	2 and 4	724	DISPLAY	
6	limit 5 to (english language and yr="1990 - 2005")	348	DISPLAY	
7	limit 6 to ovid full text available	19	DISPLAY	
8	exp TELEVISION ADVERTISING/ or exp ADVERTISING/ or advertising.mp.	6334	DISPLAY	
9	6 and 8	0	-	
10	2 and 8	25	DISPLAY	

Combine Searches | Delete Searches | Save Search/Alert

Fig. 4.30. More search history combinations. *PsycINFO* screen shots are reprinted with permission of the American Psychological Association, publisher of the *PsycINFO* database, all rights reserved. OVID interface © 2005 Ovid Technologies Inc.

set 6 at all (ANDing them together produces zero results), so we simply try combining set 8 with an earlier, larger set, 2. This combination results in twenty-five citations, a very comfortable number.

> ☑ 10. Lennon, Sharron J; Lillethun, Abby; Buckland, Sandra S. **Attitudes toward Social Comparison as a Function of Self-Esteem: Idealized Appearance and Body Image. [References].** [Peer Reviewed Journal] *Family & Consumer Sciences Research Journal. Vol 27(4) Jun 1999, 379-405. Sage Publications, US*
>
>   · Abstract
>   · Complete Reference
>   · Library Holdings
>   · ⑤ Find Text
>
>   ☐/☐Find Citing Articles

Fig. 4.31. The "Results Manager." *PsycINFO* screen shots are reprinted with permission of the American Psychological Association, publisher of the *PsycINFO* database, all rights reserved. OVID interface © 2005 Ovid Technologies Inc.

Working with Results: the "Results Manager"

The first ten results of the latest search are always listed on the main search page, starting below the Limits area (cf. Figure 4.27). Like the other databases we've been looking at, you mark the citations of interest by clicking their checkboxes. At the bottom of each page, the "Results Manager" Table (Figure 4.31) offers many options for handling your results: marked items can be printed, e-mailed, or saved, or exported to a bibliographic software application. You can choose exactly which fields to include, and even sort the records in a particular way.

Additional Feature: The *PsycINFO* Thesaurus

You can directly access the *PsycINFO* Thesaurus by going to the Search Tools interface, selecting the Thesaurus, and entering a term. You can also access it from the Mapping Display screen in the course of a search, by clicking on any of the linked subject headings (Figure 4.23 shows a good example of a list of linked subject headings in a Mapping Display). In either case, you'll get taken to the Thesaurus display for that term. This allows you to see how the term fits into the hierarchy, what "narrower" terms will be included if you leave the "Auto-Explode" box checked, what terms are broader, what terms are related, as indicated in Figure 4.32. It can be quite interesting to wander around in the Thesaurus for a bit.

Combine selections with: [OR ↕] [CONTINUE »]

Thesaurus for **Stress**
Database: PsycINFO

Select Term(s)	Subject Heading	Hits	Explode	Focus	Scope Note
▲	[Back up in List]				
☐	Stranger Reactions	324	☐	☐	◘
☐	Strategies	8946	☐	☐	◘
	Strategies (Learning)				
	Strength (Physical)				
☑	**Stress**	**24047**	☐	☐	◘
	[Narrower Terms]				◘
☐	Chronic Stress	165	☐	☐	◘
☐	Environmental Stress	905	☐	☐	◘
☐	Occupational Stress	9153	☐	☐	◘
☐	Physiological Stress	2305	☐	☐	◘
☐	Psychological Stress	5256	☐	☐	◘
☐	Social Stress	1147	☐	☐	◘
☐	Stress Reactions	7373	☐	☐	◘
	[Related Terms]				◘
☐	Adjustment Disorders	243	☐	☐	◘
☐	Adrenal Cortex Hormones [+NT]	252	☐	☐	◘
☐	Anxiety [+NT]	25808	☐	☐	◘
☐	Caregiver Burden	2279	☐	☐	◘
☐	Crises [+NT]	1304	☐	☐	◘
☐	Deprivation [+NT]	1270	☐	☐	◘
☐	Disasters [+NT]	1166	☐	☐	◘
☐	Distress	7096	☐	☐	◘
☐	Endurance [+NT]	123	☐	☐	◘
☐	Family Crises	593	☐	☐	◘

Fig. 4.32. The *PsycINFO* Thesaurus at heading "Stress." *PsycINFO* screen shots are reprinted with permission of the American Psychological Association, publisher of the *PsycINFO* database, all rights reserved. OVID interface © 2005 Ovid Technologies Inc.

Quick Recap

PsycINFO is the online version of *Psychological Abstracts*. The on-line database provides journal indexing back to 1806. *PsycINFO* is the preeminent index to psychology literature, and covers journals, books, book chapters, technical reports, dissertations, published conference papers, bibliographies, and more. Sources are international. The *PsycINFO* field structure is extremely detailed, offering sixty-three different fields (not all are searchable). Using *PsycINFO* through the Ovid interface takes advantage of the Ovid "Map to Subject Heading" functionality, which automatically provides a list of suggested terms from the *PsycINFO* Thesaurus for any word or phrase typed into the search field. Specialized functions in the Subject Heading Mapping Display are Auto Explode, i.e., automatically search the indicated term and all narrower subject headings; and Focus, i.e., restrict the search to records where the indicated term is a major aspect ("focus") of the article. The optimal search style to use in the Ovid interface is to build a search one concept at a time, and then combine sets from the search history. This is very different from the other databases considered so far. The most commonly used Limits appear in the Advanced Search interface, and many more are accessible via the More Limits link.

Exercises and Points to Consider

1. I've heard there's a bibliography of movies that had librarians in them—surely *Library Literature* would be the place to find out? This time, instead of Browsing the Subject Index, go to the Thesaurus, and look up librarians in movies. Look at the results—there's the perfect heading! What happens if you try this without the Thesaurus? Try some other approaches for this search, as if you were a typical patron.

2. Search example 2 in *Library Literature* was about chat services as part of the Reference function. Go to the database, and reproduce that search, then compare the results with what you get by simply typing in: Reference chat as a Keyword search. There are several things to notice about this. For one thing, you learn that Wilson does not automatically search multiple word entries as a phrase: it simply looks for both words, in any order. To take a devil's advocate role here: aren't these results just as good as those we got with a much more elaborate search? Carefully compare the results—Are there any records not found in the second set (the keyword search) that really would have been bad to miss? Not to undermine the more sophisticated techniques this text has been encouraging you to learn, but the reality is that most people will simply keyword search, and in some—perhaps many—cases that approach will do the job. When it doesn't work, you need to be ready with better techniques. Message: don't get rigid, either about what you're seeing, or what you're doing.

3. In ERIC, see what material you can find about language or music programs in elementary schools. Are these offerings increasing or decreasing? What languages are offered most frequently?

4. Refer back to the third search example in ERIC that was shown as an "Expert" search (Figure 4.20). Can you replicate this search in the Advanced Search screen?

5. Your sister recently had a baby, and is upset because the baby's sleep patterns aren't settling down at all—she wonders if the baby has some kind of sleep disorder, and if it's going to affect her (the baby's, not the mothers!) development.

    You start by going to *PsycINFO* and typing in: sleep disorders.

    That maps directly to a subject heading, but you're curious what might be included "under" it, or near it in the Thesaurus list. Click the subject heading to find out.

    Hey—look down there! "Sleep Wake Cycle"! That sounds good. Select that (deselect sleep disorders), and click its "Explode" box. Click the "Continue" button (top of screen).

Next term: type "infants" in the search box, and see what comes up on the Mapping Display.

"Infant Development"—that looks good. Select that and Continue.

Now combine those two searches by ANDing their search set numbers together.

Do you like the results?

6. A friend has a child with Aspergers Syndrome (a form of autism), and is worried about how this may affect his verbal and writing skills—his language development. In *PsycINFO*, what happens if you search and then combine Aspergers Syndrome and Language Development? (You don't get very many.) Maybe we could "widen our net" on the "Language" aspect of the search.

Type in the broad term Language, and see if the Mapping Display offers more subject headings we could use. Choose several.

Now combine this new (very large!) set with the Aspergers Syndrome set. It should result in a few more results than before.

5

Databases for Science and Medicine

The databases in this chapter, besides being intrinsically interesting and well-crafted systems, provide a view into their respective disciplines that goes beyond their content. Obviously, medical databases will index medical material, and science databases will index scientific publications. But the two subject databases considered here are functionally quite different, and I believe the difference reflects a basic tenet of each discipline.

Every discipline or profession has its own language: a specialized vocabulary is one of the things that unites and defines a profession (think of all the jargon we use in libraries). In almost no area is this truer than in medicine: a major part of the study of medicine is mastery of its language. The language is crucial, and *the* medical database, MEDLINE®, reflects this. One of the key components of MEDLINE records is their detailed system of subject headings and subheadings for *terms*, painstakingly applied by trained professionals. The "Mapping" functionality of the Ovid interface to MEDLINE reflects this emphasis on subject terms: whatever word or phrase you enter, the "Map to Subject Headings" function will do its best to steer you to the appropriate subject headings. Consider this, and see if you agree: the basic tenet here as a focus on "what." Medical terms represent "what:" what organ, what condition, what symptoms, what drugs, and what outcome.

In contrast, the approach taken by the scientist who developed the *Science Citation Index*® (and later similar indexes for the other disciplines), was that the *citations* were of paramount importance: the references associated with scientific papers. To me, this represents "who." *Who* was cited? *Who* was citing? Although used in other organizations, the *Science Citation Index* is a very "academic" product, and in academia, a great deal rides on who you are (which you establish by publishing your work), and who has recognized your work (by citing it). You will find that the *Web of Science*® citation indexes do not use subject headings at all.

Another way this difference in emphasis (terms or "what" versus "who") is reflected in the functionality of each database is the way they arrive at "Related records." In PubMed®, an algorithm based on words ("what") identifies related records. In the citation indexes, shared citations ("who") identify related records.

As you work through this chapter and get familiar with these databases, keep this idea in the back of your mind: that medicine is focused on "what" (terms), and the citation indexes are focused on "who." See if you spot additional aspects of the databases' functionality to support it.

MEDLINE® and PubMed®

MEDLINE

It's easy to know where to start a consideration of medical databases: it has to be with the MEDLINE database from the National Library of Medicine. The difficulty is knowing where to stop: MEDLINE is a huge, immensely detailed, highly specific and sophisticated resource for an elite professional field. So let me declare right here: this text is not going to attempt to teach you how to search MEDLINE. If you get a job in a medical library, you will get thorough training from professionals in the field. Instead, in the spirit that you can achieve *something* reasonable, no matter what the subject area, by employing the same basic strategy (engaging in a reference interview, using your searching techniques, and keeping your eyes open), what follows will be a demystifying look at MEDLINE as offered through the database vendor Ovid. We'll then take a look at a freely accessible version of MEDLINE on the Internet, where it is available through a resource called PubMed. This situation is almost unique in the database world, in that the same high quality content is available both via subscription, and for free, and thus definitely merits our attention.

About MEDLINE

MEDLINE (Medical Literature Analysis and Retrieval System Online), is a product of the U.S. National Library of Medicine (NLM), which describes it as their "premier bibliographic database" containing "approximately 13 million references to journal articles" in the life sciences, with a focus on biomedicine. Date coverage is generally from 1966 to the present, although some older material is also available. MEDLINE is a journal citation database (many citations offer links to full text, but the database itself does not contain full-text), and international in scope: it selectively covers "approximately 4,800" journals from all over the world, in thirty languages. The NLM enhances records from non-English language journals by supplying translated article titles; English translations of abstracts are dependent on the article authors. The database is updated daily, from Tuesday through Saturday, with the addition of "between 1,500–3,500" new citations each day. (Additions "each day" does not mean, however, that the contents of a journal published yesterday will be indexed and added today. The kind of detailed processing required to create full MEDLINE records does take some time.) This phenomenal effort is the result of a distribution of labor among the NLM, its international partners, and collaborating institutions (U.S. National Library of Medicine 2005, *MEDLINE*®).

A key distinguishing feature of MEDLINE is its carefully crafted thesaurus, known as "MeSH®," for *Medical Subject Headings*. (Think of it as the Library of Congress Subject headings (LCSH) for the medical world.) This highly developed, hierarchical system of subject headings is also the work of the National Library of Medicine, which has a whole branch devoted to continuous maintenance, revision, and updating of the MeSH vocabulary. The impression one gets is that this is a dynamic system, continually growing and changing in response to developments in scientific and medical research and practice. Statistics about MeSH are impressive: as of April 2005 there were 22,568 subject headings, augmented with 23,887 *see* references, and 106,651 other entry points (U.S. National Library of Medicine 2005, *Medical Subject Heading (MeSH) Fact Sheet*).

As with any thesaurus, of course, these terms are employed by highly trained indexers to describe and provide entry points for each article. As a user of this database, one important thing for you to remember is that indexers are instructed to always choose the most specific terms available. Although the MeSH system is hierarchical,[1] with broad terms such as "Digestive System Diseases" at the most general level, if an article is discussing a specific malady, such as Crohn Disease, only the more specific term will be applied as a heading. All the layers of headings between Digestive System Diseases and Crohn Disease (Gastrointestinal Diseases, Gastroenteritis, and Inflammatory Bowel Diseases) would *not* appear as additional subject headings.

Accessing MEDLINE

The MEDLINE database is leased to a number of different vendors, including OCLC's FirstSearch, Ovid, and Cambridge Scientific Abstracts (CSA). At one institution, you may find you have several "flavors" of MEDLINE available to you. In addition, the MEDLINE database is also available as part of PubMed, a free Web resource at http://pubmed.gov, which we will look at in the next section. Since we are looking at MEDLINE through the Ovid interface, which we saw in Chapter 4 for *PsycINFO*, the initial search screen should look very familiar. What is slightly different is the number and nature of the Limits available here (Figure 5.1).

These options represent the most frequently used types of limits, such as articles dealing with Human (rather than animal) subjects, English language, articles with abstracts, or full text. The other options represent article types such as various types of Reviews,[2] and journal subsets (Core Clinical Journals), as well as major "subject subset" groups: AIDS, Cancer, Complementary Medicine, Bioethics, History of Medicine, Space Life Sciences, and Toxicology. These are also all available on the full "Limits" screen, accessible via the "More Limits" link (grayed out in Figure 5.1 because no search has yet been performed).

Stepping Through a MEDLINE Search

The search topic for our walk through MEDLINE is: prevention and control of heart attacks in women who are adults, but not yet classified as middle-aged (e.g., ages 19–44). We'll start by simply entering heart attack as our search—not a very professional term, but again the excellent "map to subject headings" feature will take care of us.

Fig. 5.1. Ovid MEDLINE, initial advanced search screen. © 2005 Ovid Technologies Inc.

Select a Subject Heading

A heart attack is, of course, known in the medical profession as a Myocardial Infarction. We'll choose that term (and try not to be distracted, as usually happens, with the other interesting and related terms), and mark both the Explode and Focus options (Figure 5.2). (These options were explained in the discussion of *PsycINFO*, and also appear in the "Hints" section of this screen.) We'll choose not to "Include All Subheadings" at this point, and "Continue." By not including all the subheadings, we'll get offered the Subheadings screen to choose the ones of interest.

Select Subheadings

The Subheadings screen is something new that we didn't see in *PsycINFO*, and it provides a wonderful and fascinating glimpse into the medical worldview. The subheadings system is a standardized list of terms that reflect all the facets of how the medical profession approaches tasks or topics: does it have to do with blood? Is it a complication? A therapy (by diet or drug or in general)? Is it about epidemiology? Genetics? Mortality? Surgery? All the possible aspects are provided for in the subheadings system, but what is displayed in this screen represents only those subheadings

O V I D°	**Mapping Display**	ovid web gateway

🔒 Main Search Page | ☐ Help | ☒ LOGOFF

Your term mapped to the following Subject Headings:
Click on a subject heading to view more general and more specific terms within the tree.

ℹ️ **Any term you select will automatically be exploded to include all narrower terms. To select a term without exploding, clear the Explode checkbox for that term.**

☐ **Include All Subheadings**

Combine selections with: [OR ⬍]   [CONTINUE »]

Select	Subject Heading	Auto Explode	Focus	Scope
☑	Myocardial Infarction	☑	☑	ℹ️
☐	Hypertension	☐	☐	ℹ️
☐	Depressive Disorder	☐	☐	ℹ️
☐	Angioplasty, Transluminal, Percutaneous Coronary	☐	☐	ℹ️
☐	Middle Aged	☐	☐	ℹ️
☐	Antihypertensive Agents	☐	☐	ℹ️
☐	Antilipemic Agents	☐	☐	ℹ️
☐	Coronary Artery Bypass	☐	☐	ℹ️
☐	Hyperlipidemia	☐	☐	ℹ️
☐	Risk Factors	☐	☐	ℹ️
☐	heart attack.mp. *search as Keyword*			

❓ **Hints:**

- Click on a **Subject Heading** to view its tree - related terms that are more general and more specific.
- Select the **Explode** box if you wish to retrieve results using the selected term and all of its more specific terms.
- Select the **Focus** box if you wish to limit your search to those documents in which your subject heading is considered the major point of the article.
- If your search did not map to a desirable subject heading, select the box **Search as Keyword**.

Fig. 5.2. Ovid Mapping Display: suggested MeSH subject headings for "Heart Attack." © 2005 Ovid Technologies Inc.

that can be meaningfully used with the current MeSH heading (in this case, Myocardial Infarction). You can learn a great deal by simply studying the list (Figure 5.3).

The main intent of the subheadings system is to provide a very efficient way to get at precisely the aspect of a topic you might be looking for, such as "Prevention & Control." Without doing a second search on the "prevention" idea, we can, in one search, retrieve only those articles that deal with prevention and control of myocardial infarction. (Note that you can also choose multiple subheadings, to retrieve several aspects of your main search term at once.)

Apply Limits

We get our results (over 2,000 of them), but we haven't gotten at the "adult females" aspect of our search yet. Time to visit the More Limits screen, where we can choose Female, and Age Group Adult (19 to 44 years) (Figure 5.4). While it's tempting immediately to limit to English language, try to hold off until you've looked over the results. Titles are offered in translation, and if the perfect article happens to be in German, surely in our globalized, multicultural world, you can find someone who can translate for

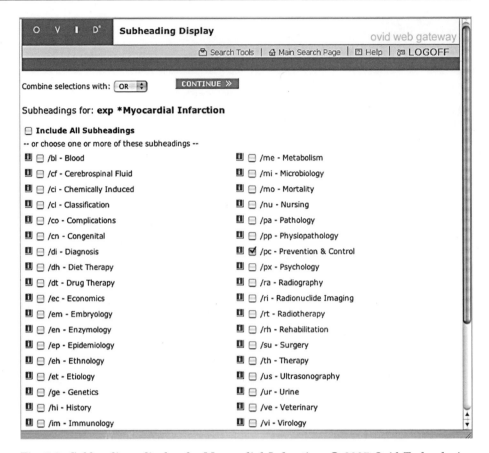

Fig. 5.3. Subheadings display for Myocardial Infarction. © 2005 Ovid Technologies Inc.

you? In any event, don't eliminate the possibility without looking through the results first.

As you can see, the Limit screen is quite long: the screen shot in Figure 5.4 is a partial shot, to show just those limits we used ("Female" toward the top of the figure, and "Age Groups" toward the bottom). While you're at this screen, note also all the other limits, such as "Clinical Queries,"[3] so specific to this database.

Results

After limiting, our results are down to a manageable 102. As you can see even in the first few results, while all of them are scholarly, the technical level of the sources varies. Some of these articles definitely will be only accessible to specialists (for example, number 6), while others, such as the one from the *Journal of Women's Health* (number 3), are more likely to be understood by an educated lay audience (Figure 5.5).

Overall, however, the results make clear that MEDLINE is very much a professional tool. Medical librarians can go through weeks of training, learning all of its functions and what they mean. As mentioned at the beginning, this brief introduction is simply meant to give you exposure to one

Fig. 5.4. Partial view of the "More Limits" screen. © 2005 Ovid Technologies Inc.

of the most sophisticated databases on the market (both in functionality and in content), and to show that if you really had to, you could certainly go in and perform *some* kind of search here. For general consumer health queries, however, there are better choices: subscription databases such as Health Reference Center (from Thomson-Gale), or free government Web sites such as MedlinePlus.gov (also a product of the National Library of Medicine).

PubMed®

PubMed—More than MEDLINE

On to PubMed (http://pubmed.gov). As a database of medical citations, you could think of PubMed as what you'd get if databases were like hamburgers: "give me MEDLINE—and super size it!" MEDLINE is the main component of PubMed, but PubMed offers a number of groups of additional material, notably:

- Older (pre-1966) citations, known as OLDMEDLINE.

Fig. 5.5. Initial entries in the Results display. © 2005 Ovid Technologies Inc.

- Citations for articles in MEDLINE journals that were not selected for indexing in the medical database due to their non-life sciences content.

- "In-process" citations: records that have not yet had full MeSH indexing applied (U.S. National Library of Medicine 2005, *What's the Difference*).[4]

PubMed is much more than a super sized database of medical citations, however. It is a portal to databases from the National Center for Biotechnology Information (NCBI)—of gene sequences, molecular structures, etc.,—and to "Services" such as citation matchers and a special interface for clinical queries, as well as "Related Resources" such as Clinical Trials and Consumer Health information. It's huge, first-class, professional information, and it is freely available on the Web. As with MEDLINE, I'm afraid we won't do more than touch the surface of the possibilities here—but at least you'll now know it exists, and you can explore further when and if the need should arise.

Introduction to the PubMed Interface

Let's take a look (Figure 5.6).[5]

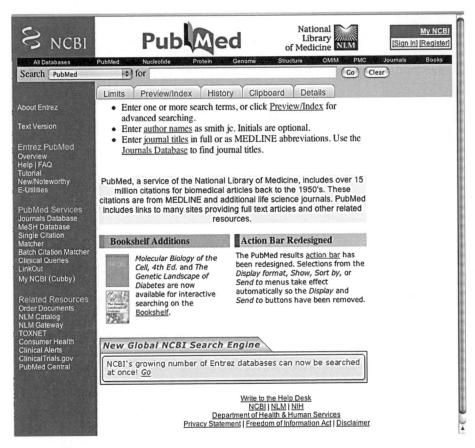

Fig. 5.6. Initial PubMed screen, as of April 2005.

Sidebar 5.1.

Beware the trap of expectation that because PubMed is a free Web resource, that somehow it will be "easier" than MEDLINE; that the content will be "easier." Not in the slightest. As noted in the opening discussion of this section, PubMed contains the MEDLINE database content, plus additional journals not indexed by MEDLINE, and links to advanced scientific resources such as the NCBI genome databases. In other words, despite the fact that this is a free Web resource, open to the world, this is probably not the place for the average mortal to try and find an answer to a medical question. If you are working with a health professional, researcher, or student in the health sciences, yes, this is the place. If you want to help your mom or your neighbor find some health information, go to MedlinePlus.gov.

Similarities to Ovid's MEDLINE

If you look around, many of the features in Ovid's MEDLINE can be found here, including the Limits (Figure 5.7): Publication Types, the age groups, Humans or Animals, Subsets, gender, and Date. The Languages Limit is available, but consists of only seven major Languages (English, French, German, Italian, Japanese, Russian, and Spanish). The History tab provides a list of previous searches, similar to the Ovid search screen, and

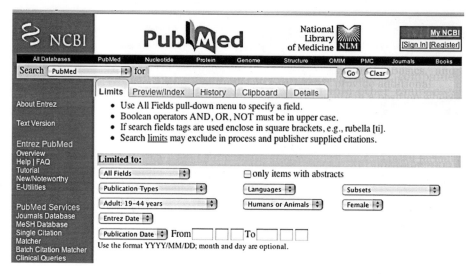

Fig. 5.7. Limits in PubMed, as of April 2005.

Preview/Index provides the ability to search in a particular field. In the drop-down list of "Search" options, and linked on the sidebar, under PubMed Services, is access to the MeSH Database, giving you access to the thesaurus to explore terms and their relationships.

Unique PubMed Features

Other features are unique to the PubMed interface, and are quite handy (NCBI PubMed, 2005):

> The PubMed query box and Feature Tabs are available from every screen, so you don't need to return to the homepage to enter a new search. A spell checking feature suggests alternative spellings for PubMed search terms that may include misspellings.

In the results lists, there are additional links to Related Articles and Links (these vary depending on the article, but take advantage of the other NCBI resources whenever possible). The Related Articles feature in PubMed makes use of a word-analysis algorithm, and is very effective: the results are almost always quite useful. In the second half of this chapter, when we look at the *Web of Science* citation databases, we'll see a different way of judging and retrieving "related" articles.

Running the Same Search in PubMed

Let's try our same search again: prevention and control of heart attacks in adult women. We can basically set up the same search in PubMed, using the Limits tab to select our age group and gender limits. Then, because we are laypeople who don't know any better, we still search on the layman's term "heart attack." Because PubMed performs "automatic term

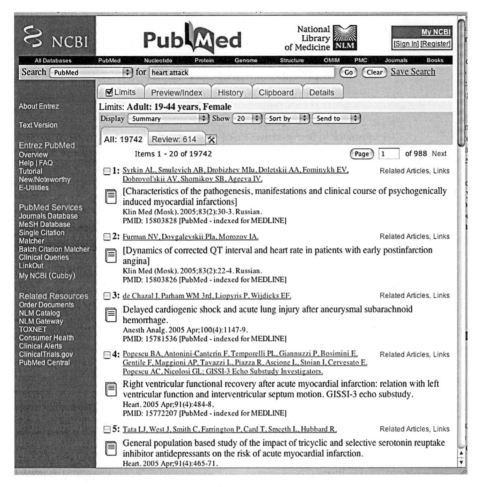

Fig. 5.8. Search results in PubMed, as of April 2005.

matching,"[6] the same process we saw explicitly in Ovid's MEDLINE is carried out here as well, behind the scenes, so that all of our results are, seemingly magically, exactly on the appropriate professional term "Myocardial Infarction," which is automatically "exploded" to include the more specific terms Myocardial Stunning and Shock, Cardiogenic. However, PubMed also searches the terms "heart attack," and "myocardial infarction," in a number of other ways, which has a significant effect on the size of the result set: this search has retrieved close to 20,000 hits—a daunting number (Figure 5.8). Information on the "Details" tab and a careful reading of the Help assist in explaining why.

Search "Details"

The Details tab provides a "query translation," an explicit rendition of how your search was executed (although you may still need the Help to translate the "translation"!) In this case, three variations of the search were "ORed" together:

Fig. 5.9. Using the Preview/Index tab to add a Subheading, as of April 2005.

- Myocardial infarction was searched in the Title and Abstract fields of journals indexed by PubMed that are not included in MEDLINE.

- Myocardial infarction was searched as a MeSH subject heading (exploded).

- Heart attack was searched as a text word in any text field.

The effect of these three ORed searches probably accounts for most of the dramatic increase. However, since we also weren't led through the screens of subject headings (Figure 5.2) and subheadings (Figure 5.3), we didn't have the opportunity to "Focus," or to choose just one subheading: "Prevention & Control." But because we now know something about how the MEDLINE database is set up, and have an idea of what MeSH Subheadings are, we can at least apply our one desired subheading.

Applying a Subheading in PubMed

The subheading functionality lives under the Preview/Index tab: we can go there, select the appropriate field, and put in an appropriate value (Figure 5.9).

Limiting to Review Articles

Applying the one subheading definitely cuts down and focuses the number of results. The "Review" tab also helps: it shows only the results that are review articles, leaving us with ninety-two results (Figure 5.10).

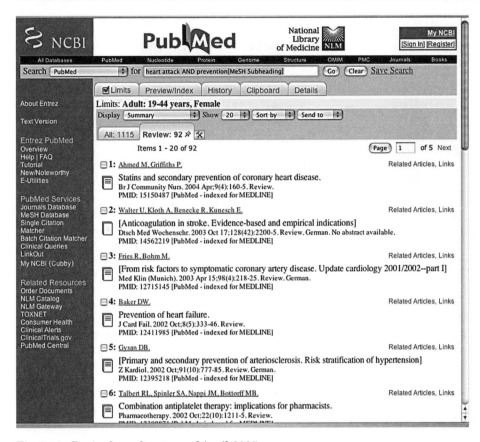

Fig. 5.10. Revised result set, as of April 2005.

Larger Result Sets in PubMed

The total number of results (1,115) is still higher than we retrieved in Ovid's MEDLINE. The records with MeSH headings and subheadings have been reduced, but the ORed text word searches are still driving the overall results up. It is possible to achieve something more like our MEDLINE search and results numbers by employing more Limits, as you'll see in the Exercises, but it's useful have an "everyman" experience first, and experience the database as ordinary users would. PubMed is more than MEDLINE, as this example has amply demonstrated.

Concern about Large Results Sets

My only (old-fashioned?) concern is that medical professionals will simply accept these huge numbers of (possibly) not the most precise results, because that is always their experience with Web search engines: thousands of results, that's the way it is. Will medical professionals notice, or bother to learn how to make use of, these filtering and refining features? They are not, generally, trained as searchers; they are trained as doctors and nurses. Our medical librarians report that PubMed is increasingly popular, however, so evidently users are finding it satisfactory. One might speculate that mastery of the language of medicine, and usually knowing what they are looking for

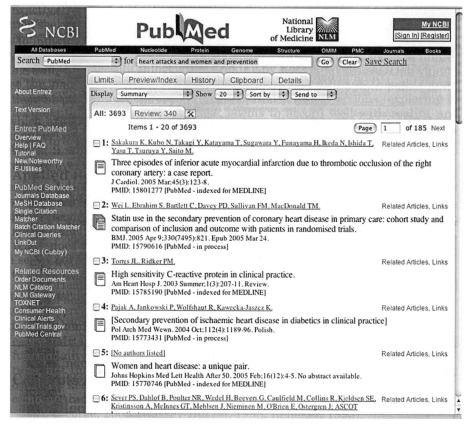

Fig. 5.11. Doing the search without using features, by ANDing terms in the search box, as of April 2005.

(rather than a broad, exploratory search such as a layman might do), are key factors that allow medical professionals to compose effective searches without sophisticated search techniques. For the layman, adding more terms to the query (for example, simply entering a word search on "heart attacks and women and prevention") seems to help produce results sets of (almost) acceptable size (recall) and precision—especially if you focus on the first couple of screens of Review articles (Figure 5.11).

Output in MEDLINE and PubMed

Ovid "Results Manager"

The Ovid version of MEDLINE has the same "Results Manager" that we saw in the discussion of *PsycINFO*, with the same functionality: formatting for printing, e-mail, save, and order (through the local library's Interlibrary Loan unit).

PubMed "Send to" and "Order" Issues

PubMed is similar, with the "Send to" drop-down in the Results display offering choices of text, file (save-type functions), e-mail, clipboard, and order. "Order" is where things can get interesting. Although it is now possible for libraries to create customized access to PubMed, if such access has not been set up, or a user still uses the public URL to go to PubMed, the Order function will take the user to an NLM function known as Loansome Doc (cute or what?)—which has nothing to do with the local library, and will charge the user for document delivery. About here is where librarians get rather anxious about users' preference for PubMed: although it is now possible to integrate PubMed with local customized link resolvers (such as SFX), this kind of personalized access is dependent on people using a special URL. If the "right" URL isn't used (and "pubmed.gov" is pretty easy to remember and type in), even though the user may be sitting right in the library not 10 feet from the Interlibrary Loan office, there is no way for the non-customized PubMed to convey the information that a local, lower or possibly no-cost, Interlibrary Loan service is available.

Getting to the Full Text

Full Text in Ovid MEDLINE

Many subscription databases that do not provide full text themselves now work with "bridging" services such as SFX, a link resolver that will make the connection between the citation database and local resources. Added to the bibliographic database, these services will offer a menu of choices depending on availability, such as: another database that does provide the full text, the local catalog (for hard copy), or a link to the local Interlibrary Loan system. The Ovid databases can be integrated with SFX.

Full Text in PubMed

Accessing full text in PubMed raises some of the same issues as Interlibrary Loan. The non-customized version of PubMed provides as many links as it can to full text, some of which are free (titles in the collection called PubMed Central), and others that are subscription based. If subscription-based, PubMed will link directly to the publisher Web site for the journal. If this is how the local library also accesses the electronic version of that particular journal, and access from the library or organization is thus "recognized" by the site, the user will get the article he or she needs. However, if the library accesses that journal via an aggregator service, there is no way to convey that information via the non-customized PubMed, and the user would be misled into thinking that either the material was not accessible, or only available at cost. If the library has set up customized access, citations will include links to the local "bridging" service, providing users with as much functionality as the subscription version of the database. Now *that's* food for thought, indeed.

The *Web of Science* and the Citation Indexes

Now we're going to take off the stethoscope, and get into the mindset of the scholarly academic researcher. Think of yourself as Joe(sephine) Bloggs, Ph.D. When you write a scholarly paper, it almost always involves a literature review, or at least a process of consulting previous articles that you can quote to support various points throughout your paper. You are drawing on past knowledge in this way, building on the ideas of previous researchers and taking them further, or moving tangentially. If we look at your list of references, we can trace the "lineage" of your ideas back in time. For

J. Bloggs, undergraduate, this is still a common and accepted way to get started writing a paper: to find a recent work that is related to what you want to write about, and trace its references. This is fairly easily done, because the references provide the information about the other articles (accurately, you hope). However...there are works in every field that achieve the status of "classic papers," that get cited by subsequent authors over and over again. What if you wanted to trace that evolution, that is, all the people who had *cited* a particular paper or book? A professor could hand you a "classic" work from 1965, tell you "that's the authoritative work in this area"—what do you do with that? A place to start would be to see who has cited that work recently, and in what context. You want to trace the evolution of those ideas *forward* in time. How in the world could you do that?

History of the Citation Indexes

The concept of tracking and indexing not just articles, but the references associated with those articles, was the brainchild of Dr. Eugene Garfield, founder of the Institute for Scientific Information, or ISI. From a concept first outlined in a 1955 article in *Science*, the oversize, print, multivolume sets known as the *Science Citation Index* (1963–), the *Social Sciences Citation Index*® (1965–), and the *Arts & Humanities Citation Index*® (1976–), have been providing researchers with a unique and powerful way to trace the evolution and impact of ideas over time. As Carol Tenopir (2001) put it: "The power of citation searching lies in the capacity to take a seminal article and uncover who the author was influenced by (who was cited) and go forward in time to discover how that seminal research affected newer works (who is citing it)." Now it was possible, albeit somewhat physically challenging (because of the size of the volumes: huge—and the size of the print: tiny) to trace "who is citing whom." As technology progressed, the Citation Indexes moved to CD-ROM, and then to the Web. And if ever a tool benefited from going electronic, it is this one. The whole concept of what a citation index allows one to do seems much easier to grasp and to explain to others in an online realization. It also makes possible many enhanced features, which we'll explore as we work through the database functionality.

Citation Indexes in the *Web of Science*

In 1992 ISI was acquired by The Thomson Corporation, which has continued to take the citation index concept from strength to strength. The *Science, Social Sciences*, and *Arts and Humanities Citation Indexes* are now all part of the *Web of Science*, which itself is one element in an overall *ISI Web of Knowledge*SM—-the total suite of research tools offered by Thomson.

Web of Science Content

In all, the *Web of Science* indexing and abstracting tools cover more than 8,500 research publications from around the world. More and more years of backfiles have been added to the database, steadily expanding coverage both back in time, as well as forward with weekly updates. Depending on the subscription package, coverage can go back as early as 1900 for the *Science Citation Index*, and 1956 for the *Social Sciences*. The institutions in my purview have opted for the "1973 to present" package. What this date cutoff refers to is how far back the records for the *journal articles* go; under a 1973 to the present subscription, you can still search a *cited reference* from any time period, but you will only be allowed to see records for articles citing that reference that were published from 1973 to the present. Keep remembering that this database has a dual nature: the cited references records, which can be from any date, and the journal article records, which are restricted depending on the subscription.

As you might imagine (if you haven't, you should), an undertaking of this size and complexity involves thousands of workers, incredible feats of programming, etc. It is big, and frankly, it's expensive. You are likely to find it only at major research libraries, but it's worth being aware of as part of your overall understanding of how research works, and how our current knowledge builds on past work. If you work in an academic environment, this is part of understanding the scholarly animal.

An Index Focused on Citations

The unique feature that the citation indexes introduced was that each bibliographic record (author, title, journal, year, etc.) also includes its list of cited references—the bibliography—for that article. The cited references are associated with their articles, but each reference is also recorded in the database as an independent, "cited reference" record, which can be searched and used in various ways. Note too that while the type of source material indexed in the *Web of Science* databases is only journal articles (not books, technical reports, etc.), the references associated with a source article can be drawn from any type of material, and thus cited reference records can be articles, but also books, reports, unpublished papers, or whatever the author has cited. (If your brain is starting to hurt, don't despair: it's actually surprising clear and easy once you get into the database.) Again, this dual nature: source article records, and cited reference records referred to in that source. What can you do with all this information?

Regular Topic Searches; Tracing *Back* via Citations

You can use the *Web of Science* databases just like any other indexing and abstracting product: to perform a keyword search to find articles on a particular topic, to find articles by a particular author, or to track down a specific article when you have only partial information. The added twist is that having identified one or more articles, you can also see the list of references from each article, and by looking at this bibliography, you can, if the items are linked (to other journal article records in the database), immediately start tracking the ideas in a current article *back* in time.

Tracing Forward, and Tracking Citations for Tenure

In addition, because you can search cited references, you can see which subsequent articles have cited a particular work. As mentioned previously, you can track the development and influence of an idea from when it was first published, to now—a way to bring research forward, from old to new. In addition to helping students and scholars in the process of writing papers, citation indexes also provide important—even crucial—functionality. Researchers can use this database to find out who is citing their work, and in what context. The "crucial" element is that in the "publish or perish" scramble for academic tenure in the United States, faculty who are up for tenure can use these databases to show how many times their papers have been cited by others, which can be a key factor in proving their eligibility for tenure.

Relating Records by Citations

As mentioned above, in electronic form, the data captured by the citation indexes can be exploited in new and useful ways, impossible in the print version. The *Web of Science* databases have built in a feature called "Related Records." Related records are articles that have at least one cited reference in common. Articles that share four, five, or more references—are likely to be discussing the same topics. This is a completely different way to locate relevant papers on a topic that may not have been found with a traditional author or subject search. Think of it: this is about as close to "searching by concept" as opposed to "searching by words" as you can get. True, you start with a word search (to produce the initial results), but then, based on shared references—shared *concepts*—you can move on into related intellectual territory. This is a powerful concept and tool.

Additional Differences in Available Fields

Present: The Address Field

The article records in the *Web of Science* databases also include an "Address" field, used to record where each author works. This is useful in a number of ways. From a librarian's perspective, it provides a quick way to get a sense of the total output of a particular department (if they publish in journals covered by the *Web of Science*), and what sorts of things they write about. Used in conjunction with the "Analyze" function (discussed as an advanced feature at the end of this chapter), it can be used to determine where your institution's faculty publish most frequently, and thus which journals to lobby hardest for during a serials review. For an academic or corporate researcher, it allows him or her to track what a colleague (or a competitor!) at a specific institution is publishing. The researcher could search on just author name, or author name combined with address (to disambiguate common names) to track known people. Using a keyword(s) and address search, the researcher could track the output of a department or unit at another institution, without knowing any specific names at all.

Absent: Subject Headings Fields

Finally, there is one thing that hasn't been mentioned about these remarkable databases. Did you notice? Having just discussed MEDLINE, where subject headings are crucial and heavily emphasized, here at the *Web of Science* we haven't mentioned them at all, because . . . the citation indexes don't use subject headings! Yes, it's true. All the databases we've looked at up to this point have used some kind of subject indexing, and I've made a big point of emphasizing it. Now we come to a set of databases that don't use added subject terms at all, but which are every bit as powerful and compelling (if not more so), than the previous databases. The determination not to employ subject indexing was another part of Dr. Garfield's vision. The labor- and thought-intensive process of having humans analyze each article and apply subject terms slowed the production of the indexes down too much for the needs of the scientific research community. He realized that as "retrieval terms, citations could function as well as manually indexed keywords and descriptors" (Thomson Scientific, 2005). (There is also an advantage that in the sciences, paper titles tend to be content-ful and descriptive, thus providing a richer source of keywords for searching.) So, you will not

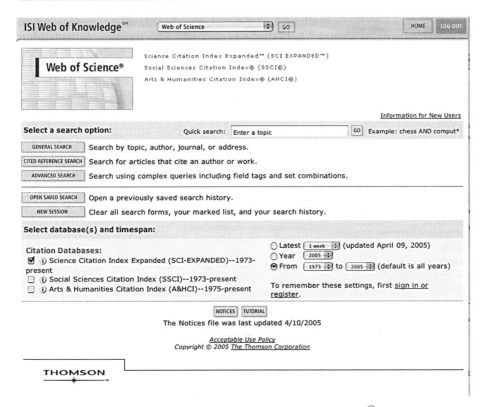

Fig. 5.12. *Web of Science* initial screen. Data from *Web of Science*®, produced by the scientific business of The Thomson Corporation.

find vendor-supplied subject indexing here.[7] But I can almost guarantee you won't miss it. Let's take a look.

Searching the *Web of Science*

Initial Settings

Figure 5.12 shows the initial screen for the *Web of Science* databases (the details will depend on your subscription, but this should be close).

As you can see, this screen allows you to choose which of the Citation Indexes you wish to search (one, two, or all three), a range of years, and a search option. We're going to start with a General Search, on a "scientific" topic, so will leave only the *Science Citation Index Expanded* checked.

"General" Searches

Clicking General Search brings us to Figure 5.13.

You can get a sense of some of the Boolean operators and other elements of our Searcher's Toolkit that are available here from the examples provided right in the interface. See the Sidebar for more details.

Fig. 5.13. Initial General Search screen. Data from *Web of Science*®, produced by the scientific business of The Thomson Corporation.

Sidebar 5.2.

Here's a quick inventory of your Searcher's Toolkit for these databases:

- Boolean operators: AND, OR, NOT

- Proximity operator: SAME

- Order of precedence: SAME, NOT, AND, OR. Use parentheses to change the order

- No need to use quotes around phrases

- Truncation/wildcards:

  - *—zero to "many" characters

  - ?—substitutes for one character, ??—two characters, etc. Can be used within a word, or at the end

- "Restrict search"—e.g., limit—there are functions to specify:

  - Language

  - Document Type

(a)

(b)

Fig. 5.14. A first, simple topic search. Data from *Web of Science*®, produced by the scientific business of The Thomson Corporation.

Sample "General" Search for a Topic

We'll get our feet wet with a simple search (Figure 5.14):

Acid rain same adirondack?—as "Topic."
Select "Article" as document type.

General Search Results

In the results, explore the one by JOHNSON AH, ANDERSEN SB, SIC-CAMA TG (Figure 5.15)—how many references does it have? How many times has it been cited? Take a look at the "Related Records"—do they seem related or useful to you?

Sample "General" Search for an Author

Another example: say you were familiar with Stephen Hawking's books, but wanted a list of journal articles by him. Use the Author search field, and, as the interface indicates, enter the name as Hawking S∗ (no comma, and do not spell out the first name).[8] How many S Hawkings can there be? But we can add Cambridge in the address to be sure it's him (Figure 5.16).

You will find that Stephen Hawking is a very prolific author, and that almost all of his articles are highly cited, as well. Note too that usually he is listed as Hawking SW, but sometimes as Hawking S—so it was good to use the wildcard symbol to be sure we retrieved both.

Cited Reference Searching

On to the special functionality of this database: searching a *Cited Reference*. Wherever you are in the database, notice the buttons at the top stay

Fig. 5.15. From the Acid Rain search results. Data from *Web of Science*®, produced by the scientific business of The Thomson Corporation.

Fig. 5.16. Search strategy for journal articles by Stephen Hawking—partial screen. Data from *Web of Science*®, produced by the scientific business of The Thomson Corporation.

with you, allowing you to change direction at any time (cf. the full screen shot in Figure 5.15). Click the "Cited Ref Search" button at the top of the screen.

Cited Reference Search Example 1

Now let us say you are interested in the classic book by James Watson and Francis Crick, *The Double Helix*, in which they described the discovery

Fig. 5.17. A cited reference search. Data from *Web of Science*®, produced by the scientific business of The Thomson Corporation.

of DNA. How many times has it been cited? Is it still being cited by current authors? In what contexts? As mentioned in the introductory notes for these databases, here is an interesting thing: we can search for who has cited a work that is both outside the year coverage (1973–current), and outside the material type (book rather than journal article), of the database. The work itself does not have to be retrievable as a record in the database; it just has to have been cited by others. You can do a cited reference search on really ancient material, as long as people are still citing it. Ponder that for a couple of minutes. We're not used to working with material that is outside of the stated year span of the database.

Cited Reference Search Input

In this case, we will make use of all the fields provided in the cited reference search screen, and boldly type in the information as given. Later on, we'll work on an example that isn't as tidy or straightforward.

As shown in Figure 5.17, type in:

CITED AUTHOR: Watson J*

CITED WORK: double helix

CITED YEAR(S): 1968

This produces a results list as shown in Figure 5.18.

Cited Reference Search Results

Yikes! A million variations! Is this all the same thing? Unfortunately, yes. This represents all the ways people have cited this work in their bibliographies. Every time somebody writes a reference a little differently (or

Fig. 5.18. Results screen for a cited reference search. Data from *Web of Science*®, produced by the scientific business of The Thomson Corporation.

even incorrectly!) that reference gets its own entry (note the "Hint" in the box of instructions at the top of the screen). Although Thomson Scientific does do a lot of clean up and "normalization" of references, it would be impossible to check and "fix" every reference for every article, and maintain the rate at which new material is added to the databases to keep them current. As a result, papers that are frequently cited produce results lists like this one. Don't panic, now you know why.

Getting to the Articles Doing the Citing

In real life, you would probably want to use the Select All* button if you wanted to be comprehensive. For example purposes, however, select (checkbox) the two entries with the most "hits" on this page, and click the Finish Search button. Now we start seeing titles of the articles that have cited this classic work, with the most recent ones listed first (Figure 5.19).

Here are ten articles selected from the first two pages of results—note the variety of disciplines referring to this work, and the international range of journals.

Fig. 5.19. Results: recent articles citing *The Double Helix* by Watson and Crick. Data from *Web of Science*®, produced by the scientific business of The Thomson Corporation.

1. Stauffer, JE
   Nutrigenomics
   CEREAL FOODS WORLD, 49 (4): 247–248 JUL–AUG 2004

2. Olby, R
   The third man of the double helix—The autobiography of Maurice Wilkins
   SCIENCE, 302 (5653): 2071–2072 DEC 19 2003

3. Kotsias, BA
   Jubilee of the discovery of the double helix
   MEDICINA-BUENOS AIRES, 63 (5): 447–449 2003

4. Semenza, G
   DNA: the double helix
   FEBS LETTERS, 544 (1–3): 1–3 JUN 5 2003

5. Silverman, M
   The discovery of DNA structure: 50 years on
   CLINICAL AND INVESTIGATIVE MEDICINE-MEDECINE CLINIQUE ET EXPERIMENTALE, 26 (2): 53–53 APR 2003

6. Huxley, H
   The cavendish laboratory and structural biology
   PHYSICS WORLD, 16 (3): 29- + MAR 2003

7. Heymsfield, SB
   Heat and life: The ongoing scientific odyssey
   JOURNAL OF PARENTERAL AND ENTERAL NUTRITION, 26
   (6): 319–332 NOV-DEC 2002

8. Wivagg, D; Allchin, D
   The dogma of "the" scientific method
   AMERICAN BIOLOGY TEACHER, 64 (9): 645–646 NOV-DEC
   2002

9. Webb, B
   Robots can be (good) models—Response
   BEHAVIORAL AND BRAIN SCIENCES, 24 (6): 1081–1094 DEC
   2001

10. Flannery, MC
    Stephen Jay Gould: An appreciation
    AMERICAN BIOLOGY TEACHER, 64 (6): 464–469 AUG 2002

We'll get to how this selected set of records was produced in a moment, when we address how to output results from the Citation Indexes. First, however, another cited reference challenge . . .

Cited Reference Search Example 2

Getting back to Stephen Hawking, say you'd like to see who has been citing his book *A Brief History of Time* recently. (The book was published in 1988.) This is basically like the previous cited reference search. We would start at the Cited Reference search screen and enter the author's name in the correct way, and the year the work was published (Figure 5.20).

Title Abbreviations and the Cited Work Index

Now—you'll be wondering why the Cited Work field was left blank. In the previous example it was given to you (*Double Helix*). But wasn't it given to you here? The book is called *A Brief History of Time*, right? Well, yes,

Fig. 5.20. Cited reference search for Stephen Hawking's book published in 1988. Data from *Web of Science*®, produced by the scientific business of The Thomson Corporation.

Fig. 5.21. Using the Cited Work List to select variants on a title. Data from *Web of Science*®, produced by the scientific business of The Thomson Corporation.

and it also has a subtitle: *From the Big Bang to Black Holes*. The issue here is that we have a Work title that is potentially many words longer, and this database is very big on abbreviations. Very big. They have to be, in order to fit all the information in. The point is that almost every cited reference title will be abbreviated in some way, and it's a very, very bad idea to try and *guess* the abbreviation. (Although you might use truncation successfully.) Note the helpful links associated with the Cited Work field: to something called "cited work index," and to the Thomson ISI list of journal abbreviations. We know this is not a journal, so we'll use the cited work index. Since I know how this story comes out, here is a hint: the favorite way to abbreviate History in this case is "Hist." The cited work index very nicely allows us to type in the beginning of what we're looking for, and jump to it in the list. If we jump in the index to "brief hist time" (because there are a great many other "brief hist's," as it happens) we find (Figure 5.21).

The first seven variations look most likely,[9] and what a handy system: we can simply click the ADD button for each one, and it appears in the selection field below, intelligently ORed together (Figure 5.21). A click of the OK button inserts this whole string into the appropriate field in the search screen. Performing the search now results in another amazing list of variations on a theme, as indicated in Figure 5.22.

Results: Example 2

Note how people citing this work have listed Hawking sometimes with just his first initial, S, sometimes as SW, and some people think he has a different middle initial altogether. The title of the work appears in various

		CITED REFERENCE INDEX						

CITED REFERENCE INDEX
Go to Page: 1 of 2 [GO]
References 1 -- 20

|◀ ◀◀ ◀ [1 | 2] ▶ ▶▶ ▶|

[SELECT PAGE] [SELECT ALL*] [CLEAR ALL] or select specific references from the list. When desired references have been selected from all pages, click FINISH SEARCH to complete your search.

Select	Times Cited**	Cited Author	Cited Work	Year	Volume	Page	Article ID	View Record
☐	134	HAWKING S	BRIEF HIST TIME	1988				
☐	1	HAWKING S	BRIEF HIST TIME	1988		65		
☐	2	HAWKING S	BRIEF HIST TIME	1988		139		
☐	1	HAWKING S	BRIEF HIST TIME	1988		140		
☐	1	HAWKING S	BRIEF HIST TIME	1988		148		
☐	1	HAWKING S	BRIEF HIST TIME	1988		174		
☐	1	HAWKING S	BRIEF HIST TIME	1988		1355		
☐	2	HAWKING S	BRIEF HIST TIME	1988		CH8		
☐	64	HAWKING S	BRIEF HIST TIME BIG	1988				
☐	7	HAWKING S	BRIEF HIST TIME BIG	1988		9		
☐	1	HAWKING S	BRIEF HIST TIME BIG	1988		103		
☐	2	HAWKING SA	BRIEF HIST TIME BIG	1988				
☐	2	HAWKING SH	BRIEF HIST TIME BIG	1988				
☐	140	HAWKING SW	BRIEF HIST TIME	1988				
☐	5	HAWKING SW	BRIEF HIST TIME	1988		24		
☐	1	HAWKING SW	BRIEF HIST TIME	1988		25		
☐	1	HAWKING SW	BRIEF HIST TIME	1988		38		
☐	1	HAWKING SW	BRIEF HIST TIME	1988		40		
☐	6	HAWKING SW	BRIEF HIST TIME	1988		53		
☐	1	HAWKING SW	BRIEF HIST TIME	1988		71		

* "Select All" adds the first 500 matches to your cited reference search, not all matches.
** Times Cited counts are for all databases and all years, not just for your current database and year limits.

Go to Page: 1 of 2 [GO]

References 1 -- 20
|◀ ◀◀ ◀ [1 | 2] ▶ ▶▶ ▶|

Fig. 5.22. First screen of results of the cited reference search on Hawking's *Brief History of Time*. Data from *Web of Science*®, produced by the scientific business of The Thomson Corporation.

ways (the subtitle is sometimes part of it), and people sometimes include the chapter or page number in their citation. As mentioned before, basically what appears at the end of an author's article is what goes into the database. Remember Reference Desk Rule #1: citations are *never* quite accurate. And if you don't believe that yet, try this: look up Hawking S* as a cited author (without any other fields filled in). Browse forward through the screens until you get to the Cited Works beginning with *Breve Hist Temps* (ah ha—this book was translated into French). Note the many variations in titles, and year (probably different editions), and this is only the Hawking, S section of the list! Imagine what might be waiting when you get to the two-initial part of the list.

Pause and Think

Again, take a moment to ponder this: all of these entries represent articles that *cited* this book. There is no general record for this book in this database, because it doesn't index books. No record for the thing itself, but endless records that refer to it. Isn't that rather interesting? Exploring the world of scholarship is lovely, but ultimately, of course, you want to identify some records and do something with them. On to output options.

E-mail, Print, Save, or Export Results

Marking and Submitting

The overall process for outputting records from the *Web of Science* can be described as: Mark, Submit, and Output. On an article results page such

Fig. 5.23. The Marked Records Output Options screen. Data from *Web of Science*®, produced by the scientific business of The Thomson Corporation.

as Figure 5.19, above, click the checkboxes for the records you want to e-mail, print, etc. In the "Sort/Mark/Analyze" box on the right side of the screen (again, refer to Figure 5.19), make sure the "Selected records" radio button is selected, then click the "Submit" button. This will start your set of selected records. Go to the next page of results, and repeat the process. The important thing to remember is that you must click Submit on *each page* as you select records. Clicking Submit causes a new button to appear in the top line of buttons: "Marked List." (Refer back to Figure 5.15 to see a screen shot that includes the Marked List button.)

Output From the Marked List Screen

When you've marked and Submitted all the records you want, click the new Marked List button. This screen gives you a number of choices (Figure 5.23):

- All the checkboxes in the middle of the screen are additional fields you can include with the records. The default is author, title, and source.

- The e-mail function is good: it lets you put in your address for "return address," and add a note to explain why you're sending the information. If you are sending results to someone else, using your e-mail as the return address, rather than a strange system e-mail, makes the message look less like spam.

Other options are to format for printing, save to file, or "export to reference software"—that is, a bibliographic management package such as Reference Manager.™

Advanced Search   (See search history below)

Selected database(s) and timespan: [CHANGE SETTINGS]
Databases=SCI-EXPANDED; Timespan=1973-2005

Search General Search fields only, using 2-character tags. Combine sets using Boolean operators. Nest terms using parentheses ( ).

Field Tags	Booleans
(General Search only)	AND
TS=Topic	OR
TI=Title	NOT
AU=Author	SAME
GP=Group Author	
SO=Source	
AD=Address	
OG=Organization	
SG=Suborganization	
SA=Street Address	
CI=City	
PS=Province/State	
CU=Country	
ZP=Zip/Postal Code	

Examples: TS=(nanotub* SAME carbon) NOT AU=Smalley RE   more examples
#1 NOT #2

[_____] [SEARCH]

Search Aids: Author Index ⊠ | Group Author Index ⊠ | Full Source Titles List ⊠

Restrict search by languages and document types:

All languages	All document types
English	Article
Afrikaans	Abstract of Published Item
Arabic	Art Exhibit Review

Search History

Combine Sets ○ AND ○ OR [COMBINE]	Results		Delete Sets [SELECT ALL] [DELETE ✓]
		[SAVE HISTORY] [OPEN SAVED HISTORY]	
☐ #5	**203**	Cited Author=watson J* AND Cited Work=double helix AND View Reference Selections Cited Year=1968 *DocType=All document types; Language=All languages;* *Database=SCI-EXPANDED; Timespan=1973-2005*	☐
☐ #4	**121**	AU=(hawking s*) AND AD=(Cambridge) *DocType=All document types; Language=All languages; Database=SCI-* *EXPANDED; Timespan=1973-2005*	☐
☐ #3	**128**	AU=(hawking s*) *DocType=All document types; Language=All languages; Database=SCI-* *EXPANDED; Timespan=1973-2005*	☐

Fig. 5.24. The Advanced Search screen. Data from *Web of Science*®, produced by the scientific business of The Thomson Corporation.

Advanced Features: Advanced Search and Analyze

Advanced Search

The Advanced Search screen offers options for you real search hackers out there: searching with field codes and detailed syntax. Or, you can choose to manipulate sets from your search history, as shown in the lower half of the screen (Figure 5.24). (Access to the search history for simple manipulations of previous search sets is also available via a button in the row at the top of the screen—see Figures 5.13, 5.14, or 5.15.)

Analyze

In everyday usage of searching for articles and tracing citations, you probably won't find yourself using the "Analyze" function that frequently. However, for tracking publication patterns, or doing general research on scholarship (Who is doing it? Where, that is, what country, which organizations? What journals are they publishing in? What subject categories does this multidisciplinary department publish in?)—the Analyze function provides a fascinating tool.

Searching only the address field for: "Cog* Sci, Rochester, NY" retrieves articles published by members of the Department of Brain & Cognitive Science at the University of Rochester. This is a highly interdisciplinary department, so it is interesting to "Analyze" the results to see what journals they publish in most frequently, and to what subject categories those journals are assigned (Figure 5.25).

Fig. 5.25. The Analyze interface. Data from *Web of Science*®, produced by the scientific business of The Thomson Corporation.

Quick Recap

The *Web of Science* citation indexes have a dual nature. They allow you search and identify articles by keywords (topic searches), author, journal title, or by the author's address. The citation indexes do not have added subject headings; topical searches are dependent on the content of the article titles and abstracts. The other side of their dual nature is that they allow you to search for current articles that have *cited* a particular work from the past. The cited work can be any material type, not just journal articles, and can be from any date. Article records include a full bibliography: all works cited by the article. These citations are in a highly abbreviated format, and it is important to use the built-in look up indexes to pull up citations (and variations) correctly. Each article record has a link to related records, which are identified based on the number of cited references they share.

Exercises and Points to Consider

1. It was mentioned that by using more Limits in PubMed, it was possible to reduce the results numbers to something more like what we obtained in Ovid's MEDLINE. Go to PubMed, and set up the heart attack Limits as in Figure 5.7. In addition, look at the "Subsets" drop-down: why, there's a "MEDLINE" subset! That should fix it, right? Choose this "subset," put in heart attack, and search. Look at the information on the Details tab afterwards, to see what was searched.

   Back to the Limits screen. Click on the drop-down with the default of "All Fields"—change this to MeSH Major Topic. (This is the equivalent of "Focus" in Ovid.) Search again.

   Finally, visit the Preview/Index tab, to add the MeSH Subheading: prevention (cf. Figure 5.9). Choose MeSH Subheading from the drop-down, type prevention in the box, and click the "And" button below the box to add it to the search.

The number of search results, especially those on the "Review" tab, should now be about what you'd get in MEDLINE.

2. Think about all the work you did in PubMed to replicate the MED-LINE results. Do you think anyone besides librarians would ever master all that? On the other hand, does it matter? What if users treat PubMed as a sort of medical Google, and simply look at the first few screens of huge results sets? On a scale of 1 to 10, where 1 is "OK" and 10 is "a disaster," how would you rate this?

3. Ovid MEDLINE versus PubMed continued: for features that are the same, but implemented slightly differently (checkboxes versus Drop-down menus, for example)—which style of implementation do you prefer? Why? Overall, which database do you find more user-friendly?

4. While you're looking at PubMed, try some of the "Related Articles" links. If you have access to the *Web of Science*, do a search there, and take a look at some "Related Records" links. Going solely by the titles produced in each case, what is your impression of how well the different databases' "relatedness" function works? That is, PubMed relates articles by a word algorithm, and *Web of Science* does it by number of shared citations—does either seem to produce "more related" results than the other? Gut impression only, no research required.

5. For fun and amazement: at PubMed, click on the "All Databases" link.[10] (In the PubMed screen shots above, the first one in the black bar across the top. If the interface has changed, look for it.) This takes you to the "Entrez cross-database search page." Put in our old friend, heart attack, or any other term you want (diseases are good). You'll see the number of hits in each database for your term. Even if you have no idea of what most of these resources represent, this is fascinating! (And you can always click the "?" to get a fairly understandable description of the database content.)

6. A search scenario: You are applying for the position of librarian for physics and astronomy at the (name of university here). You want to make points when you meet the astronomy faculty, so you see if you can find out what they've been writing about. In the *Web of Science* you search:

   Topic: galax*

   Address: (part of school name) same astron* (same state abbreviation, if needed to distinguish).

7. In the *Web of Science*, look up Hawking S* as cited author again. Note the remarkable number of variations, lots of different years, in French, etc. Select only those entries where the cite seems to be odd or incorrect in some way, then "Finish" the search and look at the articles produced—interesting titles!

8. How might you set up the Stephen Hawking—*Brief History of Time* cited reference search using truncation? See how the number of

search results changes as you change where you truncate, put in the year or leave it out, etc.

9. Now that you've finished this chapter, what do you think about the opening premise: that the medical database is about "what," and the science database is about "who." Do you find this valid? Did you see further evidence to support this theory?

Notes

1. To eleven levels of specificity! (MeSH *Fact Sheet*).

2. EBM Reviews refers to a medical movement known as Evidence Based Medicine: the application of scientific method to medical practice, i.e., making medical care decisions based on documented studies, clinical trials, etc. ("evidence") rather than tradition or intuition. (And you thought what they do was scientific already.)

3. Clinical, clinician: to do with patient care (e.g., in the clinic), a medical professional who is primarily involved in treating patients (as opposed to doing research).

4. Fact Sheet includes additional added materials, and a list of other PubMed services.

5. Note that when this screen shot was taken, the database news being highlighted is that the "Action Bar" has been redesigned (and by the time this book gets to your hands, the look and feel of this Web site will probably have changed again). Just a little reminder that the details will always be changing in this business, and you need to be ready to map the new information onto your basic search principles.

6. Note: if you use truncation (*) in your query, the automatic mapping feature is disabled.

7. Alert readers may notice in Figure 5.15 a field called Keywords Plus, and Subject Category. Does this mean the *Web of Science* is getting into subject headings? In a word, no. Keywords Plus® terms are automatically generated terms, representing words or phrases that show up most frequently in the titles of an article's *references*. Subject Category is the subject category of the *journal* the article appeared in, a value decided once and then applied automatically every time a record is added from that journal. Finally, in other records you may notice "Keywords." These are author-supplied terms, a useful addition, but the addition of these terms did not slow down the process of getting the record into the database, and there is no controlled schema for them—they are simply whatever the author provided.

8. You don't *have* to use the wildcard, you can also use initials for both first and middle names, if you're sure the author always uses the middle initial. Not sure what Hawking's middle name is? Google for "Stephen * Hawking"—you'll be able to verify his name (and anything else about him) in no time.

9. My favorite is "Brief Hist Time Bing" . . .

10. The direct URL is http://www.ncbi.nlm.nih.gov/gquery/gquery.fcgi?itool=toolbar.

6
Bibliographic Databases

From the beginning of this book, we have been focusing on "article" databases that serve an abstracting and indexing (A & I) function: databases that provide a means to identify (and often to supply), articles in periodical publications. In this chapter, our focus will shift to "bibliographic" databases, which we will define as resources that provide information (mainly) about books. While A & I databases provide information about the contents of journals, etc., bibliographic databases provide information about the contents of a particular library, or many libraries, or any collection of book titles (e.g., *Books in Print*, Amazon.com). Put another way, an A & I database is like being *inside* a collection of journals or books, seeing all the contents, while a bibliographic database is like being on the *outside*, running your eyes down the spine titles of everything (book, bound journal, video, etc.) sitting on the shelves of a library or other collection.

You have undoubtedly used a bibliographic database many times already as a student or as a regular library user: every library's online catalog is a bibliographic database. The "OPAC" (Online Public Access Catalog) is how you find out about the contents of that particular library. If you think about it for any time at all, it's easy in today's networked, everything-is-on-the-web world, to see that it would be even more interesting if you could find out about the contents of other libraries—without having to go to each of their catalogs and search. It would be incredibly useful to gather the records from many libraries, and provide them as one massive "union" catalog. Such things were at one time published in hard copy, but an electronic database version would obviously be far more powerful and useful. It would provide all the contents of all the libraries, searchable through one interface. This sounds like a totally natural idea now ... but can you imagine having this vision in 1967? That is when Frederick G. Kilgour and university presidents in Ohio founded the Ohio College Library Center (Jordan, 2003) in order to "share library resources and reduce costs by using computers and technology" (Helfer, 2002). The original idea was to establish an online shared cataloging system, which OCLC introduced in 1971, and an Interlibrary Loan system, which was introduced in 1979 (Helfer, 2002). OCLC introduced the FirstSearch interface and access to several databases, including the union catalog, dubbed WorldCat, for use as a reference tool in 1991 (Hogan, 1991). OCLC (the acronym now stands for Online Computer Library Center) was a brilliant idea, way ahead of its time.

The majority of this chapter will be devoted to an exploration of World-Cat. We'll conclude with some suggestions and reminders about what to look for in your own local catalog.

WorldCat: The "OPAC of OPACs"

To me, WorldCat is far beyond just a "union catalog;" rather, one could call it a "world catalog." In the online Help for WorldCat, OCLC rather modestly describes their product as a catalog of books and other materials in libraries worldwide. The OCLC Web site pulls no punches, however, describing it as the world's largest bibliographic database. Currently there are 9,000 member libraries, representing eighty countries (OCLC, 2005). How was it, and is it, possible to put together and maintain such an enormous resource?

Background and Coverage

Note: in the following discussion, while it is always the same body of information being referring to, *how* it is referred to will differ depending on the library context. To Cataloging and Interlibrary Loan departments, this database is usually known simply as "OCLC." To librarians and library users, the database information is presented via WorldCat. (The cataloging and ILL interfaces and programs for interacting with the database are very different from WorldCat.) When the discussion concerns Cataloging or ILL, you will see that the text refers to this resource as the OCLC database. In the context of a database used by Reference librarians and patrons, it is referred to as WorldCat. Again, it is all the same body of information.

Part of the brilliance of OCLC's vision for creating this far-reaching union catalog was to make it a distributed, cooperative effort, and one that had immediate benefit for those supplying the effort. The business model here is that libraries pay annual fees to be members of OCLC, as well as activity fees to search the database and download records for use in the library's local catalog. OCLC manages the contributed data, and provides many services and benefits based on the database information. However, a key factor in the business model is that whenever a cataloger at a member library contributes a new record, or improves an existing record, the library receives *credits*. The more the library contributes, the more credits it receives.[1] While an actively contributing library is usually also an actively "using" library (thus incurring more service fees), receiving the credits does help keep the financial relationship from being entirely one-sided. Thus the OCLC database is built by catalogers at member libraries, already experts in their field, who would need to create records for their library's holdings anyway. By contributing their work, these member library catalogers offset the costs of searching and downloading records supplied by *other* member libraries. Everyone benefits, in terms of time, effort, and efficiency. One of the great benefits is that this huge bibliographic database is made available to Reference librarians and patrons in the form of WorldCat.

The scope of WorldCat is dazzling: as of this writing, the number of records in WorldCat has passed the 60 million mark, representing works dating from before 1000 BC to the present, in nearly 400 languages. As a collaborative, contributed effort, the database is updated constantly: according the OCLC Web site, on average a new record is added to WorldCat every 10 seconds.[2] The records in WorldCat represent the whole gamut of material types, everything the contributing libraries have cataloged: books, serials, manuscripts, musical scores, audiovisual materials (videos, DVDs, audio tapes, and other "sound recordings"), maps, electronic resources (Web sites, electronic journals, e-books, etc.), and these are just the common formats. As OCLC (2005) puts it: there is "everything from stone tablets to electronic books" and more.

A Tool for Many Parts of the Library

The OCLC database is both a creation and a tool of the *cataloging* department. Original catalogers create new records that get added to the local OPAC and to the OCLC database, while copy catalogers download pre-existing records for the local OPAC, as well as adding the local library's holdings to existing OCLC records (a process known as "tagging"). As you might imagine, the OCLC database is also integral to the *Interlibrary Loan* function. OCLC supplies several services that help speed and streamline resource sharing by ILL departments.

As a *reference* and *collection development* tool, librarians can use World-Cat to:

- Explore new or unfamiliar topics presented in reference questions; get a sense of what is available in a subject area.

- Find resources in an area that your library is limited in.

- Find resources in a particular format.

- Find everything written by a particular author.

- "Test the waters" before encouraging a patron to request an Interlibrary Loan, see how many libraries own the item, and where they are located.

- Identify government documents.

- Verify citations (for titles of books, journals, etc.), check publication dates, serial start dates, etc.

- Provide an interim solution if your catalog is down (but your holdings are in WorldCat).

- Develop a collection: see what's out there on a topic, what other libraries own, and what you might want to buy.

Note that records for serial publications in WorldCat can include holdings records, that is, the dates of the journal run owned by the library. It has always been possible to use WorldCat to see if another library owned a particular journal, but until holdings records were added to the WorldCat records, there was no way to tell if that subscription was current, or stopped in 1964. This is very useful for ILL staff, as well as at the Reference Desk.

Fig. 6.1. WorldCat Advanced Search screen. Screen shots used with permission of OCLC; FirstSearch and WorldCat are registered trademarks of OCLC Online Computer Library Center, Inc.

Notes and Search Examples

Let's get into the database and start looking for our Searcher's Toolkit items, as well as getting a sense of how this database differs from the article databases. We have a number of lighted-hearted searches to try here in WorldCat. We'll go straight to the Advanced Search screen (Figure 6.1) to begin.

Advanced Search Screen Notes

We've seen the FirstSearch advanced interface before when we looked at ERIC in Chapter 4, but the WorldCat interface has several significant differences that reflect its role as an access point to the contents of libraries. The immediately visible differences have to do with Limits and Ranking possibilities. In ERIC, we could limit by Year, Language, Document Type, and by library ("Limit availability to:"). Here in WorldCat, we can also limit by Year and Language, but rather than a drop-down menu of Document Types, we have a whole section of the screen devoted to choosing *material* types (Books, Serials, Archival Materials, etc.). A new drop-down has been added that limits the search by the "Number of Libraries" that own the item: the choices are 5 or more, 50 or more, or 500 or more. (Think about this one for a moment: what is the implication here? Why might you want to use this limit?)

We also have new "Subtype" limits to define our audience, content, and format. Under audience, we can specify Juvenile or not Juvenile. Under content, we have options for Fiction, not Fiction, Biography, Thesis/dissertation, Musical recording, or Non-musical recording. The format options are Large print, Braille, Manuscript, Microform, not Microform, CD audio, Cassette recording, LP recording, VHS tape/Videocassette, and DVD Video/Videodisc. These "subtypes" say a lot about WorldCat as both a reflection of the content and a tool for *public* libraries, which also distinguishes this database from the article databases in this book. Not that academia doesn't use World-Cat constantly, it does. But WorldCat is equally useful in any other kind of library too: a database of all the libraries, for all the people. Quite an achievement!

Next on the screen we see the same "Limit availability to" function found in ERIC (i.e., the library you are in, or another library you would indicate by an alpha code), followed by a "Rank by" setting. The "Rank by" options are slightly different from ERIC's: rather than No Ranking, Relevance, or Date, the WorldCat options are Number of Libraries, Relevance, Date, or Accession Number. This is another reminder that this database is all about the holdings of libraries.

More differences become apparent when we compare the fields available for searching (the drop-down menus associated with the three text input fields in the "Search for" section). The list of searchable fields in ERIC is heavily focused on indexes to subject term fields, having one-word and phrase indexes not just for Descriptors, but also Major Descriptors, Minor Descriptors, and Identifiers, as well as Subject. Fields such as Source (and Source Phrase), Report Number, Sponsoring Agency, and Abstract also reflect ERIC's function as an abstracting and indexing database, rather than a bibliographic database. In contrast, the searchable fields in WorldCat are all about identifying books and other complete items that you would find on library shelves. There are many variations on "Author" (nicely gathered together and indented under Author), along with Publisher and Publisher Location, and specific Standard Number choices: ISBN and ISSN. We have an opportunity to search by Material Type in more detail (such as "book not URL"), or types of Musical Compositions (overtures, part-songs, etc., or phrases such as folk music, gospel music, etc.). WorldCat certainly has subject-related search fields, but subjects here are rather different: in addition to Subject, Subject Phrase, and Descriptor, we have Genre/Form, Geographic Coverage, Named Corporation and Conference, and Named Person.

"Subject" is an excellent way to start exploring WorldCat, however, in conjunction with some limits.

Search Examples

Search 1

You'd like to find some cookbooks for your friend's Korean mother, who doesn't speak English. Although your natural inclination in this case might

Fig. 6.2. Results for Subject: Cookery and Language: Korean. Screen shots used with permission of OCLC; FirstSearch and WorldCat are registered trademarks of OCLC Online Computer Library Center, Inc.

be to use the term given, "cookbooks," or perhaps "cooking," if you browse the Subject index it turns out the overwhelming majority of records use the term "Cookery" for this Subject. Clicking "Cookery" in the Subject index pastes it into the search screen, and we can then use our Language limit to limit to materials about Cookery in Korean.

Notice the tabs above the result list, shown in Figure 6.2, indicating the number of results for each type of media. Note too that there are over 1,000 records for cookbooks in *Korean*—isn't that incredible? (In case you're curious, the Sound file is an instructional cassette tape.) Remember that the results are sorted, or ranked, by the number of libraries that own the item.

Search 2

Your kids are beginning to show an interest in cooking, and you'd like to see if there are some cookbooks written for children.

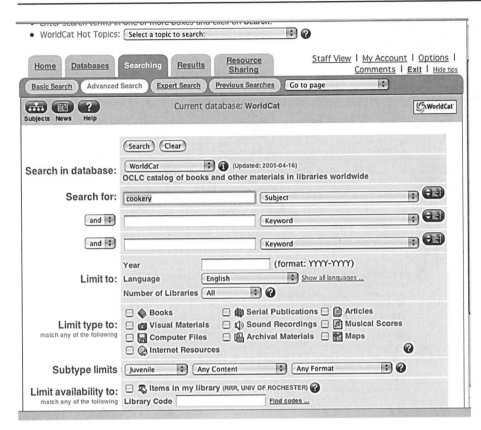

Fig. 6.3. Cookbooks for kids search. Screen shots used with permission of OCLC; FirstSearch and WorldCat are registered trademarks of OCLC Online Computer Library Center, Inc.

Returning to the search screen (the "Searching" tab is a good way to do this), we already have "cookery" set as our Subject. Any limits you set previously will also still be in effect, so remember to change the language back to English. This is the perfect occasion to use that first Subtype limit: audience, to specify we want materials for a "Juvenile" audience. Figure 6.3 shows this search ready to be run.

There are plenty of options to explore, as indicated by the number and variety of formats shown in the results screen in Figure 6.4.

Note that there is even one entry on the "Musical Scores" tab—how peculiar! Whenever you see an odd result, don't immediately assume it's a mistake. Take a good look at the record and find out why. In a carefully crafted database like this one, where your search has been set up only in terms of subjects and field search values (rather than as a keyword search), it is highly unlikely that an odd result will be a false drop. By looking and figuring out why, you'll add to your understanding of database lore in general, and discover interesting and bizarre things that may bring a smile to your face (and remind you why this profession is so much fun).

Here is why our search retrieved this "Musical Score." It's a book of children's songs and activities, including recipes, for Halloween. See the Descriptors and Notes field in Figure 6.5.

Fig. 6.4. Results for Subject: Cookery and Audience: Juvenile. Screen shots used with permission of OCLC; FirstSearch and WorldCat are registered trademarks of OCLC Online Computer Library Center, Inc.

Little witch. Old Farmer Dan. Orange pumpkins. Pumpkin, pumpkin. Popcorn ball. Skin and bones. Spin, spider, spin. Spooky Loo. That's what Halloween is for. There's a house in the middle of the wood. Three little witches. Three scarecrows. Thump! Thump! Thump! The witch rides her broom. The witches' stew.

SUBJECT(S)

Descriptor: Halloween -- Songs and music.
Halloween -- Cookery.
Children's songs.

Note(s): Songs, poems, finger plays, and recipes for Halloween./ Songs include melodic lines with chord symbols./ Includes index.

Class Descriptors: **Dewey:** 782.4215246

Fig. 6.5. Explanation of the "Musical Scores" result. Screen shots used with permission of OCLC; FirstSearch and WorldCat are registered trademarks of OCLC Online Computer Library Center, Inc.

Search 3

Continuing in a similar vein, now we'd like to find some mystery novels with a cooking theme.

Returning to the search screen, we'll keep Cookery as our Subject term, and add another field search: mystery in the Genre/Form field. We'll also want to change our "Audience" subtype to "not Juvenile."

In the results, an author named Diane Mott Davidson seems to lead the pack in terms of these cooking mysteries. Figures 6.6a and 6.6b give us a view into a full record: note the "Amazon.com-like" feature of providing the book cover and a brief blurb. In fact, the one record is really being offered two ways: the upper, generally eye-catching, easy-to-grasp-quickly section (Figure 6.6a), and then the lower, nitty-gritty, all the details section (Figure 6.6b). Even when an image of the "cover art" is not provided, the basic citation information is set off in this upper section.

Using WorldCat for Citation Verification

WorldCat is also invaluable for resolving citation problems, such as determining what the *real* title of a work is, or its publication year, author, etc. You can use it to fill in information on books and other formats, or determine what material type a title really is (a monographic series? A conference report? A serial publication?). WorldCat can be particularly useful for resolving questions about serial publications, especially esoteric titles, or titles that have ceased (and that don't appear in a periodicals directory). If we know that something existed at some time, then it is likely that *some* library, somewhere, owns it, and chances are good that that library also contributes records to WorldCat.

Search 4

A student comes to the Reference Desk and says: "My professor said I should look at some journal—it's the British journal of clinical something-or-other, I can't remember . . . but she said she knows the Health Sciences Library at Buffalo gets it . . ."

In doing any kind of citation verification or completion in WorldCat (or in an article database), the Searcher's Toolkit tools you'll want to make good use of are the field indexes and truncation symbols. If at all possible, especially in tracking down journals, try to come up with the ISSN for the publication (or ISBN, for books). Words are fuzzy and easily mistaken—but numbers don't lie. There is only one identifying number for every publication (exceptions exist, of course, but as a general principle you can depend on this). It's much more efficient and accurate to search by number than by name.

However, since we are unsure of the journal name, we can't determine an ISSN and look it up that way. Checking the Title Phrase field index for "British journal of clinical" we find the following (Figure 6.7).

Since there are obviously quite a few *"British Journal of Clinical . . ."* titles, rather than choosing anything from the index list, we'll simply return to the Advanced Search screen and enter:

British journal of clinical*

as a Title Phrase search.

(a)

(b)

Fig. 6.6. (a) Upper part of a full record display. Screen shots used with permission of OCLC; FirstSearch and WorldCat are registered trademarks of OCLC Online Computer Library Center, Inc. (b) Lower part of a full record display. Screen shots used with permission of OCLC; FirstSearch and WorldCat are registered trademarks of OCLC Online Computer Library Center, Inc.

Fig. 6.7. Browsing the Title Phrase field index. Screen shots used with permission of OCLC; FirstSearch and WorldCat are registered trademarks of OCLC Online Computer Library Center, Inc.

The patron has also told us this journal is available at the Health Sciences Library "at Buffalo." We could refine our search by finding the "Library Code" for the Health Sciences Library, and entering it in the "Limit availability to" section (cf. Figure 6.1). Clicking the "Find codes..." link opens the "Participating Institutions" search in a new window. While "at Buffalo" usually refers to the State University of New York at Buffalo, it's hard to know how that name might be abbreviated, so we'll play it very safe, and simply search Buffalo as the City, and "health" anywhere in the text (Figure 6.8).

This search gives us four results, from which it is fairly easy to pick out the appropriate institution (State Univ of New York, Health Sci Libr). Note that the symbol for each institution appears in the first column, on the left side of the screen (Figure 6.9).

We'll note the symbol, SBH, then close this window and return to the search screen. Our "mystery journal" search is now ready to run (Figure 6.10).

Upon seeing the results (Figure 6.11), the student decides it must be the first title, since it's for a Psych class.

But the student might also want to know: "is the Health Sciences Library's subscription current?" And it would be even more convenient if the journal were here, at the University of Rochester, so she wouldn't need to drive to Buffalo. There is an immediate tip-off here in the results screen: *The British Journal of Clinical Psychology* entry includes a small icon, with the notation "Univ of Rochester," indicating that the title *is* held locally. But are the local holdings up-to-date? Clicking the "Libraries worldwide" link for any of these records reveals a very useful feature noted above, in the A

Regional service providers	**Participating Institutions search**	
OCLC offices		
Participating Institutions ▸	Find a library or group of libraries, their symbols and policies. Enter whatever you know—part of a name, city, etc. To search for a group of libraries, type "or" between your search terms; for example, "DC or MD or VA".	**Also...**

The following represents the screen layout in the figure:

Participating Institutions search

Find a library or group of libraries, their symbols and policies. Enter whatever you know—part of a name, city, etc. To search for a group of libraries, type "or" between your search terms; for example, "DC or MD or VA".

Note: Some words in the Institution Name field have been abbreviated. Click here for a list of abbreviations used.

Output

Maximum Number of Hits: 50

Sort By: Symbol (Default)

[Start Search]

Search Criteria

Any Field, Any Text: Health

Fields

Institution Name:

Abbreviations

OCLC Symbol:

City: Buffalo

State:

Regional Groupings

ZIP or Postal Code:

Country:

Left sidebar navigation:
- Regional service providers
- OCLC offices
- Participating Institutions
- Abbreviations
- Participating countries
- Supplier/ILL policy info
- Regional groupings for institutions
- GAC and UL group codes
- System code definitions
- PI instructions
- Hints for PI
- PI record fields
- IFM participants

Right sidebar:
Also...

OCLC libraries
- Instructions
- Hints
- Fields
- Update my listing
- Search Participating Institutions

Abbreviations and codes explained
- Abbreviations
- Countries in Participating Institutions records
- Supplier/ILL policy information
- OCLC regional service providers
- Regional groupings for Institution Locations
- Group Access Capability (GAC) and Union List (UL) group codes
- System code definitions
- IFM participants

Fig. 6.8. Participating Institutions search screen. Screen shots used with permission of OCLC; FirstSearch and WorldCat are registered trademarks of OCLC Online Computer Library Center, Inc.

Tool for Many Parts of the Library section. Many serial records in World-Cat now include holdings information, i.e., in addition to which libraries own the title, the years and volumes owned are available as well (Figure 6.12).

In Figure 6.12, we get our confirmation: the SUNY Health Sciences Library has a current subscription, but so does the University of Rochester. A trip to Buffalo (or an ILL request) isn't necessary after all.

Quick Recap

WorldCat is different from all the other databases in this book. Rather than being an index to journal articles or statistical publications, it is a database of the contents of all kinds of libraries: public, academic, and corporate. The range of materials included and audiences that might be served by the information contained here are thus incredibly broad.

Search Results for: Any Text="health", City="buffalo"

Symbol	Institution Name & Address Network/Service Center/International Division	System Code ILL Policy IFM Full Text	USMARC Code	Groups
SBF	**LIBRARY CONSOR OF HEALTH INST BUFFALO** BUFFALO, NY 14214 UNITED STATES NYLINK	Cataloging NONSUPPLIER IFM: N	None	**GAC:** NYGC **SUL:** GCYS
SBH	**STATE UNIV OF NEW YORK, HEALTH SCI LIBR** BUFFALO, NY 14214-3002 UNITED STATES NYLINK	Cataloging $, SUPPLIER IFM: Y	NBuU-H	**GAC:** GNYS, ILLD, NE@R, NYGC, RRWG **SUL:** GNYA, NEPU, NYUL, NYWU **XG:** LAND, RSUN
VTO	**BRY-LIN HOSP, HEALTH SCI LIBR** BUFFALO, NY 14209 UNITED STATES NYLINK	SUL Only NONSUPPLIER IFM: N	None	**SUL:** NYUL, NYWU
VUK	**HEALTH SYST AG WNY LIBR** BUFFALO, NY 14203 UNITED STATES NYLINK	SUL Only NONSUPPLIER IFM: N	None	**SUL:** NYUL, NYWU

Records found: 4 Records displayed: 4

(Return to Search)

Fig. 6.9. Participating Institutions search results. Screen shots used with permission of OCLC; FirstSearch and WorldCat are registered trademarks of OCLC Online Computer Library Center, Inc.

Fig. 6.10. Search for *British Journal of Clinical** titles restricted to Library Code SBH. Screen shots used with permission of OCLC; FirstSearch and WorldCat are registered trademarks of OCLC Online Computer Library Center, Inc.

Fig. 6.11. Results: *British Journal of Clinical** titles restricted to Library Code SBH. Screen shots used with permission of OCLC; FirstSearch and WorldCat are registered trademarks of OCLC Online Computer Library Center, Inc.

WorldCat is the largest union catalog in the world, comprised of records for books and many other material types from thousands of member libraries. The database is a distributed effort, built by catalogers at contributing libraries. As a Reference tool, WorldCat can be used in many ways, such as topic exploration or collection development, finding resources in a particular format, verifying citations for books or other materials (not articles), or discovering where materials your library does not own are available, e.g., which other libraries own them. The WorldCat Advanced Search interface has a number of additional Limits (for material types) and Subtype limits (for audience, content, and formats) not found in other FirstSearch databases. The Results screen is tabbed to allow users to see all the results, or to view records by material type (serials, Internet resources, maps, etc.). Every record includes a "Libraries worldwide" link to view the list of libraries that own the item. (One can also restrict a search to a particular library.)

Your Local OPAC

Even though WorldCat is a (huge) union *catalog*, I always think of it as a *database*. On the other hand, I always think of my institution's online catalog as—a catalog, not a database. Now, why is that? Is it because WorldCat comes to us through the FirstSearch interface, as do many article databases, and our library catalogs come from other vendors—vendors who specialize in online public access *catalogs*? Whether you have the same

NY	HUNTER COL	vol: 20-23-30 1901-1984	ZHM
NY	ITHACA COL	vol: 20-40 1981-2001	XIM
NY	LEHMAN COL LIBR	vol: 20-31 1981-1992	VYL
NY	LONG ISLAND UNIV, C W POST CAM	Microfiche only v.20- 19	VXX
NY	LONG ISLAND UNIV	v.41- 1981-2003	ZLI
NY	MARIST COL LIBR	vol: 22- 1983-	XMA
NY	MOUNT SINAI SCH OF MED		VVL
NY	NEW YORK ACAD OF MED		VVK
NY	NEW YORK INST OF TECH, NEW YORK	v.20-28 1981-1989	YFE
NY	NEW YORK INST OF TECH	v.20-29 1981-1990	ZNT
NY	NEW YORK PUB LIBR, BR LIBR		BNY
NY	NEW YORK STATE LIBR		NYG
NY	PACE UNIV, PLEASANTVILLE LIBR	vol: 20-25 1981-1986	VZU
NY	PFIZER, INC, NEW YORK		PFIZE
NY	QUEENS COL	vol: 20-32 1981-1993.	XQM
NY	SAGE COL, THE	v.20- 1981-	ZRS
NY	SAINT JOHNS UNIV LIBR	vol: 26- 1987-	ZSJ
NY	SAINT LAWRENCE UNIV	v.21-v.40 1982-2001	XLM
NY	STATE UNIV OF NEW YORK, HEALTH SCI LIBR	vol: 20- 1981-	SBH
NY	SUNY AT ALBANY	vol: 20- 1981-	NAM
NY	SUNY AT STONY BROOK, HEALTH SCI LIBR	vol: 20-33 1981-1994	VZB
NY	SUNY AT STONY BROOK	vol: 20- 1981-	YSM
NY	SUNY COL AT BROCKPORT	vol: 20- 1981-	XBM
NY	SUNY COL AT CORTLAND	vol: 20- 1981-	YCM
NY	SUNY COL AT FREDONIA	vol: 20-23 1981-1984	XFM
NY	SUNY COL AT ONEONTA	vol: 20-31 1981-1992	ZBM
NY	SUNY HEALTH SCI CTR AT BROOKLYN	vol: 20-37	VVD
NY	SUNY UPSTATE MED UNIV HEALTH SCI LIBR	vol: 20-29 1981-1990	VYQ
NY	SYRACUSE UNIV	v.20-v.37 1981-1998	SYB
NY	⚷ UNIV OF ROCHESTER	vol: 20- 1981-	RRR
NY	UTICA COL	v.20- 1981-	VVV

Fig. 6.12. Holdings information screen. Screen shots used with permission of OCLC; FirstSearch and WorldCat are registered trademarks of OCLC Online Computer Library Center, Inc.

reaction or not, go now and revisit whatever library catalog you use most often. Try to look at it as if it were a new database. Examine it with the Searcher's Toolkit in mind: what fields does it offer? What limits? Does it offer a basic and an advanced search mode? Are there even other modes? Does it support Boolean searching, wildcards, or truncation? Are there stop words? What are the default search settings? Are there any special features that have been customized for *your* library?

Now compare searching your OPAC with WorldCat. Does one seem "more transparent" (in terms of how it works) than the other? Look up an item owned by your library, and then find the record for it in WorldCat.[3] How do the record displays compare? Think about what factors might be driving the needs of a remote, *union* catalog as opposed to the local catalog for one library (or library system).

In general, you may find it easy to fall into using the local OPAC just as a title look-up device, forgetting what a sophisticated search engine it really is (or, perhaps, it isn't). It's worth it to take a few moments and reacquaint yourself with this resource, which you probably feel you know so well.

Exercises and Points to Consider

1. In the section called "A Tool for Many Parts of the Library," we mentioned a couple of ways you might use WorldCat at the Reference Desk—what other uses can you think of?

2. Find some books on fast food (what's the best way to get books really on "fast food," and not food you can prepare fast?)

3. Half-remembered reference problem: a patron comes in trying to describe some books she has enjoyed. She remembers the author's name was "something-something smith," and the books are mysteries, about a female detective in Africa somewhere. Try just searching the author field for Smith, and the Genre/Form field for mystery, and see if you can identify this series of books.

4. If you have a favorite author or genre, see if you can use WorldCat to find all the records for those works in your local public library branch. (Tip: use the code lookup screen.)

5. WorldCat claims to have records for everything from stone tablets to electronic books. See if you can find examples of both ends of this spectrum. (Hints: in each case, use a combination of keywords and Limits. For the stone tablets, note the "Visual Materials" Limit, and that the "Material Type" for this sort of thing is "real object." For electronic books, you'll want to use the "Internet Resource" Limit.)

6. WorldCat results are sorted, or ranked, by the number of libraries that own the item. There are three other options, but this is often set as the default. Why, do you think? What would be advantages, disadvantages of other results display options?

Notes

1. Not all member libraries can or do contribute records, of course. Many small libraries simply pay to be able to search and download records for their local catalog, as it is still more efficient and economical than employing cataloging staff.

2. Visit the "Watch WorldCat grow" page at http://www.oclc.org/worldcat/grow.htm. It is absolutely fascinating.

3. Check the "Libraries worldwide" link to make sure you get the version of the record with which your library is associated. While the ideal might be one record per title in WorldCat, the reality is that there are often several records for the same title, because participating libraries have cataloged the item slightly differently.

7
Humanities Databases

Although people come to librarianship with all kinds of different backgrounds and with many different undergraduate degrees, from purely anecdotal evidence it seems to me that there is still a preponderance of people with undergraduate degrees in the humanities who enter the library field. Or am I imagining that large sigh of relief among you readers, now that we've arrived at the "Humanities" chapter? In any event, it's likely you'll find the two databases considered here, *America: History and Life*,[1] and the *MLA International Bibliography*, to be fun, easy to use, and a fascinating window into their respective disciplines.

As with MEDLINE® and the *Web of Science*® in Chapter 5, these two databases are excellent examples of tools that are structured specifically for their subject matter, in this case, American history, and the world of literature, language, and human communication. What is important to historians? Many things, obviously, but the foundation of history is "when" it happened: dates. You'll find that *America: History and Life* uses a unique set of index values for its date field, to support this emphasis on "dates" in a way most appropriate to the discipline. We'll compare this to the *MLA International Bibliography* "Period" index values, which reveal a rather different mindset about dates. What is uniquely important to *MLA* and its users are attributes of written (and other forms of) communication: genres, themes, influences, etc., all of which are supported in *MLA* records, and in the version of the *MLA* database described here. We'll also see a difference in approach regarding "language" (of the source, or as a topic of the source) between the historical and literature databases. As in Chapter 5, as we work through these two resources, in addition to absorbing information about functionality and content, try to be alert to aspects of each database that seem specially designed to support its subject discipline.

America: History and Life

Background and Coverage

America: History and Life, and its complement, *Historical Abstracts*, are the flagship products of ABC-CLIO, a family owned company devoted to history and social studies reference products. The company was founded in 1953, and the first volume of *Historical Abstracts* appeared in 1995. *Historical Abstracts* indexes materials on world history, while *America: History and Life*, focuses on American and Canadian history. We will work with the latter database, but what you learn about searching *America: History and Life* can be applied to *Historical Abstracts*.

As described in the online database FAQ, and the ABC-CLIO Product Information Sheet (Speck, 2002), *America: History and Life* first appeared in print 1964, but the index covers materials back to 1954, which is a somewhat unusual treat in the indexing world. The online version contains all the content of the print versions, e.g., 1954—present, making it a "date deep" resource. The historical scope of coverage, however, goes back to prehistory: that is, articles, book and media reviews, or dissertations discussing any period of American and Canadian history from prehistory to the present, are eligible for inclusion. Journal articles are drawn from a worldwide scan of almost 1,700 journals. The database is updated monthly, and approximately 16,000 entries are added per year.

America: History and Life is a true indexing and abstracting service: it contains *citations*, some with abstracts. In full records, when an Abstract is available, an "Abstracter" field is also present, to provide attribution. The addition of this field demonstrates that abstracts in *America: History and Life* are written by individuals, rather than being machine-generated. (Abstracter is a display-only field, and is not searchable.) Although *America: History and Life* does not contain any full text, it can be configured to help users get to full text. The ABC-CLIO databases are "OpenURL" compliant, that is, they support link resolvers such as SFX. A combination of these history indexes, a linking technology, and a subscription to the full text journal archive service JSTOR, would be very powerful and convenient for users.

Notes and Search Examples

If you subscribe to both of the historical databases from ABC-CLIO, your search session will start with the entry screen as shown in Figure 7.1: an easy choice between *America: History and Life* and *Historical Abstracts*.

Basic Search Interface

Clicking on the *America: History and Life* button brings us to the Basic Search screen, as shown in Figure 7.2. Yes, it is basic, and not threatening: this database is intended for use by a wide range of ages and skill levels. In "Basic" mode we have the ability to search in two of the most often used fields, Keywords or Subject Terms, and to limit the search by document type. Thus even from the Basic Search screen one could search for dissertations whose titles or abstracts contained certain keywords, or quickly locate a book review for a particular title, since the Keywords index contains all the words from the title, author, abstract, as well as Subject Terms fields. (The Subject Terms field search only checks the controlled terms in that index.)

Fig. 7.1. Initial entry screen for ABC-CLIO databases. Used with permission, courtesy ABC-Clio Inc.

Fig. 7.2. Basic Search screen. Used with permission, courtesy ABC-Clio Inc.

With the "Add/Remove Search Fields" option, one could also add only those additional search fields needed at the moment—in essence, make your own customized interface. It's actually more sophisticated than the first impression suggests. Some additional fields and functionality await us in Advanced Search, however, so let's move on.

Advanced Search Interface

Advanced Search (Figure 7.3) gives us a choice of nine fields to search, of which five have an index of values to choose from, signified by the open

Fig. 7.3. Advanced Search screen. Used with permission, courtesy ABC-Clio Inc.

book icon. Hopefully what's beginning to run through your mind is a mental checklist of the Searcher's Toolkit: we have field searching, and limits. As your mouse hovers over elements of the screen, brief amounts of "context sensitive" help are displayed. The interface points us to Help for more information, where you'll find the "User's Guide" is very up-to-date, with labeled graphics and clear explanations.

As mentioned briefly in the introduction to this chapter, now we meet the field that is so distinctly appropriate to this database's function as an index to history literature: the Time Periods field. What is unique and interesting here are the *values* for this field. If we click the book icon at the end of the Time Periods field, we go into the Time Periods Browsable Index, as shown in Figure 7.4. 1000H? 1010D? What is going on here? Well, if you're an historian, you might look at eras such as centuries (*h*undreds of years), or perhaps *d*ecades: that might be the way you usually carve up time. And that is what we have here: a controlled set of terms for historical periods,[2] nicely annotated with the number of records to which the term has been applied. Both of these points are interesting: one, that the terms for this field *are* controlled (a clue to inferring this is that the list is so "clean," there are no extraneous entries): this concept is important enough to warrant devising a specialized system and applying it rigorously. And two, the numbers of records associated with each period reveals something about the level of scholarly research activity in the various time periods. For one

Fig. 7.4. Time Periods Browsable Index. Used with permission, courtesy ABC-Clio Inc.

thing, more seems to be written about the century periods than the decades. This is immediately obvious here, in the very early time periods, but is also demonstrated in the modern time periods: if we used the search box to jump ahead to 1900, we'd find the decade periods now have record counts of over 50,000 in all cases (outliers are the 1970s, with over 90,000, and the 1990s, with under 30,000), but the count for 1900 is over 370,000. Even the record counts for materials discussing 2000 as a century are slightly ahead of those dealing with 2000 as a decade period.

We'll use the Time Periods field in a moment, but first, a simple search to demonstrate one of the common uses of this database.

Search Example 1: Finding Book Reviews

In this search example we'd like to find book reviews in history journals of Robert Westbrook's *John Dewey and American Democracy*. We'll start the search strategy with the author, Robert Westbrook. We could simply enter his name in the Authors/Editors field, but the search engine is fairly generous in how it interprets text entries: we would get every variation on Robert Westbrook, but we'd also pick up records with multiple authors, where "Robert" and "Westbrook" matched, but not necessarily in one name.

Fig. 7.5. Authors/Editors Browsable Index. Used with permission, courtesy ABC-Clio Inc.

It's just more efficient, ultimately, to jump into the index and select the name variants we'd like to search on, as shown in Figure 7.5.

The "Add Checked Terms To Your Search" button adds all our selections to the search screen, appropriately "ORed" together. Using the convenient checkbox to select "Book Review" as our document type, and a keyword from the title of the work, our search is ready, as shown in Figure 7.6. Our results appear to be right on target, judging by the first several records shown in Figure 7.7.

Some things to note about this search: in the case of a book review, "Title" always refers to the title of the work being reviewed, and Authors/Editors *generally* refers to the person who wrote the work being reviewed. If you have access to *America: History and Life*, and can replicate this search, you'll find as you go down the list of results that toward the end, the Author is no longer Robert Westbook, and the book being reviewed is not *John Dewey in America*. The "Expand Record" link reveals why: now Robert Westbrook is the *review* author, and he is reviewing other people's books about John Dewey. Thus searching an author name (John Bloggs), and review as a document type, will retrieve both reviews of works by John Bloggs, and reviews by Mr. Bloggs of other people's works. Don't let it throw you.

Search Example 2: Finding Material about a Topic in a Particular Time Period

In this search, we want to produce a list of references to works about anti-Catholic activities of the Ku Klux Klan in the 1920s. The key elements in setting up this strategy are to use the Time Periods field, and the Subject Terms index to select various Ku Klux Klan headings. The "anti-Catholic" concept can be handled in the Keywords field, and beware of being too specific here. Just because the user expressed her reference need as "anti-Catholic" doesn't mean you have to use that term exactly. You might try it,

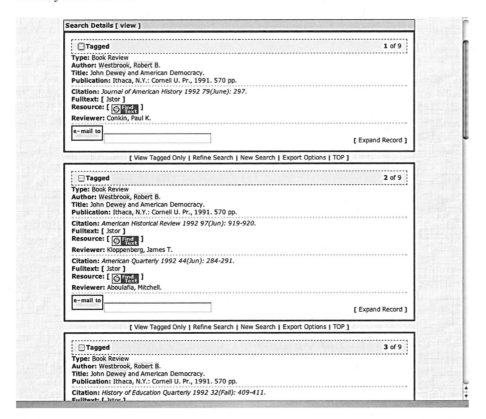

Fig. 7.6. Search strategy to find reviews of a particular book. Used with permission, courtesy ABC-Clio Inc.

Fig. 7.7. Search results list, brief display. Used with permission, courtesy ABC-Clio Inc.

Fig. 7.8. Search 2 strategy except for keyword. Used with permission, courtesy ABC-Clio Inc.

but then suggest other possibilities: "Catholic" for example, or "Catholi*"—don't forget about your wildcard tool. In this case, some general historical knowledge is very helpful: if it's about Catholics and the Klan, by implication it's "anti," you probably don't need to be specific. Figure 7.8 shows the search screen set up for this search, but lacking the keyword. Again, if you have access to this database, get in and try it yourself, and see how the results differ when you change the keyword (from anti-Catholic, to Catholic, to Catholi*).

Before we proceed with the search, however, I'd like to point out another feature on the search interface: the Display Options link (Figure 7.9). Display Options allows you to change various defaults, such as sort order, the field the results are sorted by, and number of results displayed per page, all without leaving the search interface. Although a relatively small matter, I always appreciate it when a vendor offers that last option, giving me control over the number of records displayed at once. Note that Display Options is only available from either of the search screens; it is not available on the search results screen.

Tagging and Output Options

Tagging Records

In a pattern that should be very familiar by now, you select the records from results lists by clicking their checkbox, as shown in Figure 7.10. In this

for [   ] in **Authors / Editors** ⊌
for [   ] in **Titles / Translations**
for [   ] in **Languages** ▥
for [   ] in **Journal Names** ▥
for [   ] in **Publication Dates**
for [|1920D|] in **Time Periods** ▥
for [   ] in **Entry Numbers**

limit to ☐ Articles, ☐ Book Reviews, ☐ Media Reviews, ☐ Collections, ☐ Dissertations.

Add / Remove Search Fields [hide | add all fields | remove all fields]
☑ Author ☑ Title ☑ Language ☑ Journal ☑ PubDate ☑ Period ☑ Entry#

Search History [hide | clear search history]
Select a link to restore search criteria and results...
1. AUTHOR=|**Westbrook, Robert.**| or |**Westbrook, Robert B.**| or |**Westbrook, Robert Brett.**|, DOCTYPE=**book**, TITLE=**Dewey**,

Display Options [hide]
Display results in groups of [25 ▸] entries,
in [Descending order ▸] sorted by [Date field ▸]
Automatically tag all search results ☐

Personal Profile [view]

[Content Support | Technical Support | Forum Support]
© 2006 by ABC-Clio Inc. All rights reserved.

Fig. 7.9. Display Options interface in "View" mode. Used with permission, courtesy ABC-Clio Inc.

☑ **Tagged**   3 of 45
Type: Book Review
Author: Tucker, Todd.
Title: Notre Dame vs. the Klan: How the Fighting Irish Defeated the Ku Klux Klan.
Publication: Chicago: Loyola U. Pr., 2004. 261 pp.

Citation: *Indiana Magazine of History 2005 101(3): 289-291.*
Fulltext: [History Cooperative]
Resource: [⊘ Find Text]
Reviewer: Safianow, Allen.

[e-mail to] [   ]
                                                       [Expand Record]

[View Tagged Only | Refine Search | New Search | Export Options | TOP]

☑ **Tagged**   4 of 45
Type: Article
Author: Erickson, Christine K.
Title: "KLUXER BLUES": THE KLAN CONFRONTS CATHOLICS IN BUTTE, MONTANA, 1923-1929.
Citation: Montana 2003 53(1): 44-57. **ISSN:** 0026-9891

Resource: [⊘ Find Text]

[e-mail to] [   ]
                                                       [Expand Record]

[View Tagged Only | Refine Search | New Search | Export Options | TOP]

Fig. 7.10. Some tagged records. Used with permission, courtesy ABC-Clio Inc.

database, however, you don't need to remember to "submit" or do any other extra action to save your selected records: once checkmarked, records are immediately added to the Tagged List. You can page back and forth in your result list, tagging records on any page of results, and the selected items will all be added to the Tagged List. The Tagged List is not cumulative between different searches, however; running another search will wipe out the contents of the Tagged List, so you do need to take action on your selected

Fig. 7.11. The Export Records screen, set to export to RefWorks. Used with permission, courtesy ABC-Clio Inc.

records before moving on to another search. Other details to observe in Figure 7.10: the e-mail box in every record, allowing you to immediately send something of interest to yourself or someone else, and the navigation links under every record, allowing you to View Tagged Only, Refine or run a New Search, access the Export Options, or jump to the TOP of the results list.

Export Options

Records from *America: History and Life* can be output as short or full records, and printed, saved, or sent as an e-mail message (Figure 7.11). The "Output Types," ASCII or Tab-Delimited, are both plain text; the ASCII format provides a cleaner "look" for printing, while you might want to use the tab-delimited option if you were going to keep track of your citations by importing them into a spreadsheet. If you use a bibliographic management program to manage your citations (such as RefWorks or EndNote), ABC-CLIO provides the option to export directly to those programs as well. The e-mail options give you full control over the look and feel of the message, allowing you to specify everything yourself: To, From, Subject, *and* Message. (The e-mail option under Export would be more convenient in cases where you had marked a number of records and wished to e-mail all of them at once, rather than using the individual e-mail function in each record.) In every case, the search strategy is included.

Special Features: CLIO Notes

America: History and Life provides a very useful additional pedagogical feature called CLIO Notes, available via a tab in the navigation bar across the top of the screen, directly above the Basic or Advanced Search interface. CLIO Notes provides chronologies and hundreds of brief summaries of significant historical events and themes. If you were working with a student who was just beginning research on a historical topic, this would be an excellent place to start. For a student interested in post-Civil War events, it might be helpful to start with the time period "[1865–1877] Reconstruction." A chronology of events is displayed, with major sections and associated topics, for example: "The South—Scalawags and Carpetbaggers." Each topic summary ends with three "Consider these topics . . ." questions, which could be used to help the student focus in on a specific research theme. After the suggested topics is a preset search interface that can be used to get the student started on his or her search, and thinking in terms of Subject Terms and Document Types (in addition to Keywords).

Quick Recap

America: History and Life (AHL), and its complement, *Historical Abstracts*, are major indexes to the literature of history. AHL provides citations, some with abstracts, for articles, book and media reviews, and dissertations that discuss any period of American and Canadian history from prehistory to the present (*Historical Abstracts* covers world history). The Advanced Search interface offers field searches as a series of text entry boxes, including the special purpose "Time Periods" field. Most search fields have an index of values that can be browsed, and selected terms can be "Added" to the search interface. The output options are well developed, including the most desirable e-mail features and output to citation management programs. The "CLIO Notes" feature can be used as an online historical encyclopedia (it provides chronologies and summaries of historical events and themes), and as a source for paper topics, based on the questions at the end of each topic summary.

MLA International Bibliography

Background and Coverage

The *MLA International Bibliography* is produced by the Modern Language Association of America, and is one of the longest running indexes still in existence. The Association itself was founded in 1883, and began publishing a printed index in 1921. (Materials in the online database, however, date back to 1884,[3] another example of an electronic product that has expanded beyond its print counterpart.) In a situation similar to that at the National Library of Medicine, staff of the Modern Language Association Department of Bibliographic Information Services work with outside bibliographers from around the world to produce the *Bibliography*. It is a huge cooperative effort.

The *MLA International Bibliography* is vast in many ways: the scope of topics included, sources, document types, number of records, and publication dates. Topical coverage is described broadly as "all forms of human communication:" literature, folklore (including music and art), the study of linguistics and languages, literary theory and criticism, the dramatic arts, and the history of printing and publishing. Coverage of the "history, theory, and practice of teaching language, literature, and rhetoric and composition," from 1998 onward, was added to the scope of the *Bibliography* (MLA, 2005) in 2000. As indicated in the title, sources from all over the world are reviewed for entry into the database. (The "Language of Publication" thesaurus list is probably the longest and most esoteric you will ever encounter.) Document types covered include types you would expect, such as books, book chapters, and journal articles, but also indexed are reference works, published working papers, conference papers and proceedings, citations for dissertations listed in *Dissertations Abstracts International*, electronic publications, and works related to teaching: handbooks, textbooks, anthologies, etc. (ProQuest, 2005).

The "numbers" for the *Bibliography* are equally impressive: there are over 1.7 million records in the database, and recently new additions total about 66,000 records per year. Subject terms used to describe records come from the *MLA Thesaurus*, which includes over "49,000 topical terms and 327,000 names" (ProQuest, 2005). A database about literature is, obviously, very concerned with names: names of writers, and names of characters.

The *MLA International Bibliography* is the first database we've encountered in this book that is *purely* an index. Full records are quite long due to the number of fields included, but there are no abstracts, and no full text. Like the ABC-CLIO databases, however, the *Bibliography* is OpenURL compliant: it supports full text linking technologies. It is also possible to run the *MLA International Bibliography* in concert with, or as a module in, a full text database called *Literature Online*, as described briefly below.

Relationship to Other Literature Resources

Any discussion of the *MLA International Bibliography* (MLA IB) should also mention two other major literature resources: the *Annual Bibliography of English Language and Literature* (ABELL), and *Literature Online* (LION). ABELL has a somewhat smaller scope than MLA IB, in that it focuses on just English language materials, and literature in English. ABELL also includes book reviews, unlike MLA IB. LION, the only full text database in the three, also focuses on English literature, and provides the texts of over 350,000 literary works, along with criticism and reference resources. At this time, Chadwyck-Healey, the specialist humanities imprint of ProQuest Information and Learning, is the sole publisher for LION, and is also a supplier of ABELL. With the recent addition of MLA IB to the set of Chadwyck-Healey databases, it is now possible for subscribers to all three databases from this vendor to opt for integrated access: the use of *Literature Online* as the single point of access for all three literature databases. For the purposes of this chapter, however, we will consider the *MLA International Biography* as a stand-alone database.

Notes and Search Examples

Any consideration of "humanities databases" needs to look at the *MLA International Bibliography*, but the question then is: from which vendor? At the time of this writing, there are five major database vendors offering the

Fig. 7.12. Chadwyck-Healey MLA Standard Search Interface. Copyright ©2004–2005 ProQuest Information and Learning Company.

Modern Language Association's database. I have chosen to look at one of the newest offerings, the Chadwyck-Healey version, because the interface seems to have been nicely tuned to the subject matter,[4] and the possible integration with other databases (described above) is quite compelling. Let's take a look.

Standard Search Interface

The *MLA International Bibliography* as offered by Chadwyck-Healey provides three search interfaces: Standard, Advanced, and Directory of Periodicals. We'll work with the first two here; notes about the Directory of Periodicals appear under "Additional Feature" below. The Standard Search (Figure 7.12) offers support for the kinds of searches users might need most often: a straight topical search (using Keywords or Subject—All), the ever-popular search for literary criticism or interpretation (Author as Subject, Author's Work), and the need to fill out a citation from incomplete information (using a combination of Keyword, Article Author, Journal, and Publication Year). If we are mentally ticking things off on our Searcher's Toolkit list, the ability to use Boolean operators is not obvious, although we assume

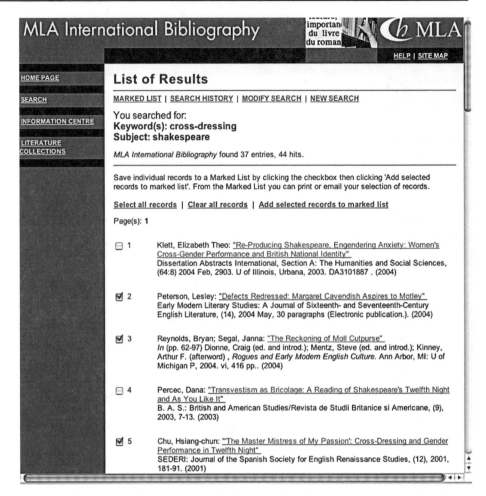

Fig. 7.13. Search results for subject: Shakespeare and keyword: cross-dressing. Copyright ©2004–2005 ProQuest Information and Learning Company.

it's there. The "Help" confirms this, along with supplying information about the other "tools" we're used to looking for, such as proximity operators and wildcards. There is an implied AND between fields on a page. A set of document types appears as an explicit "Limit," as well as fields that act in a limit capacity: Language of Publication and Publication Year.

Search Example 1

Our first search example is a topic lately of interest to the literary community: examples or use of cross-dressing in the works of Shakespeare. Figure 7.12 shows our search ready to be run.

Just the first five results for this search (Figure 7.13) start to demonstrate the breadth of coverage, in terms of document types and international reach, of this database. Represented are a dissertation, an electronic journal article, a book chapter, and articles from Romanian and Spanish journals. Two additional points to note about the results screen are:

Fig. 7.14. Full Record display. Copyright ©2004–2005 ProQuest Information and Learning Company.

- First, several of these results have been selected in the usual way, by clicking their checkboxes. Before viewing any other screens (going forward in the list, or even viewing a record), the "Add selected records to marked list" link must be clicked, or the selections will be erased.

- Second, the system reports that the search retrieved "37 entries," but "44 hits." The entries count refers to the total number of citations, or records. The second, larger "hits" count measures the number of times search terms appeared in records. A record in which a keyword appears more than once, as in Figure 7.14, will cause the hit count to go up.

The Full Record display in Figure 7.14 should begin to give you a sense of the detailed indexing performed on records in the *MLA International Bibliography*, and the degree to which the record structure in this version of the database supports and makes explicit the subject fields. In this record alone there are ten subject fields, including three Literary Theme fields, and two iterations of the Author as Subject, and Author's Work fields.

Fig. 7.15. Use of the Author as Subject field. Copyright ©2004–2005 ProQuest Information and Learning Company.

Fig. 7.16. The Author as Subject and Author's Work fields. Copyright ©2004–2005 ProQuest Information and Learning Company.

Two Additional Search Samples

Returning to the Standard Search screen, the partial screen shot in Figure 7.15 shows an example of a type of search students frequently need to do, but frequently do incorrectly. Students are used to searching for authors as authors, but when they need to find analysis or discussion *about* an author, they often fail to grasp that they must now search the author's name as a Subject. The "Author as Subject" field in the Standard Search screen is helpful for addressing this need.

Figure 7.16 is very similar, demonstrating a strategy for finding materials that discuss a specific work by an author. It also provides the opportunity for a discussion of non-English names.

Non-English Names in the Bibliography

As has been pointed out several times, the scope of the *Bibliography* is international, and among those 370,000+ names in the Thesaurus are thousands of names from scores of nationalities, including names transliterated from non-Roman alphabets. So, for example, the MLA indexers use the spelling Tolstoi, not Tolstoy, for the author of *War and Peace*. The only problem is that if you look up "Tolstoy" in the Thesaurus, there is no "see" reference to guide you to the other spelling. Working with Eastern European, Russian, and Chinese names (including place names) can be particularly tricky. For example, the controlled heading for the former leader of Communist China is "Mao Tse-tung (1893–1976)," not Tse-tung, Mao, or Zedong, Mao, forms and spellings that Westerners might be likely to try.

When working with names, be prepared to be flexible: use the Thesaurus as much as possible, but if the answer still isn't clear, try keywords, parts of names, or truncation. You are likely to find records containing the information you need quickly, and you can then "pearl grow" from there.

Advanced Search

Let us move on to the Advanced Search screen. Chadwyck-Healey has made a deliberate decision to display all the searchable database fields in a

Fig. 7.17a. Advanced Search, upper half. Copyright ©2004–2005 ProQuest Information and Learning Company.

list, rather than using drop-down menus. The advantage is that the number and names of all the fields are obvious at a glance; the disadvantage is that it does make for a rather long screen! Figures 7.17a and 7.17b provide the complete picture.

What a wealth of fields: every possible aspect of a publication has a searchable field, and now we see some of the other topical areas of this database being brought out, such as Folklore, Linguistics, and Performance. (I've left a search in the Folklore Topic field; we'll see a couple of results from that search later on.) Note that you can search by "Language of Publication," but in keeping with the Linguistics aspect of this database, there is also a field to search by "Subject Language," that is, the language being discussed in the article. For example, you could find articles written in French, on the Kumak language. Another Limit, for identifying Peer-Reviewed materials, also appears on the Advanced Search screen in this version of the database.

Advanced Search—Period Field

There is also a "Period" field that deserves a brief discussion. If you go into the Thesaurus for the Period field, your initial reaction is likely to be "*what* is going on here? How in the world are they defining 'period'?" Because many of the entries look quite strange (especially compared to the regularity of the time period index in *America: History and Life*). For example, year spans that are huge: 1–500 AD, 1–1499, 100–1999, 1699–1200 B.C., and

Fig. 7.17b. Advanced Search, lower half. Copyright ©2004–2005 ProQuest Information and Learning Company.

also not as huge, but very specific: 196–220, 1699–1792, 1700–1737, 1700–1820. There are month spans: 1–30 September 1990, February 1999; and specific dates: 2 September 1849, Sept. 18, 1981. There are also the kinds of year spans or descriptive terms you might expect: 1800–1899, 1700–1899, Belle Époque, fin de siècle, Showa period, and Ming Dynasty. What *is* going on here? It turns out that the MLA indexers use the Period field in a number of ways. Any dates specifically mentioned in a work being indexed get added as Period entries, which explain the unusual time periods. In a full record display, these appear as a Period field, with the gloss (date) before the value. In addition, such records almost always have a second Period field, with one of the broader, "controlled" types of time values, such as 1900–1999. Thus, a record for the citation of an interview with Spalding Gray that took place in February 1999, has two time period fields:

Period: 1900–1999

and

Period: (date) February 1999.

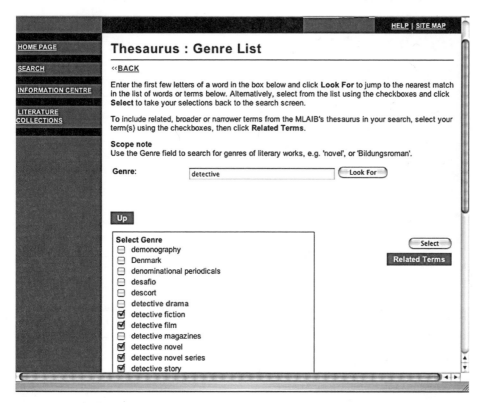

Fig. 7.18. The Genre List Thesaurus. Copyright ©2004–2005 ProQuest Information and Learning Company.

MLA places great emphasis on recording information exactly as given by an author, but also works to put the materials being indexed into some kind of broader context. In literature, the broader context seems to be spans of one or more centuries, or, occasionally, a well-recognized "named" period.

Search Example 2

Our search objective now is to find some materials discussing Swedish detective novels. We could just type "detective" into the Genre field, but it's interesting and useful to see what all the possible headings are in the Thesaurus (Figure 7.18). As we find, there are quite a few headings for "detective" genres, so why not select several—we can decide we're interested in books and films, but not in magazines. After checkmarking the desired headings, the "Select" button will transfer the information to the Search screen, appropriately ORed together. Making use of the Thesaurus for "National Literature" in the same fashion, we arrive at a search screen as in Figure 7.19. The first six of our seven results for this search appear in Figure 7.20.

In this screen, some entries have again been selected to add to the Marked List, which already has some records from various other searches not depicted in the text. Let's see what that Marked List has accumulated.

Subjects

Subjects - All:		select from thesaurus ››
	e.g. Kafka, Franz *or* realism *or* Paradise Lost	
Author as Subject:		select from thesaurus ››
Author's Work:		select from thesaurus ››
Folklore Topic:		select from thesaurus ››
Genre:	EXACT "detective fiction" OR EXACT "detective	select from thesaurus ››
Linguistics Topic:		select from thesaurus ››
Literary Influence:		select from thesaurus ››
Literary Source:		select from thesaurus ››
Literary Theme:		select from thesaurus ››
Literature Topic:		select from thesaurus ››
National Literature:	EXACT "Sweden" OR EXACT "Swedish literatur	select from thesaurus ››
Performance Medium:		select from thesaurus ››

Fig. 7.19. Search strategy for materials about Swedish detective works. Copyright ©2004–2005 ProQuest Information and Learning Company.

HOME PAGE

SEARCH

INFORMATION CENTRE

LITERATURE COLLECTIONS

List of Results

MARKED LIST | SEARCH HISTORY | MODIFY SEARCH | NEW SEARCH

You searched for:
Genre: EXACT "detective fiction" OR EXACT "detective film" OR EXACT "detective novel" OR EXACT "detective novel series" OR EXACT "detective story"
National Literature: EXACT "Sweden" OR EXACT "Swedish literature"
Update Code: 000001 to 200501

MLA International Bibliography found 7 entries, 7 hits.

Save individual records to a Marked List by clicking the checkbox then clicking 'Add selected records to marked list'. From the Marked List you can print or email your selection of records.

Select all records | Clear all records | Add selected records to marked list

Page(s): 1

☐ 1   Kirsch, Frank-Michael: "Zu S & W's Neuorientierung des Kriminalromans"
Weimarer Beitrage: Zeitschrift fur Literaturwissenschaft, Asthetik und Kulturwissenschaften, (35:12), 1989, 2079-2082. (1989)

☐ 2   Kümmel, Michael: "Der Held und seine Stadt: Anmerkungen zur Topographie in einigen modernen Kriminalromanen"
Die Horen: Zeitschrift fur Literatur, Kunst und Kritik, (32:4 [148]), 1987, 31-41. (1987)

☑ 3   Mellerski, Nancy C.; Winston, Robert P.: "Sjowall and Wahloo's Brave New Sweden"
Clues: A Journal of Detection, (7:1), 1986 Spring-Summer, 1-17. (1986)

☐ 4   Albrecht, Richard: "Sjöwall/Wahlöös Roman om ett brott: Aspekte zur bundes-deutschen Verbreitung und bundes-deutsche Aspekte zur Verbreitung"
Text & Kontext: Sonderreihe, (11:1), 1983, 118-137. (1983)

☑ 5   Benstock, Bernard: "The Education of Martin Beck"
In (pp. 189-209) Benstock, Bernard (ed.) , *Art in Crime Writing: Essays on Detective Fiction.* New York: St. Martin's, 1983. xi, 218 pp.. (1983)

☐ 6   Maxfield, James F.: "The Collective Detective Hero: The Police Novels of Maj Sjöwall and Per Wahlöö"
Clues: A Journal of Detection, (3:1), 1982 Spring-Summer, 70-79. (1982)

Fig. 7.20. Results: materials about Swedish detective works. Copyright ©2004–2005 ProQuest Information and Learning Company.

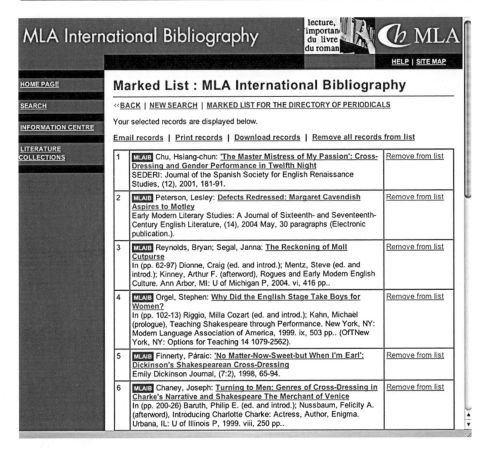

Fig. 7.21a. Marked List, beginning. Copyright ©2004–2005 ProQuest Information and Learning Company.

The Marked List and Output

The first six entries in my Marked List appear in Figure 7.21a; obviously these are all from the first "Shakespeare and cross-dressing" search. Again, note the range of sources, including one from the recently added "teaching" topical area. In Figure 7.21b, the rest of the Marked List, entries 7–10 are from a Folklore Topic search on "brewing," exemplifying the broad topical reach of the database, into culture (food) and history, and again demonstrating a wide variety of types and levels of sources. Entries 11–13 are from the Folklore Topic search on "animal tales" shown in Figure 7.17b, and the last three are from the most recent search on Swedish detective novels.

Records in the Marked List, as indicated by the links across the top, can be e-mailed, printed, or downloaded. The output interface for the e-mail function is shown in Figure 7.22, and includes a particularly nice feature: you can add an annotating note to *each* record in the list.

The download options are very bibliographic management software-savvy. There are options to export directly to ProCite, EndNote, or Reference Manager, or to RefWorks, or to download a file compatible with importing into any of these four programs.

7 MLAIB Dumpe, Linda: <u>On the Early History of Festive Beverages in Latvia: Beer</u> In (pp. 125-34) Lysaght, Patricia (ed., foreword, and introd.), Food and Celebration: From Fasting to Feasting. Ljubljana, Slovenia: Zalozba ZRC, with Department of Irish Folklore, University College Dublin, 2002. 428 pp..	Remove from list
8 MLAIB Meacham, Sarah Hand: <u>'They Will Be Adjudged by Their Drink, What Kinde of Housewives They Are': Gender, Technology, and Household Cidering in England and the Chesapeake, 1690-1760</u> Virginia Magazine of History and Biography, (111:2), 2003, 117-50.	Remove from list
9 MLAIB Larson, Carlton K.: <u>Relax and Have a Homebrew: Beer, the Public Sphere, and (Re)Invented Traditions</u> Food and Foodways, (7:4), 1997, 265-88.	Remove from list
10 MLAIB Brown, Charles E.: <u>The Brewing Industry</u> In (pp. 80-84) Leary, James P. (ed. and introd.), Wisconsin Folklore. Madison, WI: U of Wisconsin P, 1998. xviii, 542 pp.. (Reprint from 1938.).	Remove from list
11 MLAIB Ogihara, Shinko: <u>Mythology and Animal Tales</u> In (pp. 274-77) Fitzhugh, William W. (ed.); Dubrevil, Chisato O. (ed.), Ainu: Spirit of a Northern People. Washington, DC: Arctic Studies Center, National Museum of Natural History, Smithsonian Institution, with U of Washington P, 1999. 415 pp..	Remove from list
12 MLAIB Walcott, Derek: <u>Animals, Elemental Tales, and the Theater</u> In (pp. 269-77) Arnold, A. James (ed.); Walcott, Derek (afterword), Monsters, Tricksters, and Sacred Cows: Animal Tales and American Identities. Charlottesville: UP of Virginia, 1996. vii, 291 pp.. (Charlottesville: New World Studies).	Remove from list
13 MLAIB Teuton, Sean: <u>Talking Animals: An Interview with Murv Jacob</u> American Indian Culture and Research Journal, (26:2), 2002, 135-50.	Remove from list
14 MLAIB Benstock, Bernard: <u>The Education of Martin Beck</u> In (pp. 189-209) Benstock, Bernard (ed.), Art in Crime Writing: Essays on Detective Fiction. New York: St. Martin's, 1983. xi, 218 pp..	Remove from list
15 MLAIB Williams, Thomas E.: <u>Martin Beck: The Swedish Version of Barney Miller without the Canned Laughter</u> Clues: A Journal of Detection, (1:1), 1980 Spring, 123-128.	Remove from list
16 MLAIB Mellerski, Nancy C.; Winston, Robert P.: <u>Sjowall and Wahloo's Brave New Sweden</u> Clues: A Journal of Detection, (7:1), 1986 Spring-Summer, 1-17.	Remove from list

Fig. 7.21b. Marked List, continued. Copyright ©2004–2005 ProQuest Information and Learning Company.

Cautionary Note

While this section of the chapter is obviously enthusiastic about the many subject-specific search fields available in the Advanced Search screen, at the same time, do not hesitate to fall back on a simple keyword search if a field search doesn't seem to be working. For example, a search on "women" as a Folklore Topic, and animals as a keyword made sense to me, but retrieves no results. (Reversing the terms doesn't help.) Searching "women and animals" as keywords, however, retrieves many results, which can then be browsed for the most on-target citations. (Information from those citations might then be used for pearl growing a slightly better search.) The MLA indexers are governed by many principles in choosing and assigning terms for entries, as indicated in the overview provided on the MLA Web site (MLA, 2004), but an overarching theme is that the indexing is dependent on *explicit* content. That is, a term will not be assigned to a record unless it is specifically mentioned in the content of the item. As the MLA indexers have seen the materials, and you haven't, being too specific may lead to frustration. Always be ready to throw your net wider by simplifying your search.

Additional Feature: Directory of Periodicals

The third search option in the *MLA International Bibliography* is the Periodical Directory. (This is implemented in various ways by different

You are viewing records for emailing.

To email the citations for the records, fill in the details below and click the **Send** button. You will also be sent a copy of the email for your own records.

Those fields marked with a * must be supplied.

Your Name: *

Email Address: *

(If you are sending to multiple recipients, separate the addresses with a semi-colon and a space)

Subject: Chadwyck-Healey Literature Collections – Sel

Citation Format: *   ◉ Short Citation
                     ○ Long Record
                     ○ Compatible with ProCite, EndNote, Reference Manager and RefWorks
                     Note: when importing citations into EndNote, ProCite, Reference Manager or RefWorks,
                     you should select RIS format from the list of import filters.

Email Format: ◉ Plain Text ○ HTML
                 (Select HTML format if you wish durable URLs to be included in your email)

(Clear)   (Send)

MLA International Bibliography. Copyright 1963-2005, The Modern Language Association of America. All rights reserved.

MLA International Bibliography
Author: Chu, Hsiang-chun
Title: 'The Master Mistress of My Passion': Cross-Dressing and Gender Performance in Twelfth Night
Publication Details: SEDERI: Journal of the Spanish Society for English Renaissance Studies, (12), 2001, 181-91.
Publication Date: 2001

Notes (text format only):
Interesting number of cultures/
countries represented in one record.

MLA International Bibliography
Author: Peterson, Lesley
Title: Defects Redressed: Margaret Cavendish Aspires to Motley
Publication Details: Early Modern Literary Studies: A Journal of Sixteenth- and Seventeenth-Century English Literature, (14), 2004 May, 30 paragraphs (Electronic publication.).
Publication Date: 2004

Fig. 7.22. E-mail output interface. Copyright ©2004–2005 ProQuest Information and Learning Company.

database vendors: sometimes the Periodical Directory content is integral with the rest of the database, and sometimes it is necessary to search it as a separate database.) The Periodical Directory provides extensive, detailed information on over 7,100 journals and book series. The information provided is aimed both at users as *readers*: fields such as topical scope (subject), types of articles included, and subscription address, but also even more at users as *writers*, as indicated by the extensive series of fields devoted to instructions for authors: charge for submission, preferred editorial style, copyright holder, time from submission to decision, and time from decision to publication, to name just a few. If you were a graduate student specializing in Renaissance literature, the Directory of Periodicals would provide a very easy way to produce a list of journals or book series to which you might submit your work for publication. If you were an established scholar, you could quickly refresh your memory of the submission guidelines for the journal(s) in which you usually publish. Note especially all the new Limit options in Figure 7.23: they all have to do with the user as a writer.

Quick Recap

The *MLA International Bibliography* (MLA IB) is produced by the Modern Language Association of America. The topical scope of the *Bibliography*

Fig. 7.23. The Directory of Periodicals Search interface. Copyright ©2004–2005 Pro-Quest Information and Learning Company.

is very broad, encompassing almost anything that could be described as "human communication," e.g., from literature and linguistics to folklore, dramatic arts, and teaching. Types of materials indexed include journal articles, books, book chapters, reference works, conference papers, dissertations, electronic publications, and works related to teaching, such as handbooks. The MLA IB database is available from several different vendors; the version considered here is from Chadwyck-Healey, the specialist humanities imprint of ProQuest Information and Learning. This version supports special purpose search fields such as Author as Subject, and Author's Work (as subject) in the Standard interface. The Advanced Search interface offers a long list of discipline-specific search fields, including Literary Influence, Literary Theme, National Literature, and Performance Medium. An unusual feature in the e-mail output option is that a "Notes" field is supplied for *each* record being sent, allowing the user to individually annotate the citations. An additional feature of the MLA IB is the Periodical Directory, which contains detailed publication, subscription, and submission information for over 7,000 journals and book series. Authors seeking to publish their work can use the Periodical Directory to identify appropriate publications, and obtain submission instructions.

Exercises and Points to Consider

1. What are the stop words in *America: History and Life*?

2. What are some archival sources being used by current historians that can provide a *Mexican perspective* on the U.S. war with Mexico (1846–1848)? Think about this carefully for a few moments: How are you going to get at that "Mexican perspective" part of the search? See the Endnotes for a Hint.[5]

3. Go into the CLIO-Notes. (Use this suggested topic, or any historical topic of interest to you.) Select "World War II 1939–1945" from the navigation bar on the left side. Browse through the chronology, and under "The Economic and Social Impacts of War," click on "Conscription and Women Workers." Use the form provided in the CLIO-Notes interface to set up a search for the third question provided:

   > How did enlisted women contribute to the war effort during World War II? What duties were they asked to undertake? What duties were they not allowed to perform? Why?

   Notice how the form changes as you select and deselect checkboxes, and what operator is used. Did you find this interface helpful, or were there pitfalls? Now go to the Advanced Search interface and experiment with setting up a search strategy for the same question there. Compare the results.

4. Compare the version of MLA described here with the version at your school, if available. What are advantages/disadvantages of each?

5. In the MLA Subject list (Thesaurus), how is the author of *Huckleberry Finn* listed? As Samuel Clemens, or his pseudonym, Mark Twain? Compare this to your OPAC—which name is used there?

6. Consider the name of this Spanish author who was active in the late sixteenth and early seventeenth centuries: Lope Félix de Vega Carpio, often referred to simply as "Lope de Vega." Experiment in the MLA Subject list until you find how his name is indexed.

7. How many people have written their dissertation on Tolstoi's *War and Peace*?

8. Look up Saul Bellow as an Article Author, then as the Subject of other people's articles, and note the difference in the number of results. Explore the longer list, and come up with a way to focus your search.

Notes

1. Note that it's not "America*n*: ..." This is a mistake people frequently make.

2. You might be wondering about the order you see in the initial entries of the Time Period Browser: 00H, 0D, 1000D, 1000H, 100H ... This order simply reflects how computers sort values. If you go to Excel and type in a selection of the values you see

in Figure 4, and then Sort them, you'll see exactly the same results. It's not exactly a feature, but be assured it's not a bug, either.

3. The MLA deep date coverage isn't just lip service, either: if you search simply the date range 1884–1885, there are forty-five entries! (as of August 2005).

4. Each vendor, of course, has its own user interface that is based on that vendor's field structure, so your experience searching the same database offered by different vendors can vary a great deal. If your institution subscribes to MLA from a different vendor, you will see distinct differences between that version and the one described here. For example, other versions may not offer as many document types, or as many search fields, such as the specialized search for "Author as Subject." Another difference you might notice is that other vendors implement field searching as drop-down menu choices (e.g., FirstSearch), rather than listing out all the fields. Be ready for differences, and use them as a constructive exercise: which implementation seems to work better, either for specific types of searches or overall?

5. Hint: If you were writing about something from the Mexican perspective ... what language would you probably be writing in? Then use the Subject index to find and select all variations of "Mexican War."

8
Numerical Databases

This chapter will take us into some very different territory. Rather than citations to textual materials, we're going to explore the idea of searching for numerical information: data, statistics—*numbers* about things. There are very few commercial databases that have tackled the issue of providing numerical information, but a great many Web sites have done so. We'll look at one of the major players in the commercial world, LexisNexis *Statistical*, and two free government Web sites, American FactFinder (from the Census Bureau), and the Bureau of Labor Statistics. Before leaping into the databases, however, let's set the stage with some thoughts about "finding numbers."

Finding Numbers

If you are not a specialist with years of experience—and even sometimes when you are—reference questions that involve finding statistics or data are probably the most challenging ones you'll face. Let's be honest: for most of us, numbers are scary! There was a reason we weren't math majors. But don't be discouraged. "Numbers questions" don't always have to give you that deer in the headlights look: like all of the other subject areas, my intent in this chapter is to try to give you some basic tools to approach the question in an informed fashion, and to increase your chances of connecting the patron with the information requested. To begin with, I'm going to share with you my worldview about some basic "number" concepts: what determines the collection of numbers, how they can be categorized, who does the collection, and what sources to try for various categories.

Sidebar 8.1. Numerical Terminology

Data refers to individual numbers, for example, the original computer file of all the numerically coded responses to a survey, which usually looks like just a series of numbers. This is a *data* file, usually called a data set. Data are actual values. One value in a data set is a data point. When you process data, grouping like data points and expressing them as percentages, then you have:

Statistics, which are groups of numbers, usually expressed in terms of percentages. The data (number) and the statistical percentage it represents both appear in the sentence: "Almost 9 million (data) young Americans, or about 15 percent (a statistic) of all children, are overweight."

In my experience, people who are not in "numerically oriented" fields (such as economics, business, sociology, etc.) tend to use the terms "data" and "statistics" almost interchangeably: they will ask for "data" about something, when they are really interested in statistics. (This is good, because statistics are usually easier to find.) But if a person really does want a series of values to analyze, then he or she really does want a data set. A person in this position will usually be quite aware of the difference between data and statistics, and you should be, too.

A more detailed discussion of "Data or Statistics" is available as part of the Social Science Data Services Web site at the University of Rochester: http://www.lib.rochester.edu/index.cfm?PAGE=473.

Concepts About Numbers

Collection of Numbers

First and foremost in working with a numerical question is to consider whether or not it will have been worth someone's time and effort to collect the information, and to make it available in the way the user desires. "Numbers" take a lot of time and effort to collect: real effort, often by real people. For example, the year 2000 Census cost a total of $4.5 billion, or $15.99 per person counted (Gauthier, 2002). The first reports based on Census data only began to appear in March 2001, because collecting the numbers is only the beginning. Next, the data have to be analyzed and formatted into some kind of useful reports that either benefit the collecting organization (for planning or allocating, say), or that are interesting enough to outside parties that they'll pay money for them.

In my experience on the job as a "data librarian," I am frequently faced with people who feel they have an absolutely reasonable and rational numerical request, and that "certainly the information should be 'out there.'" And while what they're looking for might sound reasonable and rational to me too, it doesn't mean the information actually is out there, or that it exists in exactly the way they envision. If the government doesn't have it (our best free source), and a nonprofit or possibly trade organization doesn't have it, then it means it would have to be information collected by a for-profit organization. Obviously, it was collected to help the company make that profit, so they have no incentive to freely disseminate it while it is still relevant. If the information isn't strategically vital or tactically important, and the company thinks they can sell data (or reports based on the data) for more than the cost of collecting and analyzing the information, then those "numbers" may be available (for a fee). Again, as stated at the beginning of this section: if it's not worth somebody's time and effort, it probably won't be counted, and then exactly *because* it's worth time and effort, it may not be freely available.

Categories of Numbers

It can be helpful to think of collected numbers as falling into three broad categories: People, Business, and Financial. Numbers that get collected about People are things such as population counts, demographics (race, income, etc.), and vital statistics (births, deaths, etc.) Business numbers include broad information *about* business, such as numbers of companies, production, and workers in various industries, as well as numbers related to *doing* business, e.g., market research, or sales figures for a particular company. There are certainly "business numbers" that are financial (historical stock prices, for example), but my third category, financial numbers, has to do with money or monetary equivalents (e.g., stocks) in a broader sense: information such as GDP, banking data (total currency in circulation, total value of money in savings accounts, etc.), exchange rates, and aggregate numbers associated with the stock market, such as the Dow Jones Industrial Averages.

Fitting a "numbers question" into one of these categories helps organize my plan of attack, because the categories tend to be associated with certain kinds of collection agents. This means I'll get some ideas of where to look first, and also means I'll have a sense of whether the information might be freely available, or fee-based.

Who Collects Numbers

In the United States, the U.S. government is probably the largest collector and publisher of "numbers." This can probably be said of other developed countries as well. These organizations are termed the "public sector," and usually the information they make available is free (your tax dollars at work).

Then we have the "private sector:" trade or business organizations, professional associations, market research companies, and polling and surveying organizations. Usually information produced by a private sector organization isn't free, although some trade and professional groups may provide some statistics on their Web sites. In general, however, numerical information collected by the private sector ranges from possibly affordable (say, from $20–500, which would probably be acceptable to a small business owner, or to a library buying a reference book), to prices meant for large corporations, e.g., $4,000 market research reports.[1]

Try the Public Sector for...

When a reference question involves numbers to do with people, my first move would be to try a government source (as long as the question is about people as people, and not as *consumers*). A government exists to govern over people, and governing bodies are quite interested in information about their constituents. Governments are also very interested in the businesses in their countries: these companies are, after all, what keep the country solvent. So for questions involving numbers of businesses, shipments of product X, employment, etc., try government sources. There are public sector sources for some financial numbers questions as well: for questions involving monetary figures in a nationwide sense, try the Federal Reserve Bank, or the Bureau of Economic Analysis for economic data.

Try the Private Sector for...

As mentioned above, the government is my first choice for questions about people as people (heads that get counted). If someone wants to know about people as consumers, however, or what people are thinking, then it's more likely the answer will come from a private sector source: a market research report, a survey report from a company such as Harris Interactive, or perhaps a Gallup Poll. (And it will probably cost money.)

Questions about numbers for specific businesses almost always come from private sector sources: trade organizations or publications that specialize in a particular line of business. Who cares most about home appliance manufacturing? The Association of Home Appliance Manufacturers (AHAM). Hosiery? The National Association of Hosiery Manufacturers (NAHM). Oil, airlines, and milk: they all have trade associations devoted to (among other things) collecting numbers pertinent to their mission, purpose, etc. Certain private sector publishers specialize in trade reports: Crain Communications (thirty trade publications), Ward's Communications (*Ward's Automotive Yearbook*), and Adams Media (beer, wine, and liquor handbooks). For any line of business, remember to consider associations as a source of information. This is perhaps especially true for service businesses, i.e., any line of work that does not involve producing a product: be sure to check for a related professional organization, as this may be the only source of statistics about the profession.[2] (For example: want to know what butlers earn? Try the Web site of the International Guild of Professional Butlers at http://www.butlersguild.com/.)

There are a couple of types of "business numbers" that are, surprisingly, freely available on the Web. One is stock quotes for particular companies: current quotes are available from any of a number of Web sites, and Yahoo! Finance offers a remarkably deep historical stock quote reporting system (the catch is that it only works for companies currently in business and trading on U.S. stock exchanges). Also accessible on the Web are the financial statements of public companies, which must be filed with the Securities and Exchange Commission (SEC), and are public documents. This information is available in a number of places including the SEC's Edgar system (http://www.sec.gov/edgar.shtml), and the company's own Web site, where the figures appear in the company's Annual Report.

Financial number questions that will probably involve a fee-based source tend to be ones that require a series of historical values (e.g., an exchange rate for a particular currency over a 30-year time period), or financial information for another country, or a combination of the two (a table of 20 years of debt values for Nigeria, for example). The sources for such information are often organizations such as the United Nations or the World Bank (not commercial in the ".com" sense), but they still can't afford to give away their data for free.

Quick Recap

It takes time and effort to collect, format, and publish data or statistics. Without a financial or other strong motivation to prompt the process, data are unlikely to be collected. If information has been collected, it may not be available for free. In the United States, the government (the "public sector") is probably the largest collector and provider of freely available data about people, industries, and economics (national level financial information). "Numbers" relating to business that can also be found at no charge on the Web are financial statements (e.g., balance sheet, income statement, etc.) for public companies, and current stock quotes. Information that is rarely if ever free includes market research, and data about specific businesses, which are most likely to be collected by survey companies, trade associations, or trade publishers (the "private sector"). One exception is trade associations, which occasionally make data related to their organization available on their Web sites.

A Comment About Searching for Numbers

One of the frustrating things about searching for numbers is that all too often, whatever the person asks for, the numbers you can find won't be exactly the ones the patron wants:

You: "Here are some great figures about spotted hyenas!"
Patron: "Oh. Thanks, but I really wanted *striped* hyenas ..."

Remember that this does not represent a failure on your part: if you have done a rigorous search, it probably means that no one has cared enough yet about striped hyenas to collect and publish numerical data about them. Don't let it get you down. It is amazing, on the other hand, what numbers you *can* find! Let's go learn about the first of the three sources we'll cover, LexisNexis *Statistical*.

LexisNexis® *Statistical*

Background and Coverage

Originally known as "Statistical Universe," Mary Ellen Bates first reviewed this database in 1998, describing it as a "recently created" joint effort by LexisNexis and Congressional Information Service, Inc. As Bates says, the new database addressed "the need for value-added access to Web-based information" (Bates, 1998). Indeed: LexisNexis saw how useful it would be if the wealth of statistical material produced by the many agencies and offices of the U.S. Government could be brought together under one search interface, enhanced with indexing, and the tables provided in a format that would keep their integrity intact (e.g., GIF images rather than ASCII renditions). Even though much of this information is freely available on the Web, the task of locating it amidst the plethora of government Web sites can be frustrating and difficult. In addition, the need to preserve and continue to provide access to earlier editions of files is not consistent across all government Web sites. Putting the materials into a database increases the chances of preserving an historical series of reports. And a print indexing and abstracting service for U.S. government statistics already existed: the Congressional Information Service *American Statistics Index* (ASI). By adding GIF images of the tables cited in the index, the service would give users immediate access to the information. Adding in selections from the Congressional Information Service's two other statistical A & I subscription

series: *Statistical Reference Index* (SRI, which indexes statistical information published by state governments, private sector publishers, and universities), and the *Index to International Statistics* (IIS, which covers international intergovernmental organizations, such as the United Nations, World
Bank, and OECD), would add depth of coverage and take the concept even
further. Most of the materials indexed by ASI, SRI, and IIS are available in
their attendant microfiche collections, thus a database product incorporat-
ing the information from these A & I services would provide an electronic
index to the wealth of material locked up in endless drawers of fiche. Truly,
this was an excellent idea whose time had come.

LexisNexis *Statistical* is still, as of this writing, the most broadly based
"numerical" database on the market. Tom Kmetz (2003), mentioned Gale's
TableBase as the only similar product he was aware of in 2002, and this still
seems to be true as of 2005. Several other sources for international information exist, but they are all much more narrowly focused than LexisNexis
Statistical. (Gail Golderman and Bruce Connolly provide an excellent review
of the current resources for "international numbers," including LexisNexis
Statistical, in the Spring 2005 *Netconnect*.)

Subscription Options

There are three subscription options for LexisNexis *Statistical*: the
Base Edition, the Research Edition, and the Abstracts modules. The Base
Edition draws mainly on materials from ASI, but some materials from state
governments and intergovernmental organizations (e.g., SRI and IIS contents) are included as well. The Base Edition is the equivalent of a full text
article database, for numbers: all records provide a table, and the number of tables keeps expanding: in 2002 the Base Edition included "around
30,000 tables" (Kmetz, 2003). In accordance with the database's stated aim
of adding 30,000 tables annually, the number of tables had risen to "over
90,000" according to product literature issued in June 2004.

The Research Edition comprises all the material in the Base Edition,
with additional titles and the associated tables drawn from all three indexes
(ASI, SRI, and IIS). Materials from private sector sources indexed by SRI
represent the most significant content "upgrade" in the Research Edition.
Again, it is "instant gratification," as every record includes a table.

The "Abstracts modules" represent the full ASI, SRI, and IIS index and
abstract books in electronic form. These are a real boon to libraries that subscribe to one or more of the A & I services, and to the microfiche collections
that can accompany them: finally, an *electronic* index to the microfiche. A
library with a subscription to the ASI, SRI, and IIS volumes and fiche sets
might choose only the Base Edition and the Abstracts modules, since the library has even more full text back up (the fiche collections) than is provided
in the Research Edition. The only challenge in this situation is that getting
to the sources (the microfiche) isn't quite as convenient.

Date Coverage

"Date coverage" has somewhat different connotations in a numerical
database than in a bibliographic or citation database. The range of *publication* dates: how "far back" the database goes—is not necessarily as important, because in the world of numbers it's very common to find recently
published material that deals with the distant past, for example, "crop los-
ses ... 1948–1997" (published in 1999), or "acres harvested ... 1930–1994"

(published in 1997). There may be times when someone needs "numbers published in a particular historical time period," but often it doesn't matter so much *when* the document was published, as long as it has the right data. That said, to make the description of this database consistent with the other chapters, we'll note that date coverage (in the sense of when the materials were published) in the Base and Research Editions is generally from 1995 onward. (Bates, 1998). However, those materials may contain information that is much older, so if you need the price of corn in 1970, this is the place to go. The Abstracts modules include the full date coverage of the hard copy indexes, that is: ASI, 1973–, SRI, 1980–, and IIS, 1983–. Again, these represent the total possible depth of *publication* dates; the dates of the information covered in the publications can be much older (gold prices back to 1815, anyone?). Even the way the Publication Date limit field works recognizes this difference: you can set it to, for example, 1930–1940, and the publication dates in your results may range from 1960 up to the present, because the information *in* the publication meets the date requirement you set. This is a far cry from the typical date limit field in a citation database, so pause and ponder it for a few minutes.

Notes and Search Examples

The version of LexisNexis *Statistical* used in the following discussion follows the subscription model described above: a combination of the Base Edition and Abstracts modules.

Search Options

The Home screen for LexisNexis *Statistical* (Figure 8.1) lays out our three options very clearly: Search Tables Base Edition, Search Abstracts, or List of Links. Search Tables is our instant gratification mode, since it provides tables right in the records. As mentioned above, the Search Tables Base Edition subscription is drawn mainly from U.S. government statistical publications, including my perennial favorite, the *Statistical Abstract of the United States*.

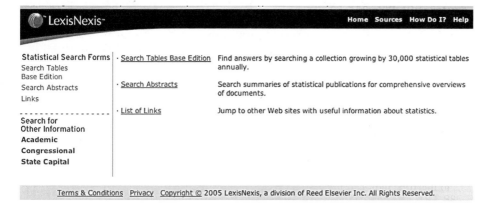

Fig. 8.1. LexisNexis *Statistical* "Home" screen. Copyright 2005, LexisNexis Academic & Library Solutions, a division of Reed Elsevier Inc. All Rights Reserved.

The Search Abstracts mode is the one that functions as a full electronic version of ASI, SRI, and IIS. As the title implies, and reflecting the content of the print A & I volumes, results in this mode only offer abstracts (some may also provide a links to online tables). However, LexisNexis offers a customizable "Locate a Copy of This Publication In Your Library" link for the Search Abstracts mode, so that libraries can direct users to microfiche collections or other local resources for obtaining the tables.

If you would still rather "go to the source" and look around for information yourself, the "List of Links" section provides a useful set of links to selected government, university, and nongovernment Web sites that are good for "numbers." Although there are now some other good "portals" and search engines for government sites,[3] this list, especially as it includes some nongovernment sites, provides a nice, controlled, less overwhelming way to approach the plethora of statistical Web sites.

Search Tips for the Base Edition

Records in the "Search Tables Base Edition" section of LexisNexis *Statistical* contain brief bibliographic citation information, a GIF image of a table of figures, and Subject Descriptors added by the LexisNexis indexing staff. The tables have also been scanned with an optical character recognition (OCR) program, so that words in column and row headings can be indexed and are keyword searchable. Taken altogether, this amounts to many words to search on, but the overall experience is subtly different from a database of articles or article citations. We are in a different place: we are finding numbers, not literature. The following suggestions represent basic strategies that are useful for getting the most out of LexisNexis *Statistical*:

- Choose broad terms to search on, if possible. Choosing from the Subject List can help—but don't be afraid *not* to use the Subject List too. For example, you will only find tables with information about "eye glasses" by Keyword searching that phrase. The Subject heading used for a table with this kind of data in it is "Medical supplies and equipment."

- Then refine the request by choosing one or two limits from the many check boxes.

- If you really want or need to put a pretty specific term in the search box (such as eye glasses), hold off on adding elements from the limit check boxes until you see what your results are like.

- As always ... if you get zero hits, eliminate search limits or terms one at a time until you start getting something. If you get too many hits, be equally methodical about adding limits or terms.

Let's go into the Base Edition Search Tables section and get a feel for what searching for numbers is going to be like.

The "Base Edition" Interface

As you can see in Figure 8.2, instead of an emphasis on text fields, as we have seen elsewhere, the emphasis here is all on limits. We do have one text input field, which we can set, if desired, to search in one of four specific fields (Table Title, Subject Terms, Table Text, or NAICS Code). There is also a link to the Subject List, so we know a set of controlled vocabulary is available,

Fig. 8.2. Search Tables Base Edition search interface. Copyright 2005, LexisNexis Academic & Library Solutions, a division of Reed Elsevier Inc. All Rights Reserved.

and we can browse the list. The "Enter Keyword(s)" bar also includes a search suggestion: *"Try 2 or more keywords (e.g. corn and Iowa),"* alerting us that Boolean operators can be used here. But what are particularly exciting and helpful here are all the possible limits, offered as checkboxes.

Limits

The "Limit to a Region" options actually represent sources: "International" is material from IIS, "U.S. Totals" is material from ASI, and "State & Local" refers to information from SRI. As the interface most frequently used by patrons, the terminology used here is much more accessible than referring to the sources by their names. The "Narrow Your Search by these Breakdowns" limits reflect how statistics tend to be published, thus subtly guiding you into the right frame of "search mind." This is exactly how you want to be able to search for numbers. Note there is even an option to "Limit to documents with Excel spreadsheets." The Excel files are sometimes offered in addition to the GIF image of the table, and are useful for users who want to experiment with manipulating the data themselves. The familiar Date limit is also available, either as a set of values in a drop-down menu (ranging from "previous year" to "previous twenty years," or "all available dates"), or by setting a date range of your choosing. LexisNexis is very accommodating in terms of date formats: this field will accept dates in almost any format, e.g., 07/24/97, Jul 24, 1997, 07/97, July 1997, or 1997). It's a small detail, but I always appreciate not having to remember and follow one particular date format.

Fig. 8.3. Looking up a term in the *Statistical* Subject List. Copyright 2005, Lex- isNexis Academic & Library Solutions, a division of Reed Elsevier Inc. All Rights Reserved.

Fig. 8.4. *Statistical* Subject List results. Copyright 2005, LexisNexis Academic & Library Solutions, a division of Reed Elsevier Inc. All Rights Reserved.

Search Example 1

What "numbers" can we find about librarians?

Using the Subject List

Let's start by checking the Subject list. We can type in the beginning of a word (e.g., "librar" as shown in Figure 8.3), and jump into the hierarchical list of terms at that point (Figure 8.4).

Note the many helpful *see also* and *use* references in Figure 8.4, as well as information on *Broader/related* terms. Always be willing to take an extra few seconds to run your eyes over a list like this, because it can help extend your knowledge of a topic, or provide new options if your original strategy isn't working. You can choose the term(s) you wish to use, and the "paste to search" button will enter them into the search form (Figure 8.5).

Using Geographic Limits

The search shown in Figure 8.5 has been set to retrieve tables that organize their data "By U.S. State," which returned twenty-two results at the time of this writing, all having something to do with school systems. Changing the limit to the Region "U.S. Totals" changes both the number and nature of results: it produces 134 results, with a broader set of topics represented (including "Occupations With a Greater-than-Average Number of Workers Aged 45 Years and Older, 1998–2008"—sigh).

Iterative Use of the Subject List

Let us say you wanted to focus only on salaries for librarians. Look up "salaries" in the Subject List, and you'll find that LexisNexis instructs you to use other terms. These can still be check boxed and "Pasted" to your search (Figure 8.6).

Anytime you iteratively choose terms from the Subject List and paste them to the search screen, LexisNexis will default to putting "OR" between the terms. Simply change the operator to AND if that is what you want to do, as in this case: "Earnings" AND "Librarians." Figure 8.7 shows the initial results from this search.

Sidebar 8.2.

If you look up "salary" in the Subject List, the search produces no results: there are no exact matches for "salary" (singular). You'll get told no matches were found, but the only button provided is the "Return to Search Form" button. To try another Subject List search, you'll need to use the browser's Back button. What would be ideal would be a choice: "Try another Subject Search" *or* Return to Search Form.

Results Page Options

Take a moment to study the results display in Figure 8.7; there are several useful features here. If our search had returned a large number of results, we could immediately "focus" the search by adding another keyword here, without having to return to the search screen. (Note that if your search will return more than 1,000 results, the system will tell you this, and will not provide results until you've whittled your numbers down a bit.) If you do want to get back to the search screen, however, there is the Edit Search link.

Fig. 8.5. Search form with Subject term, one limit. Copyright 2005, LexisNexis Academic & Library Solutions, a division of Reed Elsevier Inc. All Rights Reserved.

Print and E-mail options, which we will cover a little later, are right there. One of the most interesting features, however, is the "Table View" tab: going to Table View lets you page through the full records—which in this case, means each table. It's a wonderfully quick way to scan and compare these graphically presented results.

Search Example 2

This example is actually an interactive exercise. It depends on your having access to LexisNexis *Statistical*, and being able to get online and experiment. The suggested search statement to use as a starting point is: "Earnings" (a Subject term) OR salar!—in case there is pertinent material out there, only accessible by the keyword "salary" or "salaries." (The indexers are good, but you don't want to miss any possibilities.)

Time to Experiment

With the suggested search statement, now try checking various options under the Geographic, Demographic, and Economic limits. Can you find earnings by City? By County? Does any organization track earnings by Educational Attainment? Marital status? If a limit (or combination of limits) produces no results, simply try another, or switch that category back to "any."

Fig. 8.6. Guidance to other terms in the *Statistical* Subject List. Copyright 2005, LexisNexis Academic & Library Solutions, a division of Reed Elsevier Inc. All Rights Reserved.

Multipart Reports in Results

Figure 8.8 shows a specific instance of the OR search, in which it is limited by both County and Educational Attainment. Look at the four results in Figure 8.9 carefully: at first they almost look like all the same thing. What is different? What do these results represent? What you are seeing is typical for searches limited by county or by state: the results frequently appear as multipart reports. There will be several hits that represent consecutive sections of one large report, broken down alphabetically (a–e, f–h, etc.).

Search Example 3

Now suppose we really wanted to find the average commute time (travel time to work) in various U.S. cities. Still in the Base Edition, we could try looking up "commute" in the Subject List. By truncating the term to "commut," we would find that commuting is a subject. "Travel time" is too specific, however, and there are no matches. Trying:

   commut! AND work

as a keyword search, and adding various Geographic limits (Cities, County, or Metro Area) produces some results, but not as recent or as detailed as we'd like. Let's extend the scope of what we're searching by changing to

Fig. 8.7. Results: Earnings AND Librarians search. Copyright 2005, LexisNexis Academic & Library Solutions, a division of Reed Elsevier Inc. All Rights Reserved.

the Search Abstracts section. Hold this "search thought" while we introduce Search Abstracts.

The "Search Abstracts" Interface

The "Search Abstracts" interface (Figure 8.10) looks a lot like the Search Tables interface, with additional text entry search boxes (connected by Boolean operators), because we are now searching content with, in the words of Golderman and Connolly (2005), "meticulously detailed abstracting." The source limits for searching are also more clearly identified as the three major statistical publications published by LexisNexis (ASI, SRI, and IIS).

Getting to Full Text for Abstracts

If you're at a library that doesn't have a subscription to the microfilmed documents referred to by these indexes, getting to the source materials could be frustrating. However, sometimes the records contain links to online full text, or the documents indexed may be available in hard copy in your library: anything with "book" in the title would be worth looking for in your OPAC.

Rerunning Search Example 3

Here in Search Abstracts, a search on "Commut! and Work" by City doesn't produce that many results (fifteen, as shown in Figure 8.11); by

Fig. 8.8. Two term OR search with two limits. Copyright 2005, LexisNexis Academic & Library Solutions, a division of Reed Elsevier Inc. All Rights Reserved.

Fig. 8.9. Results showing multipart reports. Copyright 2005, LexisNexis Academic & Library Solutions, a division of Reed Elsevier Inc. All Rights Reserved.

Fig. 8.10. "Search Abstracts" interface. Copyright 2005, LexisNexis Academic & Library Solutions, a division of Reed Elsevier Inc. All Rights Reserved.

Metro Area even fewer. The first item in Figure 8.11 is the *2004 Public Transportation Fact Book*. (The title is 2004, but in the "Content notation" you'll notice this is 2002 data. Does that seem old to you? This refers back to the point about the time it takes to assemble and publish "data." Getting 2002 numbers in 2004 is acceptable turnaround; this is "recent" data.)

A "Public Transportation" fact book doesn't sound like it will have information about individual drivers, though. Besides, we're librarians. We like to search, and once a question sucks us in, it can be hard not to keep trying. Let's wrap up our tour of *Statistical* with an overview of output options, and then see what it's like to go directly to some of the sources for governmentally produced "numbers." We'll see if we can pursue our commuting time question there.

Working with Results: "Tag" and Output

Tag for Delivery

As you can see in Figure 8.11, the results lists in *Statistical* have the familiar checkboxes, for selecting those entries you wish to output. This marking function is called "Tag for Delivery" in the LexisNexis databases.

Print and E-mail

Having "tagged" your records, you can now choose the Print (which also includes a "Save" option) or E-mail tabs. However ... prepare yourself for a

Fig. 8.11. Results: Search Abstracts commuting search. Copyright 2005, LexisNexis Academic & Library Solutions, a division of Reed Elsevier Inc. All Rights Reserved.

slight frustration. If you select multiple records and choose Print, only the citations (and, if you specify "Expanded List," some indexing terms) will be printed, not the tables. In order to get hard copy output of the tables, you'll need to print the full records one at a time. The E-mail function has a similar limitation: the GIF images of the tables are not included in the e-mail output (even if it's only one record). The image would have to be saved on the desktop, and then attached to a regular e-mail message. The E-mail function allows you to put in the "To" address, naturally, but does not allow you to provide the "From" address (e.g., from you) or a Subject line. It does allow you to include a note in the body of the e-mail. If you wish to send records from *Statistical* to someone else, it can be useful to send the information to yourself first, and then forward it to the other person, putting in your own Subject line. Coming from your e-mail, rather than the vendor's, and with your Subject line, helps to keep the message from getting caught in a spam filter.

Going from LexisNexis *Statistical* to Web Sites

The LexisNexis *Statistical* "List of Links" page (Figure 8.12) gives us an easy way to connect to the government Web sites you'll want to use most often. Our first stop will be the Bureau of Census (http://www.census.gov), home of American FactFinder.

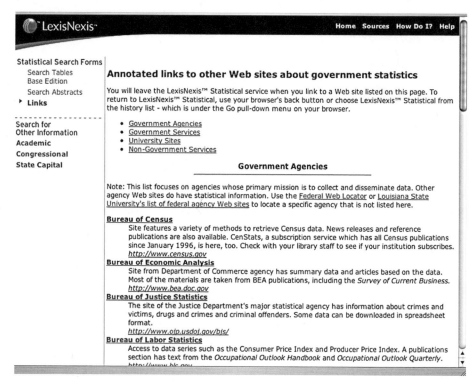

Fig. 8.12. List of Links page. Copyright 2005, LexisNexis Academic & Library Solutions, a division of Reed Elsevier Inc. All Rights Reserved.

Caveat

As LexisNexis warns on the Links page, following any of the Links means we are moving from the world of commercial databases to the free Web. There are several implications in this move. Commercial database vendors, while continuously working on their interfaces, still tend to roll out changes in a scheduled, controlled fashion: once a year, for example. An established, paying user base tends to create a certain amount of inertia: users are not crazy about constant change. Vendors tend to respect these feelings. On the free Web, however, if a Web site owner gets an idea for changing the Web site, it's far more likely he or she will simply go ahead and change it. You'd think government bureaucracy would impose a lot of inertia on government Web sites, but it's not necessarily so: some government sites have changed very little over periods of *years*, while others are quite yeasty, making little (or sometimes large) changes every few months or so. (The IRS site is different almost every time we visit it: "hey, it's FUN to pay your taxes!") While I am trusting that the screen snaps from the commercial databases in the rest of this book will not have changed beyond recognition by the time you read this, nothing can be promised about the appearance of free Web sites, so screen snaps of those will be used somewhat sparingly. The *functionality* being described should still exist, and since they are free, these sites should remain available to everyone. This discussion will provide some guideposts, but you are encouraged to go and see for yourself what these Web sites look like by the time you read this.

American FactFinder

Background and Coverage

At the Census Bureau Web site, one of the "variety of methods to re-trieve Census data" referred to in the LexisNexis *Statistical* annotation is a wonderful database called American FactFinder. This is a good tool that keeps getting better: it was one of Péter Jacsó's "Picks" (e.g., positive review) in 2000, and it has only gotten easier to use and understand since then. (Us-ing American FactFinder ca. 2000 was good—but still confusing from time to time. Now it's even clearer and simpler to use.) The folks at the Census Bureau deserve a lot of credit for continuing to work at understanding their users better, and making the incredible, complex wealth of information they collect more accessible to the public.

The data accessible via American FactFinder includes the latest Cen-sus information, but also information gathered in more frequent studies, such as the annual American Community Survey, and the Economic Census, which is taken every 5 years. The "advanced mode" of American FactFinder includes data from the 1990 census, additional economic surveys such as the Annual Survey of Manufactures, more years of the American Commu-nity Survey, and annual Population Estimate reports.

Getting to American FactFinder

The U.S. Census Bureau homepage has a lot of options, but laid out clearly enough to be navigable (Figure 8.13). It's very hard not to comment on all the other interesting things available here, but I'm going to try and restrain myself. (Don't hesitate to explore on your own, however, especially some of the links associated with "Special Topics.")

The link to American FactFinder is located in the list of buttons down the left side of the page. The American FactFinder homepage, as of June 2005, is shown in Figure 8.14.

Search Example 1

You'd like to know how well you "fit in," (statistically, at least) in your community.

Getting A Community "Fact Sheet"

It is interesting to examine statistics that have been gathered about the community you live in, and see how you "fit"—in terms of age, marital status, income, etc., in the place you call home. The American FactFinder Fact Sheets provide a good profile of every community in the United States. On the American FactFinder page, get a Fact Sheet for the place where you live. If the Fact Sheet text entry box is on the homepage, as in Figure 8.14, simply type in your zip code. (Otherwise, find a link to the "Fact Sheet" page, which will have this functionality on it.)

If you want to look up a place for which you don't have a zip code, type in the city or town name, with a state abbreviation to make it clear which one you mean (e.g., Richmond, VA, or Richmond, MI ... or MN ... or MO ...). If the name still matches more than one geography, you'll get to choose the place you want from a list.

Fig. 8.13. The U.S. Census Bureau home page, as of June 2005.

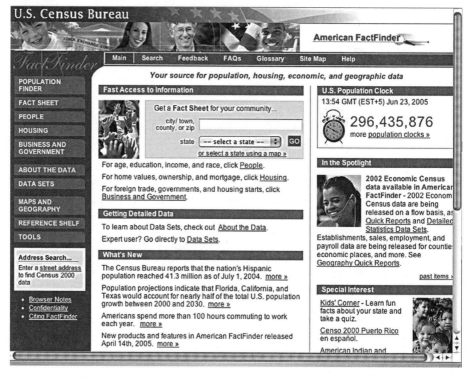

Fig. 8.14. The American FactFinder home page, as of June 2005.

Fig. 8.15a. American FactFinder Fact Sheet for Austin, TX, upper half, as of June 2005.

Fact Sheet Contents

And look at what you get! Figures 8.15a and 8.15b show the Fact Sheet for Austin, TX. In this version, as you move your mouse over the rows in the table, the highlight moves with you, helping you see clearly which figures go with which heading. For example, highlighted in Figure 8.15a is the "Median age" group 65 years and over. The total number of people in this age group in Austin is 43,905, or 6.7 percent of the Austin population, or about half the percentage in U.S. population as a whole, where this age group represents 12.4 percent of the total population. So Austin is a "young" city demographically. This view is showing data gathered from Census 2000, but note there is also a "2003" tab. Austin, TX was part of the annual American Community Survey in 2003, a source of even more current data.

Using the Fact Sheet retrieved by your zip code, what can you find out about your community? Spend some time looking through this information, and experiment with the various links: the "map" links take you to detailed, color-coded and interactive maps, the "brief" links associated with many of the data items are PDFs of nicely produced, short ("brief") Census publications on the topic. The "show more" links associated with the major categories will take you to more detail on that topic for your geographic area. Note: for the "map" and "show more" links, be sure to use the browser Back button to go back.

Commuting Time to Work Question—A Clue

Note that these Fact Sheets include a data category that relates to Search Example 3 from the LexisNexis section, about commuting time in U.S. cities. Thus, there must be a survey that asks this question, there must

Household population	636,432	96.9	97.2%	map	brief
Group quarters population	20,130	3.1	2.8%	map	
Average household size	2.40	(X)	2.59	map	brief
Average family size	3.14	(X)	3.14	map	
Total housing units	276,842	100.0	100.0%	map	
Occupied housing units	265,649	96.0	91.0%		brief
Owner-occupied housing units	119,102	44.8	66.2%	map	
Renter-occupied housing units	146,547	55.2	33.8%	map	brief
Vacant housing units	11,193	4.0	9.0%	map	

Social Characteristics - show more >>	Number	Percent	U.S.		
Population 25 years and over	401,137	100.0			
High school graduate or higher	334,626	83.4	80.4%	map	brief
Bachelor's degree or higher	161,937	40.4	24.4%	map	
Civilian veterans (civilian population 18 years and over)	46,762	9.2	12.7%	map	brief
Disability status (population 21 to 64 years)	63,935	15.3	19.2%	map	brief
Foreign born	109,006	16.6	11.1%	map	brief
Male, Now married (population 15 years and over)	120,264	44.4	56.7%		brief
Female, Now married (population 15 years and over)	112,698	43.4	52.1%		brief
Speak a language other than English at home (population 5 years and over)	189,889	31.1	17.9%	map	brief

Economic Characteristics - show more >>	Number	Percent	U.S.		
In labor force (population 16 years and over)	376,704	71.9	63.9%		brief
Mean travel time to work in minutes (population 16 years and over)	22.4	(X)	25.5	map	brief
Median household income (dollars)	42,689	(X)	41,994	map	
Median family income (dollars)	54,091	(X)	50,046	map	
Per capita income (dollars)	24,163	(X)	21,587	map	
Families below poverty level	12,993	9.1	9.2%	map	brief
Individuals below poverty level	92,011	14.4	12.4%	map	

Housing Characteristics - show more >>	Number	Percent	U.S.		
Single-family owner-occupied homes	104,794	100.0			brief
Median value (dollars)	124,700	(X)	119,600	map	brief
Median of selected monthly owner costs	(X)	(X)			brief
With a mortgage	1,181	(X)	1,088	map	
Not mortgaged	381	(X)	295		

(X) Not applicable.
Source: U.S. Census Bureau, Summary File 1 (SF 1) and Summary File 3 (SF 3)

Fig. 8.15b. American FactFinder Fact Sheet for Austin, TX, lower half, as of June 2005.

be data available on this topic. Can you find the "mean travel time to work" for the place where you live?

Advanced Search Example

The Fact Sheets are wonderful for easily finding lots of information about one location at a time. But what if you wanted one item of information for many places? As you recall, the original question in the LexisNexis *Statistical* Search Example 3 was about commuting, or travel time to work in *various* U.S. cities. The answer can be found here (finally), but requires working more directly with the original data sets. Luckily, the FactFinder creators have even made working with the original data sets manageable for nonspecialists. Go get online, and see if you can walk through getting this data set with me. If the Census Bureau should change the look of the interface, I'm afraid it will make this exercise even more confusing, so I'm going to stick to words to explain the process. The terms won't change, even if the "look" does.

1. From the American FactFinder homepage, find the "Data Sets" link. (In Figure 8.14, it appears both as a button on the left, and a link in the middle section, under "Getting Detailed Data.")

2. The next page, where you must choose which data set you want to work with, is the hardest part of the whole process.[4] (Hint: go read the Endnote.) The data set we need to work with turns out to be Census 2000 Summary File 3—Sample Data (SF3). How did we

arrive at that decision? A basic rule of thumb for choosing among the Census data sets is: "100-Percent Data" is the Census Short Form that *everybody* completes, which asks only a few, very basic questions. Anything more esoteric will have been collected via the "Long Form," which only a random *sample* of people are asked to fill out. Since our question involves information beyond what is collected in the Short Form, we'll need data collected with the Long Form, or sample data. Comparing the descriptions of SF3 and SF4, it looks like SF3 may include a wider range of topics, while SF4 looks more focused on race and ancestry. Thus, my decision to try Summary File 3. When you click the radio button for SF3, an associated list of links appears, asking you to "Select from the following" series of Tables or Maps. Let's select "Detailed Tables."

3. The next step is to select the "Geography" for our report. The "Census-ese" for what we're interested in (cities) probably best translates to the choice "Metropolitan Statistical Area/Consolidated Metropolitan Statistical Area" (MSA/CMSA). Choosing this causes the screen to reload, and we now have a choice of individual MSAs, or "All Metropolitan . . ." Highlight the "All" choice, and click "Add" to add it to your "Current geography selections." Click the Next button.

4. Now we get to select the subject of our data set, as it were: the item of information for which we want figures. We're presented with a list of "tables," and if we scroll down the list, we'll find "P31. Travel Time to Work for Workers 16+ Years." Click this entry to highlight it, and the "Add" button, to select it. All that remains is to click the "Show Result" button.

5. And there you are: a detailed set of data for travel time to work in every major metropolitan area of the United States. (Figure 8.16) You can page through it on the Web (it's arranged alphabetically by the name of the city), or, as the interface indicates, download the whole set of information as one file, using the Print/Download function. The data can then be loaded into Excel for further analysis.

See, you can do numbers! And isn't it interesting?

From "People" to "Workers"

The Bureau of Census keeps track of the state of "people" in the United States. That is, how many people there are, how old they are, what sex they are, what race they belong to, where they live, and so forth. The Census Bureau notes whether people are employed or not, their income, and whether they are below the poverty level. For more detail about "working America," however, we need to go to the Bureau of Labor Statistics.

Bureau of Labor Statistics

The Bureau of Labor Statistics, or BLS (http://www.bls.gov) tracks and provides exactly what the name says: everything about labor—working—in the United States. And it does mean *everything*; as of this writing, a myriad array of links were offered under sixteen major headings, plus additional

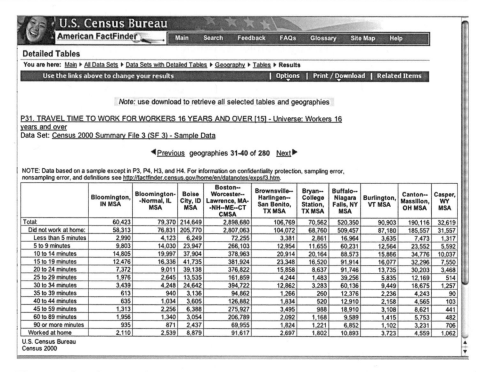

Fig. 8.16. Results: travel time to work in major U.S. cities, as of June 2005.

"call out" boxes, on the BLS homepage, as pictured in Figures 8.17a and 8.17b. Dearly as I love the BLS (how can you not love a government agency that uses a little green dinosaur icon to indicate "historical" data?), admittedly this page is pretty overwhelming to look at. However, if you invest some time in studying it, you'll find that some of the links repeat under different categories, and you'll start to get used to "the blizzard." You will almost always find something new and useful, too.

For our first example, we will focus on one section, about wages.

Wages, Earnings, & Benefits at the BLS

Search Example 1: Part 1

Suppose the person closest to you announced that as soon as you get done with your MLS, he wants to go back to school and pursue *his* lifelong dream of becoming a registered nurse. This causes you to wonder about job prospects, and especially salaries for nurses.

On the BLS homepage, find the "Wages, Earnings, & Benefits" section, which should include the "Wages by Area and Occupation" link. The next thing to decide will be what geographic area you want wage information for: national, regional, state, or metropolitan area. When you're doing research for a particular person, it makes the most sense to look at data for a particular "metropolitan area," since you'll be living and working in some specific place. (The other categories are more appropriate for more theoretical, comparative research purposes.) So let's try the "metropolitan statistical areas

Fig. 8.17a. Bureau of Labor Statistics home page, upper half, as of June 2005.

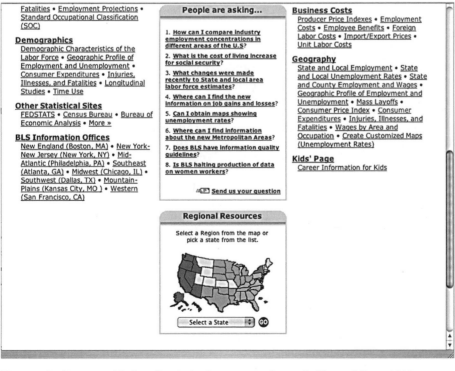

Fig. 8.17b. Bureau of Labor Statistics home page, lower half, as of June 2005.

Fig. 8.18. BLS links to Occupational Employment and Wage Estimates for Providence, RI, as of June 2005.

(MSAs) and primary metropolitan statistical areas (PMSAs)" option. Clicking this link takes us to a straightforward page where you simply have to scroll to the state you want and choose a city name. For instance, the "Employment and Wage Estimates" Web page for Providence, Rhode Island, is shown in Figure 8.18.

Oh no! more numerical codes and broad category headings to choose from—or is that really true? Note how tiny the scroll bar is in this screenshot, indicating that this is a very long Web page. Here is a beautiful thing: you *don't* have to figure out that Registered Nurses fall under the heading "29–0000 Healthcare Practitioner and Technical Occupations." All you need to do is search the page for the word "nurses," using the Web browser's "Find" function. (Find is listed under the Edit menu, or can be invoked on a PC with "Control-f", on a Mac with the Apple (or splat) key-f).

Occupations at the BLS

Search Example 1: Part 2

Continuing with the search example started above, your other concern was about the job outlook for nurses.

On the BLS homepage, find the Occupations heading. The first link listed should be the *Occupational Outlook Handbook* (OOH). There are

Fig. 8.19. *Occupational Outlook Handbook* entry for Registered Nurses, as of June 2005.

various ways to use the *Handbook* depending on your interest, e.g., if you have a specific position in mind, as in this case, or you only want to browse a job category to get ideas. The "OOH Search/A-Z Index" is usually the quickest way to finding information on a specific line of work. If you are looking for a very specific job title, or the sorts of trendy titles that crop up in the tech industry ("chief creative officer"), you may not find an entry in the *Handbook*. But for a great many occupational titles, it will bring together an extremely useful package of information: Nature of the Work; Working Conditions; Employment; Training, Other Qualifications, and Advancement; Job Outlook; Earnings; Related Occupations; and Sources of Additional Information.

Searching "Registered Nurses" rapidly brings us to the entry pictured in Figure 8.19, and the encouraging news that "More new jobs are expected to be created for registered nurses than for any other occupation." This could be a good career move!

The only bad news is that this information is provided at the "nationwide" level only. Finding information on "job outlook" by state or city is, regrettably, beyond the entry-level scope of this text, and you are encouraged to go talk to your friendly local business librarian.

Quick Recap

LexisNexis *Statistical* is one of the few databases that act as an indexing and abstracting service for "numerical" information. The database content is drawn from three hard copy A & I services: *American Statistics Index* (ASI), *Statistical Reference Index* (SRI), and the *Index to International Statistics* (IIS). LexisNexis offers three subscription options: the Base Edition, Research Edition, and Abstracts modules. The Base and Research Editions represent a basic and extended set of records from ASI, SRI, and IIS. These editions provide a GIF image of the associated data table with each record (the numerical equivalent of "full text"). The Abstracts modules act as an electronic version of the entire contents of the ASI, SRI, and IIS indexes, and can be used to point to the source document microfiche collections associated with these indexes. LexisNexis *Statistical* includes numerical information in all subject areas, although it is strongest in the type of information collected by U.S. Government offices and agencies. Publication dates in the Base and Research Editions are generally from 1995 on, but current publications often contain many years of historical data. A general search strategy for *Statistical* is to start with fairly broad terms (either from the Subject List or as keywords), and experiment with the many limits offered. The database also offers a List of Links to carefully selected government Web sites.

American FactFinder is an easy to use interface to find information from the latest Census, and other more frequent surveys, collected by the Census Bureau. You can search by zip code, or by city/town, county, and/or state, to retrieve a Fact Sheet on a particular place. Fact Sheets offer data arranged under the headings General (gender, age, and race), Social (education, disability status, married, etc.), Economic (employed, travel time to work, income, etc.), and Housing (ownership, value, etc.) Characteristics. Advanced queries, such as retrieving the same information about many places, can be carried out via the "Data Sets" interface.

The *Bureau of Labor Statistics* tracks and provides information about employment and occupations in the United States, as well as limited international information. The BLS home page has sixteen major topical areas, each with many links. Some of the density of links is caused by the same links appearing under more than one topic. We looked at only two of the hundreds of resources at the BLS: wage information by occupation, based on geographic location (e.g., salaries for librarians in Boston versus Omaha), and the *Occupational Outlook Handbook* (OOH). The OOH pulls together a range of useful information for each job described: Nature of the Work, Working Conditions, Employment; Training, Other Qualifications, and Advancement; Job Outlook, Earnings, Related Occupations, and Sources of Additional Information.

Numbers and the Reference Interview

"Numeric Reference" is a bit of a specialty, involving a lexicon all its own. Information from surveys gets turned into data sets, which are then defined in terms of four distinct characteristics. The following are four specific things to try and find out during a reference interview with a patron who wants "data."

- The *population*, often referred to as the "universe" in data-speak: Whom is the patron interested in? All the people who live in rural areas of the United States? Nurses? Railway workers in the nineteenth century?

- *Date*: Most current available? One particular date (usually a year) in the past? Or a "time series:" a set of values over a time period? (e.g., GNP for the United States from 1948 to now).
- *Frequency* (for a time series): Annually? Quarterly? Monthly? etc.
- *Place, or geographic region*: The whole United States? Alabama? Spain?

It would be nice to provide you with a succinct, complementary list of actions to take based on the answers to these questions, but it would probably require a book unto itself. Suffice it to say that these definitely *are* the questions to ask, and that eliciting information about these four things is useful in a number of ways, both practically and psychologically:

- The answers to these questions should help to determine if the patron really does want a data set, or just some statistics.
- If the request is vague, obviously the questions should help clarify it, and asking them collects useful information, while also buying some time in which to rack your brains.
- Going through the process also provides a structured approach to fall back on (e.g., go back and ask the *right* questions), if you thought you understood the question, and could get an answer pretty quickly, but your first resource isn't working out.
- Finally, answers to these questions are intended to help *you* decide where to go looking for the information—but they will be equally helpful if you need to refer the patron to someone else in the library. Capturing the answers is a useful thing to do that will make the patron feel that a "help process" has been started, and forwarding the information will make the next librarian's task much easier, as well as saving time for both the librarian and the patron.

Exercises and Points to Consider

1. In the opening to this chapter some broad categories of the following types of "numbers" were mentioned. If you are using this book in a class, have a class discussion and see how many specific types of the following sorts of numbers or statistics you can come up with:

   "People" type

   "Business" type

   "Financial" type

2. Fact-checker exercise. Working from an everyday newspaper article that mentions some statistics, see if you can verify the information, either by going to the source listed (if it is), or by searching on your own. The *Wall Street Journal* is an excellent source of this type of article, and is good about listing the sources for its figures.

Suggested Readings

Berinstein, Paula. 2003. *Business Statistics on the Web: Find Them Fast—At Little or No Cost*. Medford, NJ: CyberAge Books. Chapter 2, "Statistics Basics," and Chapter 3, "Who Generates and Publishes Statistics?" provide additional excellent background information for this topic. If you are in a position where you get "number" questions frequently, I recommend having a copy of this book close by to use as a reference.

Farrell, Megan S. 2000. By the Numbers: Finding Business Stats. *Library Journal* 125 (18): 49–51. A very useful annotated bibliography of sources in all formats for finding this frequently requested type of "numbers."

Notes

1. What one might call the "ha ha, you must be kidding!" price category.

2. Obviously, Google does a good job finding Web sites for organizations, but *Associations Unlimited*, the database equivalent of that reference staple, the *Encyclopedia of Associations*, is handy for identifying associations—especially the international ones, where their Web site might not be in English.

3. FirstGov.gov is "the U.S. Government's Official Web Portal" and is actually fairly usable. FedWorld.gov (http://www.fedworld.gov/) is both a portal and a search tool; Google Uncle Sam (http://www.google.com/unclesam), and SearchGov.com (http://www.searchgov.com/) are good "government" search engines.

4. This time, of course, you are being told what to do, but how in the world will you know for any other question? The answer is, you probably won't: so ask for help! Enlist the aid of a government documents librarian, or a librarian who specializes in data, political science, or economics. Or simply try different data sets, and see what happens.

9
Focus on People

This entire book so far has been concerned with the mechanics of databases: what they are, how to use them, and how they differ by discipline. But at any time it's important to pause and reflect on the ultimate reason *why* we're interested in learning this: in order to assist other people in their research process. Understanding the people who may benefit from using these databases and how they feel about doing research (there are a lot of emotions involved, it turns out) can inform how you interact with them. This chapter provides an examination of the general theoretical underpinnings of what your users are going through: the whole process of "information seeking." Indeed, "information seeking" is all around us, "always embedded in the larger tasks of work, learning, and play" (Nel, 2001). Whether you're motivated by the question of locating the nearest coffee shop or a desire to find information on a rare form of cancer, while you might not have thought of it this way, those who study information seeking behavior see you as engaged in a process to purposefully change your state of knowledge (Nel, 2001). If you are a librarian trying to facilitate information seeking, it's important to have the process in the back of your mind as you engage in a reference interview. Understanding the information-seeking process also helps explain the usefulness of considering your whole strategy of questioning in the reference interview (e.g., the use of "open" and "closed" questions), which will help ensure greater satisfaction on both sides: librarian and patron.

This chapter is based on selected articles and other sources from the library literature that I have found helpful for conveying the major points I wished to make. These articles range from scholarly and erudite to down-home and practical: often the informal, one or two page pieces offer some of the best, down-to-earth advice. This is, however, by no means a comprehensive review of the literature. The information seeking literature is vast and continually being added to: as of April 2005, there were 442 records that had been assigned the pure Thesaurus subject heading "Information

Needs" ("used for: information-seeking behavior") in *Library Literature & Information Science*, dating from 1982 to March 2005. However, "Information Needs" was used on its own, or as part of other subject headings, in a total of 1,664 records! The interest in the topic goes back much farther than that, as demonstrated by a study of the reference interview dating from the nineteenth century (Green, 1876). Countless other studies have followed, continually analyzing how people go about fulfilling information needs, and how librarians can better assist in the process.

Part 1: Information Seeking Behavior

The information seeking literature can generally be characterized as belonging to one of two groups: the theoretical, which discusses the topic in abstract terms and seeks to define it in terms of structured models; and the applied, which discusses it in terms of real world observations and interactions. This section will provide an introduction to some of the theory and the applied studies on people's information seeking behaviors.

Some Theoretical Background on "Information Seeking"

Robert S. Taylor's 1968 article is a classic in the area of theoretical information seeking studies. In it, he presents a model that identifies four levels of questions:

- Q1 the visceral need
- Q2 the conscious need
- Q3 the formalized need
- Q4 the compromised need

That is, information seeking can range from an unconscious, not even expressible "information need," to a very fuzzy but vaguely discussible need, to a point at which the person can clearly voice the question, and finally—the compromised need is the question "*as presented to an information system*" (emphasis mine). An example of "the question as presented to an information system" is what a person types into the Google search box. (The source quoted lists library or librarian as the first kind of possible "information system," but as we know and is amply demonstrated in the literature, after friends or colleagues, the Web is by far the first choice of information seekers today.)

In his article from 2001, Johannes Nel surveys the subsequent theoretical literature and the models of information seeking, with an emphasis on the emotional states that accompany the various stages of the search process. He describes a model of the "information search process" by Carol Kuhlthau (1991) in detail; it has many stages and affiliated emotions, as indicated in Table 9.1.

Taken overall, this process amounts to quite an emotional roller coaster for the poor information seeker. Looking over the stages, we could envision it as in Figure 9.1.

A study by Ethelene Whitmire (2003) demonstrates that when it comes to undergraduates faced with writing research papers, Kuhlthau's model fits

Table 9.1. Information search process stages in Kuhlthau's model

Stage	Task	Emotions
Initiation stage	Recognize a need for information (result of awareness of lack of knowledge)	Uncertainty, apprehension
Selection stage	Identify and select general topic or approach	Optimism (upon achieving task)
Exploration stage	Need to locate information about topic, become informed, integrate new information with previously held constructs, reconcile sources providing inconsistent or incompatible information	Confusion, uncertainty, discouragement, frustration, sense of personal inadequacy
Formulation stage	Focus, personalize topic by identifying and selecting ideas from all the information retrieved	Increased confidence, sense of clarity
Collection stage	Gather information related to the restated, focused topic; clearer sense of direction allows for more efficient, relevant interactions with information systems	Confidence increases, interest in project increases, uncertainty subsides
Presentation stage	Prepare presentation of findings	Relief, satisfaction (or disappointment if search has not gone well)

Fig. 9.1. The research roller coaster.

exactly. This model also fits with my own experience with academic information seekers, although the process doesn't necessarily progress steadily from one stage to another: they frequently go through several iterations of the "select, explore, formulate, collect" stages. Kulhthau's model has also been applied to adolescent information seeking by Ross J. Todd (2003). His figure of the model also pulls in the associated cognitive processes (thoughts: from vague to focused to increased interest), and physical actions (exploring to documenting). Theory, in this case, seems to accord well with reality, and the "reality" of information seeking behavior is a favorite topic of library literature.

Applied Research on Information Seeking Behavior

There is a vast quantity of literature on information seeking behaviors in academic settings. These studies have a long history, and include both specific and broader groups, such as:

- Veterinary students (Pelzer, Wiese, and Leysen, 1998)
- Health sciences faculty (Curtis, Weller, and Hurd, 1997; Owen and Fang, 2003)
- Nurses (Cogdill, 2003)
- MBAs (Abels, Griner, and Turqman, 2004)
- Undergraduates in general (Novotny, 2004; Prince, 2003; Valentine, 1993; Whitmire, 2003)
- "Academics" in general (Ellis, 1993; Jankowska, 2004; Marcum and George, 2003; Massey-Burzio, 1998; Reneker, 1993).

School media specialists and public librarians have also actively contributed their observations and advice about the information seeking behaviors they observe in the clientele of their libraries (Eisenberg, 2005; Loertscher and Woolls, 2002; Lorenzen, 2001; Minkel, 2004; Shenton and Dixon, 2003, 2004; Todd, 2003; Vesey, 2005).

In 2004, the June and July issues of the *Journal of the American Society for Information Science and Technology* were devoted to papers on information seeking research. Topics of research included various medical settings, everyday users at home, and computer scientists and software engineers in Israel (Spink and Cole, 2004).

Scanning the literature, other groups ranging from arts administrators (Zach, 2005) to scientists (Hallmark, 1995; Murphy, 2003) to lawyers (Booth, 2004) to genealogists (Duff and Johnson, 2003) to fishermen in Nigeria (Njoku, 2004), have all been the objects of scrutiny of their information seeking behaviors.

Information Seeking in the Internet Era

The recent applied research on information seeking behavior in "wired" societies has consistent themes: people tend to turn first to the Internet, or to friends or colleagues, when they have an information need. Much as they love the Internet, they still do like interacting with humans. However, given the choice between someone they know: a friend, a teacher, or a colleague, and a librarian (whom they do not know), they'll start with the former.

Another finding has to do with time: in the studies, users consistently complain about lack of time. Information seekers will try to save time whenever possible, which leads to opting for "convenience over quality." Although a major obstacle to doing research that is repeatedly mentioned is "knowing where to start," at the same time, elementary school children, teenagers, and undergraduates, consider themselves skilled and quite capable of doing their own research. Users are also more and more aware of the enormous amount of information available, and, in conjunction with the "lack of time" problem, complain about information overload (Young and Seggern, 2001).

Participants in Young and Seggern's (2001) study described a "dream information machine" as something intuitive (a mind reader); a thing they can interact with in natural language. Their dream information machine is also a single source: comprehensive, complete; which is portable and provides access 24 hours a day, 7 days a week (24/7). Commenting on this, note that librarians are some of these things, but we are not: portable, 24/7, and we tend to point you at several sources rather than one that has everything (we are, however, sometimes rather good at mind reading). Given this description, however, it's impossible not to pause and consider why people love the Internet.

Why People Love the Internet

According to the literature, at the beginning stages of the research process the information seeker is anxious and nervous (unless they are teenagers or undergraduates, born into the Web world and quite confident of their abilities to find things). One of the big problems is starting: an information seeker gets very discouraged and may even quit if he or she doesn't get results. They'd like one source, they want it fast, and they want it everywhere, all the time. On the Internet:

- You do it on your own; among other things, your thoughts don't have to be as clearly formulated as they would be to express your question to someone you don't know well.

Therefore embarrassment is avoided, and:

- Starting is easier since you simply type something in, and almost always get results.

- Anxiety is immediately reduced, because you got something (you probably have gotten way more than just "something"—you may have gotten thousands of hits—but it is better, quite literally, than nothing).

- You feel like you must know what you're doing. Confidence is increased: you got something(s), so you don't need help.

- It appears to be "one source" because you can get something on practically any topic from one search engine.

- It's fast, it's available 24/7, and it's almost ubiquitous, especially now that you can get to it on your PDA or cell phone.

What's not to like? Yet there are also plenty of negative emotions connected with searching on the Net.

Downsides of Internet Searching

Some of the negative emotions and aspects of doing one's own searching on the Internet include:

- Doubt, uncertainty
- Confusion
- Frustration
- Time pressure
- "Infoglut"—being overwhelmed with results (Young and Seggern, 2001)
- Never knowing when you're finished, if you've "found it all"

You have undoubtedly encountered many of these negative emotions yourself when searching the Internet. (Even Google is only as good as the search you give it.) Having to sift through long lists of results, visiting various pages, evaluating, clicking deeper within a site to try and figure out why it was included in the results, then backtracking and trying not to get lost—can definitely elicit all of these emotions. From the literature and my own experiences with users, the user mindset appears to be something like this:

> Web searching can be very frustrating, but at least you suffer in private. You don't have to confess or try to explain your topic to a stranger: a librarian (especially if it isn't totally clear to *you* yet). Or perhaps you've been working on this idea for a while, and feel like you're quite on top of it: how could someone (a librarian) totally unfamiliar with it be any help? You'd have to explain so much, and that would take too much time. Besides, you got results, so you obviously know how to search, and you're sure the information you want is out there. You want it, it sounds reasonable to you that such information should exist, therefore—it must be there, because you can find anything on the Net, right? Somewhere. It must just be a matter of trying again, and trying again, frustrating as it is.

Effect of the "Internet Mindset" on Information Seeking

The most recent literature about information seeking behaviors scarcely questions that users go straight to the Internet; that is a given. Now what is studied is how the "Internet mindset" impacts their information seeking, or search, habits. The patterns that seem to be emerging are the use of very simplistic searches involving only one or two keywords, and many iterations: search and scan (the results), search and scan again, and again. Rather than trying to evaluate or analyze why a search didn't work, users immediately change a word and try again, rapidly abandoning searches that don't appear to work (Novotny, 2004). Users rarely if ever take advantage of advanced search features, and Boolean logic doesn't even enter the picture: presented with an advanced search interface, they still simply enter keywords (Minkel, 2004; Novotny, 2004). Users don't know how to refine large result sets, instead scanning quickly for one or two likely looking titles. Overall, current search habits seem to be characterized by a trial-and-error approach (Minkel, 2004), and a general lack of any kind of critical, analytical skills (Todd, 2003). The title of Eric Novotny's 2004 article captures it exactly: "I don't think I click."

Is all this a death knell for the powerful, sophisticated interfaces developed for subscription databases? My hope is no: that features such as Boolean operators and field searching will continue to be available, to be used by those who know how. At the same time, one can already see that the way keyword searches are handled "behind the scenes" in these databases is getting better and better, so that simple keyword searches in a sophisticated database produce useful results. Is there any hope of teaching students and others to use more effective search methods—synonyms, Boolean, limits? In my opinion, on the large scale, that is, teaching whole classes to be expert searchers, is probably not realistic. But one-on-one, as "teaching moments" arise, introducing just one or two of these concepts, with the appropriate hooks: "this will make your searching much more efficient—it'll be much easier to get the information you need, and you'll get a better grade on your paper"—that, in my experience, is possible. Woo them gently—the carrot is much more effective than the stick. And the occasion for most of these "teaching moments" will be in the reference interview, our next topic.

Quick Recap

The information seeking process has been described in the theoretical literature with various models. Taylor's model uses levels of questions, while Kuhlthau's model describes it as a series of stages and tasks, each with a good deal of emotion attached. Applied studies of academic users support these models, and show two major trends: a person seeking information will tend to consult the Internet, or friends or colleagues, before turning to the library. Searching the Internet has many very appealing aspects for information seekers, as well as frustrations. The predominance of Internet usage has affected how "the Net generation" searches for information, their new habits characterized by speed, reliance on keyword searches rather than anything more sophisticated, and trial-and-error.

Part 2: The Reference Interview

We hardly even need the authority of "the literature" to tell us about how people look for information, however, because the evidence from all of our lives probably bears witness to the reality every day:

People go straight to the Internet.
Or ask other people.

Where do libraries and librarians fit in, then? It appears, for better or worse, for most people we have become the resource of last resort. Indeed, in a recent survey of MBA students (Abels, Griner, and Turqman, 2004), the answer with the highest response rate to the question: "Means of Contacting the Librarians" is "Would not consult a librarian." (Ouch.) The exception is a person you have worked with and helped before: once someone has experienced a "good search" that produces useful material in 5–10 minutes, he or she is likely to consider returning to you rather than continue to engage in marathon, fruitless sessions on the Internet. Even if the answer with the librarian is a Web search, it may well be more efficiently done and produce the needed results faster. Being a resource of last resort means we do not, perhaps, get asked as many questions (chronically overworked reference librarians can throw things at me now), but the ones we do get asked are more difficult. Most of the time this makes the job more interesting. (The rest of the time—well, every job has its frustrations. It's better if you don't bash your head on the desk when people can see you, though.) Being a resource of last resort and having to deal with more difficult questions means, however, that the topic of this section of the chapter, the reference interview, has only grown in importance, rather than lessened.

In order to sort out these more difficult questions, and elicit useful information from people who are convinced they are already good searchers who have done everything possible, you need all your best communication and people skills. Indeed, the oft-quoted dilemma as phrased by Robert Taylor in 1968 still applies:

> Without doubt, the negotiation of reference questions is one of the most complex acts of human communication. During this process, one person tries to describe for another person not something he knows, but rather something he does NOT know.

What's the Real Question?

One of the most challenging things about the reference interview is simply that people do not ask for what they really want. This is a recurring theme in the literature: "inquirers seldom ask at first for what they want" (Taylor, 1968), and "librarians have long recognized the tendency of library users to pose their initial questions in complete, often unclear, and sometimes apparently covert terms" (Dewdney and Michell, 1997). Mary Ellen Bates (1998) expressed this succinctly as "Finding the question behind the question." Catherine Ross (2003) is strongly in favor of a reference interview in "almost every" transaction, because even a very brief exchange helps people to "clarify in their own minds what their question really is." In some musings about his work on a reference desk, Sean Scott (2004) has a humorous example of the type of question that makes any reference librarian's blood run cold: "Do you have anything on that gal who died?" (It turned out to be Anne Frank.)

Why is this asking of a question so difficult? Why don't people simply ask what they really want to know? It turns out there's a lot more to *asking* a question (let alone answering one) than meets the eye. For example:

- The question may be used as a way to make contact, to see if you're "available." Indeed, it has been suggested (Dewdney and Michell, 1996) that the initial question actually be treated as "four unspoken questions:"
  - Am I in the right place?
  - Are you available to help me?
  - Are you listening and willing to help me?
  - Have you understood my topic (in general)?
- People all have worldviews, and their own ideas (mental models) of how things work, even if they have no actual experience on which to base that idea. Because of this, they will ask a question they think

you can answer—they'll couch their need in terms of something they think you can provide. This is what Taylor meant by his fourth type of question, the "compromised need." The person deliberately recasts the question "in anticipation of what the files can deliver" (Taylor, 1968), or in the form they think "is the sort of thing one should ask" (Fister, 2002).

- As illustrated by the extended quotation from Taylor toward the beginning of this section, people don't ask an exact question because they may not themselves know very well what they want, or any better way to phrase what they want. If you were a 6-year-old trying to ask your school librarian for something to read that would explain why your parents always seemed to be taking your older brother to the doctor, how well do you think you'd express it? You may discover that a lot of people become about 6-years-old on approaching a Reference desk.

- Communication barriers can interfere in asking questions: barriers because of age, language, jargon, or mishearing or misinterpreting what was heard.

- There are many questions that can sound quite reasonable…but just aren't. When you start to examine them more closely, they turn out to horribly broad and impossible.

- The exact information need may not be expressed because of embarrassment at having to ask, or because of the nature of the question.

- Even stronger than embarrassment, having to ask a question may bring up feelings of fear: fear from not knowing what to expect when they ask (what if it's a really stupid question and you get angry, or say something belittling?) You can well imagine that a person in that situation would be very careful about what question they asked, and that it might be a long way from what they really want to know (Fister, 2002).

Examples of "Not the Real Question"

Here are some examples, drawn from real life and from the literature, of questions that get asked based on the motivations described above, or questions that are open to a number of interpretations.

The totally misdirected question: "Could you read my paper and tell me if my arguments are right and if I've made any mistakes?" In reality, it turned out she wanted some better, more scholarly sources.

The question they think you're more likely to be able to answer: "Where are the issues of *Mergers & Acquisitions*?" The real question: the student's professor had suggested a particular article in *M&A*, and the student was going to browse until he found it.

Here is a wonderful example of six possible situations that could be lurking behind the very simple question: "Where are the cookbooks?" (Peterson, 1997)

1. Polly wants to browse a wide range of cookbooks to get different recipe ideas.

2. Edna is looking for a specific recipe on authentic Italian *alfredo* sauce.

3. Mary is considering modifying her diet for health reasons and could really use some books on health and nutrition.

4. Jenny is conducting a cooking seminar and needs information on how to structure her classes.

5. Joe wants to be a chef, but he really needs books on job-hunting strategies.

6. Marty is looking for *The Anarchist's Cookbook*, which is not a cookbook at all and is located in a completely different section.

The question that sounds reasonable and isn't: "I need a list of the top fifty undergraduate programs in Math, Computer Science, and Engineering worldwide." There are directories of such programs (in the United States), and one frequently sees lists in *Business Week* and similar publications of the "Top 50" or "Top 100" this or that . . . so it seems like this is a reasonable request. (But it's not: don't try it!)

The failure of communication question (mishearing the original information): the undergraduate who asked for Oranges and Peaches, by Charles somebody, who gets more and more upset as the librarian can't find it . . . until he finally happens to say "but my professor said it was the Bible of evolution!!" and the librarian realized what he meant was *Origin of Species*, by Charles Darwin (Dewdney and Michell, 1996).

Question Negotiation in the Reference Interview

It is possible to get at the "real" question, however. A combination of good communication skills, emotional intelligence, practice, and experience are the keys. The major component of good communication skills for the reference interview is known as "question negotiation."

Question negotiation, while definitely not a simple thing, sounds simple: you try to elicit information by asking questions. The questions have a particular style, known as "open" and "closed." Open questions invite your interlocutor to tell you more, to expand on the topic in a freeform way (like the famous interview question: "tell me about yourself"), while closed questions are used to request a specific piece of information, and usually require only a yes or no, or a one- to two-word response.

Open and Closed Questions

Here are some examples of open questions that are good to use in the reference interview (they tend to begin with words such as how, where, what, why, and the useful phrase "can you tell me . . . "):

- Can you tell me something more about (the class assignment, the topic, etc.)?
- How much material were you hoping to find?
- What would you like to find out (about the topic)?
- How are you intending to use the information?
- What have you tried already?
- What else have you found? or: Do you have any papers on this topic already that we could look at?
- Where did you find (example, if presented)?

Similar to the above, but with some interesting variations, here is a lovely set of questions suggested by Mary Ellen Bates (1998), a notable authority on searching:

- What do you mean by ___?
- What do you already know about ___?
- What do you expect me to find?
- Are there any sources you have already checked or that you would recommend?
- If you were writing an article about this subject, what would the headline be?
- If I can't find exactly ___, what would be second-best?
- How will you be using the information?
- So, in other words, what you'd like me to find is ___, right?

Some examples of closed questions:

- Are you looking for a specific item or a list of materials on a topic?
- Do you want a comprehensive search, or a few good items?
- Did you try (the catalog, the Web, or a particular database)?
- When do you need this by?
- Do you need scholarly (research, journal) articles or are popular (*Time*, *Newsweek*) articles okay?
- Are you looking for recent information or are you doing historical research?
- Have you used (particular resource) before?

Both open and closed questions are important and useful in question negotiation; don't fall into the trap of equating "open" with "good" and "closed" with "bad." Open questions are a good way to get things going, to start developing a big picture, and to get the user talking and thus providing subject words. Closed questions are useful for focusing the topic, making sure the interaction proceeds efficiently, and helping to rule out courses of action. Strive to avoid a question negotiation session that uses only closed questions, but rather to employ a mix of both. If you encounter a situation where closed questions seem to be all that is required, don't feel guilty, however. It can happen, especially around basic questions, or in an instant messaging environment. What you want to avoid is getting into the habit of only asking closed questions through laziness or disinterest.

In coming up with questions, it helps to keep in mind the ultimate goals for the reference interview:

- Understand the problem and its literature—the topic
- Find out what the person has already done (if anything)
- Develop search vocabulary and alternatives (synonyms)
- Determine limits (date, etc.), levels (research or popular literature?)
- Retrieval goals (How much/How many? How soon?)

- Develop an overall strategy to help you select appropriate resources (database, Web, etc.)

Overall, the question negotiation process in the reference interview should help you understand the problem context, that is, *who* and *why*. Who is your questioner: a 5-year-old, your mom, an undergraduate, or a sales manager in your company? Your choice of words, your questions, your suggestions, and the amount of time spent—every part of your interaction should be adjusted based on whom you are talking to. For example, most of the "open" questions suggested here aren't very appropriate for an elementary school student. The second primary part of the context is *why* are they asking—what is motivating the search? Is it just exploratory, personal interest? Or is it specific, a class assignment or preparation for an upcoming interview? Again, this will affect the whole nature and direction of the search.

Interpersonal Communication Skills in the Reference Interview

Having lists of questions to ask will only take you so far, however. A successful reference interaction also requires a healthy amount of good interpersonal communication skills, such as:

- Active listening: verbally or nonverbally indicating interest, attentiveness ("uh huh," nodding), and empathy (facial expressions that mirror the other person's feelings, "ouch"), even humor (this seems to come up particularly in an instant messaging type of exchange (Fagan and Desai, 2003)).
- Paraphrasing: "so you'd like (xyz), is that right?"
- Giving positive nonverbal cues: projecting an approachable attitude, using welcoming body language: smiling, eye contact, and an "interested face." The emotional underpinnings of the whole situation cannot be emphasized too much, and thus the need for "emotional intelligence" in conducting the exchange (Eidson, 2000). People generally pick up on tones of voice and negative body attitudes quickly and unerringly (Ross, 2003), and will be more satisfied with a helpful and friendly, even if incorrect or incomplete, answer than one that is correct but cold (Fagan and Desai, 2003; Radford, 1999).

As Tyckoson (2003) says: "It is the interaction, the process of communication, which is often more important than the content or a specific answer."

A school librarian's list of important communication skills emphasizes the following points, which are definitely applicable to any situation (Riedling, 2000):

- Positive, respectful responses
- Encouraging words
- Avoid premature answers

The last point deserves extra attention, because it is a trap that is so easy to fall into. Even if students have been asking for the same thing for a week, it's important to treat each instance as if it were new. Because you never know—the fifteenth time it might actually be something a bit different.

In discussing communication skills and pitfalls, a public librarian is emphatic about not using library jargon, and points out terms that people frequently either mistake, or use in a different sense from the "library" sense (Cramer, 1998):

- Bibliography for biography
- Reference book for nonfiction work
- Equating "fiction" with "not true," and thus pejorative
- "Check out" for "look at"

This point also bears some further elaboration. We need to remember that we use a very specialized professional vocabulary that is unfamiliar to most people outside our profession. For many people, "entering a library is like going into a foreign country, where a foreign language is spoken." We need to ask questions and provide an atmosphere that allows them to "describe their information need in their own terms" and in their own language (Ross, 2003).

Concluding the Reference Interview

One of the most important criteria of a "successful" reference interview is how it is concluded. It is crucial to leave the user with the feeling that the door is open to further interactions, by saying "if you don't find it, come back" or "if this doesn't work, come back, we'll try again." If you have the opportunity of seeing the person a bit later, asking a follow-up question such as "did you find it?" or "how did that work out?" is also very powerful in terms of the user's sense of satisfaction—even if the question wasn't answered! Willingness and interest seem to count for as much, or even more, than accuracy in a reference interview situation. What you want to avoid is "negative closure:" simply sending someone off to another part of the building to "browse," not conducting any sort of question negotiation to determine the real need, not offering any sort of follow-up option, or any of a number of other negative verbal or body language tactics (Ross and Dewdney, 1998).

Know When to Stop

Finally, while you may now have the impression that every reference interview will be a huge affair, that you'll need to ask all kinds of questions, and should follow up on each one if possible.... Relax. They definitely won't all be like that. Some will be quite simple and brief, and even so, satisfying to both you and the patron. It's not only important to know about all these skills, but also to employ them wisely. Use your emotional antennae and your ability to read the other person's body language, and don't go overboard if they are obviously in a hurry or not very interested. Give them what they seem to need and let it go. Something that is every bit as true today as when it was written in 1982 is: "Part of the skill in conducting an effective interview is to know when to stop" (Somerville).

Beyond the Face-to-Face Reference Interview

There are many "modes" in which the reference interview can take place nowadays: the in-person reference desk still exists, and of course the phone, but now reference interviews are also carried out via e-mail (an asynchronous exchange), and virtual reference, a.k.a. reference chat, which uses instant-messaging software (a synchronous exchange). Each move away from the face-to-face situation presents both hurdles but also, surprisingly, some advantages.

Reference Interviews on the Phone

On the phone, you have no visual cues, but the auditory ones are still there: you can tell a lot about people's ages and situations by their voices, and since it's usually easier to talk than to type, you can ask, and receive, more information. On the negative side, you may find that conversing with a nonnative English speaker over the phone seems much harder than in-person; perhaps we unconsciously rely much more on visual cues, facial expressions and the like, when it is difficult to understand what we are hearing. It can also be more cumbersome to explain a process (such as navigating through various computer screens and interacting with an interface) over the phone, but it's not terrible if the other person is sitting in front of their computer. On the plus side, you don't have to control your facial expression as rigorously as you do in person (some questions really do make you wince)! Also, there seems to be something about our "phone" expectations: people are usually quite accepting of an offer to be called back if you aren't finding what they need immediately. This gives you time to think and explore without the pressure of being watched, or knowing that they are on hold.

Electronic Reference Interviews: E-mail and Chat

With e-mail and reference chat, even the auditory cues are gone, and all you have is words on a screen, which does present quite a challenge for nuanced communication. So, you have no body language or gestures, and no voice intonation or accents. What do you do? In both e-mail and reference chat, you can use emoticons[1] and descriptions of gestures, and language that is more like how you would speak than write (Ronan, 2003). E-mail gives you plenty of time to think, and compose a thoughtful, structured answer. You can attach files with screen snaps to help explain something if needed. You can check your "script," and always remember to have positive closure by adding "let me know how this goes" or "ask again if this doesn't work out, we'll think of something else." In e-mail, the requestor may very well follow up with you, and depending on the e-mail system, all of your exchanges may stay listed in the message, so you can quickly review what you've said and done so far. The typed environment can actually be a plus for people having to communicate in a foreign language, as accents are not in the way, and both sides of the conversation have time to study the words to figure out what is being said. This typed environment is also such a part of our lives now that it is more nuanced than you would think: frustration and humor come through fairly obviously, and appropriate responses can be given. "[T]one and mood words, capital letters, and repeated punctuation reveal a lot about the writer's state of mind" (Fagan and Desai, 2003).

Reference chat implies a greater sense of immediacy than e-mail, but that may not necessarily be so: either by asking up front "do you need this right away" (Ronan, 2003), or by frequently communicating to the user that you are working on the question, the person at the other end may turn out to be fairly patient (Fagan and Desai, 2003; Kern, 2003). After all, it's likely that if the person is of "student age," they are doing several other things at the same time, and not just waiting on you (Carter, 2003; Oblinger, 2005). The RUSA Guidelines for Behavioral Performance of Reference were amended in 2004 to address the additional electronic forms of reference encounters (ALA, 2004). Ronan does an excellent job of showing how to meet the RUSA Guidelines in a "chat" environment. She describes how to use the same time-honored techniques: open and closed questions, encouragement, interest, and follow up, but modify them for the medium. For example, try to keep both your questions and responses brief and relatively informal (Ronan, 2003). You'll probably end up using mostly closed questions: that's all right, it's appropriate here. However, throwing out a big open-ended question can be a useful way to stall for time while you are thinking or looking, and provide additional useful information as well (Carter, 2003).

Both e-mail and reference chat also offer some significant intangibles: gone is the embarrassment at having to approach a desk, where other people can see and possibly hear the interaction, gone is the reluctance to interrupt someone busily at work at something else. (If you're the chat operator, that's all you're doing, right? They can't see that you're multitasking as well.) While there aren't visual cues to use in positive ways, those same visual cues aren't there to influence either party in negative ways either: the librarian can't see that you have twenty-nine body piercings, and you can't see that the librarian looks like the neighbor that always yelled at you for playing ball in the back yard—someone who can't possibly understand you. That anonymity can be very freeing.

Can a True Reference Interview Happen Online?

Librarians have questioned whether a decent reference interview can occur at all in the online situation, but more and more voices have come out in support of it, saying that it can (Fagan and Desai, 2003; Tyckoson, 2003). As the Oblingers (2005) point out, "Personal does not always mean 'in person' to the Net Gen. Online conversations may be as meaningful as one that is face-to-face." My own experience bears this out as well. You are simply meeting the users where they are, instead of making them come into your physical space: it's convenient, it eliminates some of the worst impediments to asking questions (fear and embarrassment), it can definitely work, and the key remains communication. Communication in the different media is different, but skills exist that can make it equally effective. Verbal, non-verbal, and textual: all offer ways to communicate effectively and positively. And "[s]uccessful communication . . . regardless of the medium over which that communication takes place—implies success in the reference process" (Tyckoson, 2003).

Why is the Reference Interview So Important?

For one thing, obviously we can't all be subject specialists in everything, but we need to gain the patron's confidence enough that they will work with us. Being attentive, asking questions, and taking an interest, will help with this. You are a specialist in the search field, and the person you are working with is, at the moment, the "specialist" in their field, while you are a layperson. You can still "achieve an intelligent and collegial interest" in their work, and this is "the level the search specialist should try to achieve" (Harter, 1986, 149). This situation calls for good communication skills and rapport, because you're depending a lot on the person you're working with to supply the terminology describing their search need. You need to get as much out of your patron as you can. You then work with him or her to think of synonyms, and using that knowledge, try to match the terminology against an appropriate database's thesaurus, or simply try the terms given you as keywords in a multidisciplinary database (or the Web), and proceed to pearl grow—but the initial set of terms describing the topic usually needs to come from the patron.

The reference interview is how you are going to connect people to the information they need. Through an exchange of questions, you help them clarify what their question really is, which ultimately saves their time, because you haven't, through misunderstanding or lack of probing, pointed them at something that is not useful (Kern, 2003). Tyckoson (2003) sums it up by saying: "The reference interview is the most important skill that a reference librarian can learn. Tools and sources will always change, but the process will always begin with the reference interview."

To me, it's really all about one simple thing:

You want them to come back.

And a positive reference interaction—in person, on the phone, or online (accurate or not) will help that to happen.

Quick Recap

For a number of reasons, the questions people ask in a reference situation frequently do not represent their real information need. The reference interview is meant to identify the "real question," and suggest terminology that can be used in a search. A good reference interview includes question negotiation, involving a good mix of open and closed questions, and good interpersonal skills: a positive, encouraging attitude, welcoming body language, and awareness of specialized vocabulary. How the interview is concluded, and knowing when to stop, are also important. Reference interviews over the phone, by e-mail, or by "chat" each have their pro's and con's, but techniques can be employed to make non-face-to-face encounters equally successful. A good reference interview will leave the patron with positive feelings, and more likely to return to the library with future questions.

Exercises and Points to Consider

1. School media specialists: what would be a good list of questions to use with your "clientele"?

2. Communication barriers were mentioned in a general way in this chapter, and a couple of examples were given (language, age differences). Can you elaborate on these? How many other "communication barriers" can you think of?

3. What would "welcoming" body language look like? How about unwelcoming?

4. How would you feel if you asked a question at a reference desk, and the librarian responded by turning immediately to his or her computer and typing?

5. Have you had many interactions with reference desks where you were the patron? Which ones do you remember? What do you remember about them?

6. Say you were at the reference desk, and a woman approached and said she was looking for information about sign languages used with children who are *not* deaf. What are some questions you might try asking her? What are some other things you might do?[2]

Notes

1. Emoticons: also known as "smileys" are facial expressions created from punctuation, e.g., :-) :-(:-p or "abbreviated" forms, without "noses" :) :(

2. Skilled questioning, or even more likely, a session with appropriate databases employing good pearl growing tactics, are needed to recast this question as: methods of nonverbal communication used with autistic children. Unless you're an expert in this field (in which case presumably you don't need help finding such information), this is not the language you are likely to use in everyday speech. But in order to get the best results, most efficiently, it helps tremendously to get the question reformulated into this language.

10
Choosing the Right Resource for the Question

By this point in this book, or in your course if the book is being used as your textbook, you may be feeling a bit overwhelmed: there are so many databases, and there's the whole Internet—how are you supposed to know what to use when? Specifically, you may wonder:

1. Should you always try to use a database first?
2. Is it "wrong" to use the Web?
3. Are there guidelines for when you should use a database and when you should use the Web?
4. Where do you start?

First and foremost: don't panic. Everybody feels this way at some point in his or her library school career, and frequently during the training on their first (and second, and third . . .) job as well. While there are no hard and fast rules for "what to use when" (like so many things, with time and experience you'll develop a style that is effective for you), there is an answer to the first two specific questions. Question 1: Should you always try a database first? Not at all, you should start with whatever seems most appropriate for the question, and where you feel most comfortable starting, given the resources you have available. In answer to Question 2: It is never "wrong" to use the Web, as long as you also use database resources if the question suggests they might be helpful (and you have databases available to you).

The rest of this chapter is meant to help answer Questions 3 and 4. We'll address them in reverse order so as to begin at the beginning, and because the question, "Where do I start?" has a simple and direct answer.

It's the same answer that applies to anything in reference service: Start with a good reference interview.

Start With the Reference Interview

The reference interview, whether it is in depth or only a two or three line dialogue, is the key to everything that happens next. That is how you find out what the patron wants, which should then suggest to you what resource(s) would meet the need. The reference interview should reveal factors such as:

- What is the subject area?
- What is the person looking for? For example, a specific factoid, a few good articles, an overview, or some statistics ... ?
- Does he or she want current or historical information?
- How much material is needed—a great deal, or, again, a "few good articles"?
- Does the person require "research" level material (also known as scholarly or peer-reviewed), or popular material?

And so forth: these points are discussed in the reference interview section of Chapter 9. Your reference interview should also have provided some keywords or phrases to start your search. You now have a body of information to work with (context, guidelines, intent, and subject), and can make an initial decision as to whether it sounds like a database question or a Web question. Note that I said "initial decision"—you can always change your mind and take a new approach as you work on the request; you don't have to get it right the first time.[1]

Now let's tackle the harder issue—guidelines for using databases or using Web search engines. What should you be looking for in the information you gather during the reference interview to help address that issue?

Questions for Databases

When trying to decide when to use databases and when to use a Web search engine, remember that people are using the Web to answer a lot of questions on their own, and by the time they approach a librarian, it's likely that more sophisticated techniques are called for. That said, in this section you'll find the hallmarks of questions that indicate *to me* that a database might be the answer, and questions for which a Web search might be a better approach. Never get the impression that any of this is cast in stone. As you gain experience, you will undoubtedly come to identify further or different indicators based on the clientele you are serving that will whisper to you: "database" or "Web." You will find yourself making good choices most of the time, instinctually.

Overview

Why choose a database over a Web search engine? The reasons are basic: authority and credibility. Databases can contain material with errors, but in general, there is a presumption that the material has been vetted somewhere in the process, and part of what you are paying the database vendor for is taking some responsibility for the quality of the material. Nancy Bloggs, writing Web pages in her bedroom, doesn't necessarily assume any responsibility at all. You can be more confident providing patrons with information from a commercial database than the free Web in many cases. Even for things such as a formula from a *CRC Handbook* or a dictionary definition, which may be readily available on the Web, if this information is being provided to *someone else*, it is better if it can be printed out from a database and handed over. No one is left wondering, "Who wrote this? Can I trust it to be right?" in situations where the patron really wants to be sure of getting credible information. The Web is a useful tool for getting searches started, but it is not usually the provider-of-choice for content to hand over formally to the patron as a final product.

Inevitably in the following descriptions you will find that Web searching is mentioned as well. It really is impossible to draw hard and fast lines between the two types of resources, because so often they do complement each other well, but I have tried to keep the discussions as focused as possible on databases.

Requests that Involve Articles

If your reference interview has shown that *articles* are involved in any way, it is usually a strong indicator to try a database. Articles represent content that has been formally published, usually in hard copy, and then distributed and made available for a fee. The publishers of the magazines, journals, and newspapers the articles appeared in are (usually) not giving them away free on the Internet. Yes, it's true that on the Web you can find papers that authors have posted on their Web sites, or archived in their organization's "institutional repository."[2] If you're after a known item, the Web may work. But it's not as organized, efficient, and comprehensive as a good, commercial database; there is just no comparison (yet—for some subject areas, Google Scholar is getting there).

For example, in an academic situation involving a student writing a paper, in almost every case your best choice is an article or encyclopedia database. The ability to search by subjects, to use various limits, and the knowledge that the material you'll retrieve has all made an appearance in the commercial press all firmly call for such a database.

Another way articles can be involved is as citations. In any setting, if someone were trying to track down a citation, or flesh out an incomplete citation, you should try appropriate databases first. (If it seems to be a history article, try a history database.) If you don't find what you need there, however, turn to the Web (see notes in the Questions for the Web section, below). If the patron wants to see who has *cited* an article recently, this is clearly a database question (and which database is pretty clear as well).

Articles, of course, come from journals. While patrons seldom ask, "where is the *Journal of XYZ* indexed?" this often becomes an implied question for the librarian in the course of answering the question they did ask. Usually the most efficient course of action is to check the *UlrichsWeb* database to see where the journal is indexed. (Of course, you can also simply go to a likely database and use its "publication browse" feature, to see if the needed journal is listed.)

Requests for an "Overview Article"

Patrons often want an article that provides an *overview* of some topic. There are a couple of problems with such a request. One is, you hear the word "article," and you do think database, which is right. The problem is, it is not that easy to find general, overview-type articles in the periodical literature, unless the author is writing a "review of the literature" or a "tutorial" on the topic,[3] or the topic falls within a discipline that publishes special-purpose "survey" journals, such as *Computer Surveys*. In general, articles tend to focus on a particular, finite topic rather than providing a broad introduction. A better source for an introductory or overview treatment of a topic is often an encyclopedia entry. There are database versions of encyclopedias now, and a commercial encyclopedia database could indeed provide an authoritative, trustworthy "overview."[4]

Book Questions

With the advent of mega online book vendors such as Amazon.com, Barnes & Noble (at http://www.books.com), or Powells.com (which covers the gamut of new, used, and out of print), the line between whether to use a database or a Web resource for "book" questions has grown much more indistinct. Obviously if the patron wants to know if your library owns a particular book, you'll go to your library's OPAC. After that, it may depend on what resources you have available. If you have access to WorldCat and *Books In Print*, try those databases first for other book-related questions (verifying or completing book citations, finding books on a topic, identifying a particular title that may be old or unusual). Because the databases are not trying to *sell* the books, there is less screen "noise" to ignore, and thus they are more efficient. You cannot beat the comprehensiveness of WorldCat, which helps avoid the possibility of having to look at several online book and out-of-print vendor Web sites. On the other hand, if the patron is a student who wants a textbook (and is surprised you don't have all the textbooks on Reserve), head off to Amazon.com immediately, to show him the deals on used copies.

Business Questions

Just by the nature of the beast, if it's a "business question," it is usually safe to assume that the answer is worth money, and thus is less likely to be freely available out on the Internet. Business questions frequently involve articles, which we have already discussed as a "database indicator." Another typical business query is the request for lists of companies in a certain line of business, or in a specific geographical area. Although there are free phone directories and such on the Web, the best directories for companies are commercial databases, such as the *Million Dollar Database*, or *Business and Company Resource Center*. Business documents such as market research reports or analyst's reports almost without exception come from subscription or other fee-based resources. The one major exception to this general rule of "databases for business questions" is in the case of certain business "numbers," which we encountered in Chapter 8. Stock quotes and the financial reports (e.g., Annual Reports) of current, public companies can usually be found on the Web.

Law Questions

In this highly specialized area of reference, official legal databases are definitely your first choice. Although it is possible to find the text of some states' statutes (e.g., Texas Statutes) or law (often referred to as "code," as in U.S. Code or N.Y. Code) online, it will probably be easier to find the information needed using a commercial legal database. Especially in this topic area, the authority of a commercial, subject specific database is very important.

Medical Questions

Things get somewhat fuzzier when it comes to helping patrons with medical questions. Because, as with law, we are again dealing with a very serious and specialized topical area, you should start with databases if possible, to take advantage of their authority and credibility. If you are working with medical professionals or medical students, obviously you'll use MEDLINE® or PubMed®. There is also a database, called CINAHL, specifically aimed at nursing professionals. For the lay public, there is a very nice Gale database called *Health Reference Center*. However, there is an immense amount of medical information available on the Web that people are more than happy to tap into on their own, usually without recognizing the risks involved: the need to be very aware of the credibility of the source, the date of the information, etc. We'll revisit this issue in the Questions for the Web section.

Quick Recap

Questions for which you will want to try to use databases are hallmarked by an underlying need for authority and credibility. Requests that mention a need for articles, either for research purposes such as writing a paper, or tracking down a specific citation, are usually best answered by appropriate databases. Requests expressed as a need for an "overview article" are often better served by material from an encyclopedia entry. Questions about books are sometimes answered equally well by subscription databases and free Web sites, such as Amazon.com. Business-related questions usually involve material that has been expensive to collect, and such questions will be better addressed with commercial databases. Preference should also be given to commercial databases for law and medical questions, due to the specialized and serious nature of the topic areas. The particular need in those situations for authority and credibility demands that only professionally produced and professionally acknowledged resources be used.

Choosing a Database

If you're faced with a question that seems like a database question, you could be in one of three situations: having lots of databases at your disposal (the assumption so far in this book), a few databases, and none at all. In this section we'll look at the issue of making a choice in light of those three scenarios.

Scenario 1: An Embarrassment of Riches

If you're at an institution that subscribes to literally hundreds of databases, the natural question is: How do you decide which one to use? Determining which database to start with involves a lot of the factors you use to *evaluate* a database (a topic addressed again in Chapter 11):

- What subjects does the database cover? (If the topic is well defined, definitely in one subject area, a subject-specific database such as *Art*

Index or *EconLit* could be the right resource. If the topic seems fuzzy, or interdisciplinary, a multisubject database such as ProQuest *Research Library* may be a better answer.)

- What types of material are included? Magazines? Scholarly journals? Books or book chapters? "Working Papers"? Other materials? Or do you need a numeric, or directory database?

- What *level* of material? (Is it "popular" level or research level?)

- What is the date coverage of the database? Does it cover the right time period? If you are trying to find or verify a really recent article, you'll want to check how frequently material is added to the database you're thinking of using, and how up-to-date it is.

- If the database does not provide full text, are the sources mostly available in your library (or in another database)?

- How "searchable" is the database: Does it offer controlled vocabulary to focus your search, or does it offer keyword searching of all fields, if you need to find a needle in the haystack? What fields are searchable? If you only have one piece of information, but that field isn't searchable in the database you've picked out, you have a problem . . . or if you're looking for a particular *kind* of article, like a book review, you want a database that offers a search by article type feature. Is it possible to limit by scholarly or "peer-reviewed" articles, if that's what you need?

You don't have to pick just one database, either. You could identify two or three candidates, and test your most specific search term in each one to see which shows the most hits. Especially if you're venturing into a new subject area, try your most specific term in the database you've chosen, and see how many hits there are. If the database has a subject list or thesaurus, look up your term to see if it is listed, and how many records are associated with it.

This list of factors to consider probably sounds like it would take far too much time, while the patron is sitting there expecting immediate action. As you gain experience, you will find that you can do this "database or the web?" analysis quite quickly, however. If you're at a major university or large public library that subscribes to a large number of databases, it's very likely that the library staff have already created Web pages that organize the databases into groups by subject, and often by whether or not they are full-text. Start by looking at databases by Subject, or at Guides developed by librarians that might suggest the best databases for different subject areas. Quickly scan the descriptions of the databases' *coverage, currency,* and *material* types. Go into the database(s) that seem most appropriate and test them for subject coverage, availability of appropriate fields and limits as mentioned in the bulleted list above. This will all come across as "action on the question" to the patron, and results will probably follow pretty quickly.

And of course you have the free Web as well. Even when you have hundreds of subscription databases at your fingertips, it's a perfectly acceptable strategy to run a quick Web search, just to see if the term is "out there," and what context it is used in, especially for an unfamiliar topic area (think of this as a "reality check"). As mentioned before, the two can complement each other well.

Scenario 2: A Few Good Databases

This scenario could apply to a school library with a handful of databases available, or to a corporate, law, or other special library as well. In each case, the limited number of databases will have been chosen for the appropriateness to your clientele and your mission, so in a way, you could consider this an advantage: some preselection has taken place, and these should already be the "most likely" databases for the questions you expect to encounter. Given this, you can still look at your databases in light of the factors discussed above. Which one(s) might be most appropriate, given their *coverage*, *currency*, *searchability*, and *ability* to identify *research*? You can jump into one or more and test your search terms. Frankly, in many ways you have the advantage over the libraries that have hundreds of databases, because you can be thoroughly familiar with each resource you have, and have a much better idea which one will be most useful for any given question, without any testing or analysis at all. And, of course, you have the free Web as well.

Scenario 3: No Subscription Databases at All

It would certainly be sad, and frustrating, after learning about all these nifty fee-based resources to find yourself in a situation where you don't have any subscription databases available. No point in grousing and hand-wringing, however: let's assume that at least you have an Internet connection. Two U.S. Government agencies provide free versions of their database content on the Web: PubMed from the National Library of Medicine, and ERIC from the Department of Education. OCLC offers a version of World-Cat called Open WorldCat: use the special syntax "Find in a library" along with a keyword in a search at Yahoo! or Google to come up with Open World-Cat records. Google Scholar provides a way to search for peer-reviewed articles from scholarly journals; the effectiveness of this search engine varies according to the subject area of your search, and the time period. You should be able to trust the authority of Web sites from the government (.gov), such as MedlinePlus.gov, or ones run by reputable organizations (.org), like the American Cancer Society (http://www.cancer.org).

Actually, you may find there are some (subscription) databases provided at no cost to you through your local public library system. This is something to have explored ahead of time, so you'll have some idea of what is there, and what you need to do to gain access (a current library card with a barcode number, for example).

Each of these scenarios has included the Web, the last one relying solely on it. This seems the natural time to look at "what questions are best answered by the Web?"

Questions for the Web

One is tempted to say "what *isn't* a question for the Web?" since it seems like no matter what keywords you search for, they'll have appeared in some Web page, somewhere. However, there are certainly topics that are much more likely, or only, answerable by a Web search.

Personal Uses of the Web

We use the Web endlessly for personal "research:" finding books at Amazon.com, getting weather reports, checking crossing delay times for the bridges to Canada, making travel plans, checking movie times, buying an answering machine (buying anything), or trying to find an answer to a software question. It's quick, it's easy, and it's not the sort of information you'll find in databases. (But for a review from *Consumer Reports* about something we're thinking of buying, we wind up back at a database, because that's an article.) Since it's just for our personal information, we take the responsibility for deciding how authoritative the information is, and whether or not that's important.

Professional Uses of the Web

Popular Culture, Local Information, and People

At the reference desk, questions having to do with popular culture ("Who is the highest paid player in the NFL?"), or with daily life or local information ("Where are all the HSBC bank branches in (city X)?" "Can I get a list of all the choral societies in (city Y)?"), or—a favorite—identifying the source of a song, poem, or quotation from a small fragment—are definitely "Web search" material. For anything to do with films, a part of popular culture, the Internet Movie Database (IMDb) is my resource-of-choice. The Web is also amazing (a little frighteningly so) for finding people. It doesn't always work, but we all know some pretty incredible stories about locating people by searching for them on the Web.

Citation Disambiguation

The Web is useful for tracking down citations. If you're not finding a citation in a database (even after leaving out part of what the patron has told you), don't hesitate to drop parts of the citation into Google (or your favorite search engine) to try and figure out where the problem lies. In doing a Web search, you are looking for the citation to appear on someone else's Web page (where it's correct and complete, hopefully), or at least to gain some sense of context that would indicate, for example, that you have chosen to look in a database in the wrong subject area. Maybe you can even find the author's Web page and see how he or she referred to the work in question. Try anything you can think of to provide a clue.

Rare or Obscure Topics

You can also start with a Web search when the patron indicates that what he is looking for is quite obscure, and you want the biggest haystack possible in which to look for that needle (think of the desperate parents in the movie *Lorenzo's Oil*). Of course, the patron has probably already searched on the Web, but perhaps you can do it better. Do a quick Web search if the topic is obscure *to you*, just to try for a quick sense of context, and possibly some additional useful keywords.

Medical Questions from Laypeople

If you are working on a medical question with a patron who is not a member of the health services professions, it is hard not to use the Web in your research. As mentioned in the section about Medical Questions that appeared above, the patron very likely has been searching the Web on her/his own, and one can't deny there is a great deal of medical information available there. What is imperative is that you impress on the patron that a great deal of it is incorrect, misleading, and outright dangerous, unless it comes from a reputable source. Depending on the resources available in your library and the skill level of the patron, your approach may be to encourage a change not in *source* but in *methodology*. Rather than simply doing Web searches, you can try to get the patron to *browse* reputable sites, such as MedlinePlus.gov, or WebMD.com, and the sites of, again, reputable organizations. Use Web searches to find those associations and organizations, but then urge the patron to go into those sites and browse or search within the site. If at all possible, however, databases such as *Health Reference Center* or the *Virtual Reference Library*, both from Gale, would be preferable.

Standard Facts and Statistics

For someone looking for a specific, standard fact (e.g., what year did the Berlin Wall fall?), the authority of an encyclopedia database is attractive, but you may well just try a Web search, because it may be quicker and just as useful. (It's a standard date, after all—if the page comes from a credible source, it might be right.) Of course, if the patron then wanted historical background for the falling of the Wall, you should get back to the encyclopedia or article databases very quickly. The area of quotations and definitions can be equally murky: in a situation where it doesn't matter that much, you can probably just do a Web search. At the Reference Desk, if you have a resource such as *Oxford Online*, it would be more authoritative and professional to use that.

As we found in Chapter 8, government agencies provide quite a wealth of statistical, numerical information on the Web. There aren't as many databases available in this area, so I often find myself using the Web as an equal partner when a question requires statistics or "numbers" to answer it. (But again, if I have access to an appropriate database, it will almost always provide a much more *efficient* way of getting the information, and usually be more authoritative as well.)

Quick Recap

Although you can certainly find academic material on the Web (papers, lectures, reports, etc.), organized, academic research is not yet its strongest point. (There are exceptions, of course, such as the arXiv site for high-energy physicists.) The overarching themes in this Questions for the Web section have rather been issues of daily life, popular culture, people, and connecting with the "informal college," that is, tapping into the "web" of other people's knowledge (e.g., for software questions, obscure topics, or "fragment" questions—lyrics, quotations, etc.). The Web is useful for providing clues, context, or a reality check. It is amazing—what *did* we do before?

Exercises and Points to Consider

1. What do you use the Web for? Try keeping a journal for a week in which you record every time you use the Web to answer a question, either at work or in your personal life. Can you detect any common themes in your Web use?

2. "Search madness" activity: if you are using this book as part of a class, have the group come up with a list of questions that they have encountered in a library, in their studies, or in their daily life.

Then add in questions from earlier chapters in this book, or from search assignments. For questions that required databases before, try them as Web searches. For the questions submitted by the class, decide which seem suitable for the Web, and which for databases. Spend a session just searching and comparing results.

Suggested Reading

Tenopir, Carol. "Sorting Through Online Systems." *Library Journal* (May 1, 2002): 32, 34.

This is the shortest, sanest set of tips and advice for keeping the plethora of databases "straight" in your head. Even though some of the names have changed since 2002, the advice still applies. A must read.

Notes

1. For the record, this is a sea change from the early days of searching on systems like Dialog, where you paid by the minute, and often by each record displayed, etc. Then you really did do your homework thoroughly before "going online," and it was generally expected that you would get it right the first time. The advent of databases on CD-ROM, and now on the Web, has totally changed this aspect of searching (for the better).

2. Google for "institutional repository" +DSpace or +Eprints for more information on this topic.

3. This varies a great deal by discipline: tutorial articles (which may also appear under a title of "Review" or "Survey") are common in the Engineering and Computer Science literature. There is a standard format for articles in medical journals that includes a literature review, and the more scholarly library science articles have this as well. But a literature review may not be the same as an overview, and certainly in subject areas such as business, a real "overview" is fairly rare.

4. Unfortunately, I often find it hard to convince my patrons—who are generally undergraduates or grad students—that an encyclopedia entry is a valid resource or way to start. I'm trying to point them at a specialized encyclopedia, but they seem to relegate anything with "encyclopedia" in the title to "little kid" status.

11
Evaluating Databases

This chapter provides a detailed list of issues to consider when evaluating a database: information to gather, factors to assess, and suggestions for benchmarking. It concludes with advice about how to use this information effectively in putting together a database purchase request. The previous chapter, on choosing the best resource for the question, also draws on this material; don't be surprised if you find yourself going back and forth a bit between these two chapters.

In real life, occasions requiring an in-depth formal evaluation of a database are not going to arise that frequently. Institutions don't change their database subscriptions that often: getting anything new usually means giving up an existing service, and changing between relatively equivalent products tends to be held in check by the overall community's resistance to change. (Users generally prefer a *status quo* they are familiar with, rather than frequent changes. A replacement has to demonstrate obvious and significant improvements in ease of use or content, to be accepted.) At the same time, you will want to remain up-to-date on new databases in your subject area, and so familiarizing yourself with new and changing products may become a fairly steady undercurrent to your job (depending on the volatility of products in your subject area). Another motivation for doing a thorough study of a database is in order to write a review of it. While reviewing is an excellent way to start getting published, it isn't something you do every day. Finally, you will obviously want to master a database completely before teaching others about it, even though (as you'll find in the last chapter), you will want to be judicious in how much of what you learn you choose to pass on to your audience.

Thus the position of this chapter in the book: almost at the end of the sequence, rather than at the beginning. It's important, and hopefully useful, but it is not information you'll need to work through in its entirety very frequently. Note "in its entirety"—the information here is intended to be a fairly comprehensive list, for the special situations listed above. Some of these are major considerations, some are minor, and some you may not be able to find any information on, but it's still interesting to be aware of all the potential factors. You'll certainly find that you use selected elements from this list regularly, in your daily reference activities, as mentioned in the previous chapter. Factors of "database evaluation" such as topical coverage, date range, availability of full text, and usability of the interface, you'll find yourself assessing almost automatically, and memorizing for databases you use frequently. For those situations requiring an exhaustive review, however, the following two sections offer a list of categories and associated factors to consider in evaluating and testing databases.

Basic Facts and Figures

Initial Factual Information to Gather

Database Vendor(s)

Like anything else, the same databases are often available from different vendors, and it can pay to shop around. Vendors get the data in a raw format, and then format and load it according to how they structure their database, what fields they want to use, whether those fields are searchable, etc. The search capabilities (and obviously the user interface) will vary depending on the vendor, and you can have a really different experience searching the same database offered by different vendors. If you are seriously looking at a new database, and more than one vendor provides it, be sure to try them all. It's a big investment, and you owe it to your organization, and especially to your users, to get the version that will best meet *their* needs.

Existing Reviews

Has anyone already written a review of this database? A thorough database review is a large task, requiring hours of research and testing. Although you may still need to check the latest facts and figures (number of sources, etc.) if the review is a few years old, and you will always want to do your own testing, someone else's review is a useful place to start. The *Charleston Advisor* is an excellent source of reviews. If you are using a database such as *Library Literature & Information Science* to locate reviews, look for document type "review," and author names such as Mary Ellen Bates, Péter Jacsó, Mary Dee Ojala, Barbara Quint, and Carol Tenopir. If the database is offered by more than one vendor, look for comparative reviews, or individual reviews for the different versions.

Coverage

There are many aspects to "coverage," including:
Subject Coverage. This is also referred to as "scope." What is the subject emphasis of the database—what topical areas does it cover? Or is it multidisciplinary? For the subject, what is the *level* of the material covered, that is, who is the intended audience? K-12 students? College students? Graduate students? Faculty? Specialists? Or the lay public?

Material Coverage. What types of material and formats are included? If only periodicals, what types? Popular? Scholarly? Trade journals? Or Newspapers? Is there one type that is emphasized, that is, are there many more popular or trade journals, with only a few scholarly titles? For articles containing tables or graphics, are these included? If yes, how are they reproduced? (A formatted table reproduced in plain text can be almost impossible to interpret.) If other kinds of documents are covered, what are they? (Possibilities include books, book chapters, theses, conference proceedings, government documents, speeches, audio transcripts such as NPR interviews, and photos or visual materials such as would be found in an image archive.) Are any primary materials included? What formats are offered for full text— HTML, PDF, or both?

Source Coverage. How many sources are indexed? What is the *selection policy*: are the source publications indexed cover-to-cover, or only selectively? Is this policy universal for all titles in the database, or does it vary by title? How much information is provided: citations only, citations with abstracts, or citations and full text? This is also referred to as the breadth and depth of coverage: more source titles would indicate greater *breadth*, and cover-to-cover indexing would provide greater *depth* of coverage.

Date Coverage. Does the database provide current, or retrospective coverage, e.g., how far back in time does indexing for most of the titles go? Does the database use a "moving wall" date coverage system, wherein titles are covered up to a set number of years in the past (e.g., JSTOR titles are covered from, usually, the first issue, up to issues from 3 to 5 years ago. Each year one more new year is added, but current issues are not available.).

Geographic Coverage. Does the database index just U.S. publications? Or is the source list international? If international, are the materials in their original language? How many and what languages are represented? Are article titles and abstracts (if available) offered in translation?

Availability of Sources

A major consideration for any database is how accessible the material it indexes will be to your users. How many, or what percentage, of the sources are available in full text? If the records are mainly or all citations, does the database support linking technologies such as SFX? (Is your institution running such technology, and do you have other databases that might offer the content cited in the database you are evaluating?) If offered by multiple vendors, which ones support linking? Whether or not you can use a linking technology with a database that provides only citations, how many of the sources indexed are physically available at your library? Interlibrary Loan is always an option, but people often prefer to be able to put their hands on what they want locally.

Currency

How often is material added? How soon after a journal is published do records for its content appear in the database? Are there embargoes on certain titles (e.g., the publisher has decided not to make the most current issues available)? How many titles are embargoed, and for how long? (Weeks? months? a year? or more?). If there are embargoed titles that will be of significant interest to your library, do you have subscriptions to the print versions, or a separate online access arrangement, so that users will have access to the current issues? Here again, if the database is offered by more than one vendor, check the updating and embargo schedules for each one. Both of these factors can vary considerably by vendor.

So far this discussion has focused mainly on periodical databases, but what about a directory database? A list of associations might remain fairly stable, but matters in the corporate world are fairly dynamic: companies change their names, get bought, sold, and merged into other companies. For both associations and corporations, names of officers, their titles, phone numbers, etc. are likely to change. You will want to try and find out how often such a directory type of database gets updated (and where do they get the information from)? For example, if you live in an place where the area code has changed, and records in a business or association database don't reflect that change after a year, this is a red flag that there may be problems with the vendor's updating system.

Size

How many records does the database contain? How fast is it growing? If the database is very large, is it divided up into multiple sections? Are the sections by date (e.g., current, backfile), or by subject or material group? A database broken into sections can be annoying to use if you have to rerun your search in each section. Last, a fairly infrequent concern: if the database is one that you load locally on your own server, how much space does it require?

Errors

Are you surprised to see this heading? Remember, databases are ultimately human creations, so errors are definitely a possibility. Unfortunately, errors or error rates in a database are hard to determine empirically. You need to keep your eye out for them as you work with the database, and decide for yourself if you're seeing too many.

Generally, there are three kinds of errors: factual, typos, and indexing errors. Factual errors are nontypo mistakes in numerical or other data, e.g., a date, an address, a phone number, or a name. Typos are things like transposition of letters or numbers, or inadvertent dropping or doubling of words. Usually fairly benign, typos become a big problem when you can't pull up an article because there's a typo in the title or author, etc., or if there is a typo in a "stable URL" link, so that the link does not function. Indexing errors are errors of judgment in assigning terms or categorizing records. This type of error is almost impossible to find deliberately; it is only mentioned here so that someday when you're looking at a record and thinking: "Why in the world did they assign *that* term?"—it could well be an error. Some errors are acceptable, but when they start interfering with searching, or mean that the resource is simply providing wrong information, obviously you are moving into the "unacceptable" realm.

Unfortunately, it is very difficult to "test" for errors. In doing test searches, you can watch for typos to appear, or you can try keyword searching for words that are frequently mistyped (e.g., serach for search). In a directory database, you could randomly sample a few records, and try to check the names and phone numbers against another source. Otherwise, the best thing to do is to tap the experience of all the other users out there: look for articles, even if not review articles, which mention the database. Do they say anything about errors? Or post a question to an appropriate newsgroup, and see what anecdotal evidence other users have to offer.

Database Aids

Database Aids include both online and physical resources that provide help in using the database, teaching others to use it, and promoting it. You'll want to find out: Does the database have an online Help function? Is it easy to find, easy to understand, and easy to use? Is the help context-sensitive, that is, different depending on what screen you are on, or always the same? Note that context sensitive is not necessarily always better than static: the system's interpretation of your "context" may leave you scratching your head and wanting to start at the beginning instead. Is there an online tutorial, and is it useful? Is there a printed manual? (Usually not, but it never hurts to ask.) Are there "quick start" or similar brief "how to" cards or leaflets that the vendor will provide? Will the vendor send you promotional materials to help market the new database? Does the vendor offer any "train-the-trainer" services, either in person or via "Web cast" seminars?

Cost and Vendor Support

Vendors are regularly experimenting with new pricing models, so this can often be a more intricate question than you might think. In academic situations, the database cost is frequently based on "FTE," that is, how many *full-time equivalent* students there are on campus. Such a charge model usually then means there is no limit to the number of people who can use the database at the same time. At the other end of the spectrum from this model, some databases charge by number of simultaneous users, or "seats," you opt for, meaning that only one, two, three, etc. people will be able to use the database at the same time. Another model is to charge by the search, or to sell "blocks," or sets, of searches. When the number of searches in the block is used up, access is suspended until you purchase more. A database with deep date coverage may be divided up into sections, and it may be worth checking to see if you can purchase only the most recent section (if that would meet your needs). Price negotiation can be full of wheeling and dealing: discounts may be available based on the number of years you sign on for, or by the number of databases purchased from same vendor. No matter how you cut it, though, database subscriptions are expensive. Many libraries now participate in library consortia, which act together to negotiate pricing with vendors. Because there are so many possible factors, database prices are seldom (if ever) posted on vendor Web sites or listed anywhere. The best way to determine the cost for a particular database is to start with the Collection Development or Acquisitions Librarian in your library. If you are not currently in a library, call the vendor directly and speak with a sales representative.

It's also useful to explore what kind of support the vendor offers, in particular for usage statistics. Are usage statistics available? How detailed are they? How do you access them, or can a report be automatically sent to you on a regular basis? Do the statistics adhere to the standards suggested by Project Counter? (See http://www.projectcounter.org.) Standardized statistics will allow you to really know what you are looking at, what has been counted and what it means. If you decide to invest the money, it's very important to be able to get some idea of how much the database is getting used.

Other vendor support issues to explore are the nature and availability of technical and search support (by phone? e-mail? Web form? 24/7, and 365?), and, as mentioned above, train-the-trainer services. During your database trial period, besides working with the database itself, be sure to test the technical and search support services, not once, but a few times. Is it easy to reach a knowledgeable person? Were your questions answered, accurately and in a timely fashion?

Finally, check to see if the database has any special platform (PC, Mac, Unix, or Linux) or Web browser requirements. If any of these would mean upgrades or new equipment in order to offer the database, it puts another cost consideration into your evaluation and planning.

Testing and Benchmarking

As mentioned above, prior to initiating a subscription request, you will want to get a database trial (or multiple trials if the database is offered by more than one vendor). This will be a key component in your evaluation. I have never encountered a vendor who wouldn't offer some kind of trial access to their products. Do not abuse their good nature in this regard: don't ask for a trial if you aren't serious about the database for some reason (either for purchase, or for review-writing purposes), or if you don't have the time to evaluate it properly. And while you have the trial, make good use of it: if necessary, deliberately schedule several time slots on your calendar over the course of the trial to devote to working with the database. As they say, pound on it! You really need to know what you're talking about if you are going to recommend it for purchase. Below are aspects of the database to look for, assess, and compare (benchmark), during your database trial (your test period).

Testing

Record and File Structure

This topic takes us all the way back to the material in Chapter 1. Factors to assess include: What fields are available? Are the fields appropriate and useful given the subject matter of the database? Sometimes when vendors simply apply their standard interface to a new database, the result is less than optimal. Of the fields you see in a full record display, how many are also searchable? (Some fields will be "display only.") Another way to think of this is: how many ways can you look up same record, that is, how many "access points" do the records have? More fields aren't always better but can be helpful. Do the searchable fields each have their own index list, and can you browse that list? Think of the FirstSearch databases, and their many indexes, which even distinguish single word from phrase indexes. More indexes are great, but not always better. The questions to have at the front of your mind at all times during an evaluation are "Does this make sense for this database? Is it helpful? Does it help get me to better results more efficiently?"

Linking is an aspect of record and file structure that you can divine simply by observation. In a record display, are there fields that are linked e.g., Author or Subject, which allow you to immediately pull up all other records with that author or subject? Are there other linked fields in the record, and what do they link to?

Indexing and Cataloging Practices: "Searchability"

Don't be put off by the heading of this section: it is not a suggestion for you to actually try to find out the interior policies and work practices that the vendor uses. Rather, there are many things you can observe during testing, or find out from the documentation, that will reveal something about how the vendor has set up the indexes, and how much human intervention (cataloging) has been applied to the records. These things can be dubbed "searchability," and you will again find many of them familiar from earlier chapters:

- Are there stop words?
- Can you adjust the date range of your search?
- What limits do you have available? Are they useful?
- Controlled vocabulary:
  - Does the database use a set of a controlled vocabulary, e.g., subject terms?
  - Is it a subject list, a straight alphabetical list of terms, as in EBSCO's *MasterFILE Select* or ProQuest's *Research Library*?
  - Or is it a thesaurus: a hierarchical system, with "broader," "narrower," and "related" headings, that shows relationships between terms, as you find in *Library Literature* or ERIC?
  - If it is a thesaurus, who created it – the original database *producer* (such as the American Psychological Association), or the database *vendor*? (Remember these are often two very different organizations.)
  - With any kind of list of subject terms, can you browse the list?
  - Is there any kind of "mapping" functionality to help you get to the right subject terms?
  - If subject terms are assigned to each record, how many are assigned? (2–3? 5? 10? Or more?)
  - Are subjects assigned consistently?
  - Are the subject terms broad, or really specific? (What is the "specificity" of the indexing language?)
  - Consistency of indexing: has the subject list grown, changed over the years? If so, and if there are "discarded" headings—how is that dealt with? How do you know if a term has been discontinued?
  - Has some form of mass search and replace been performed, or do you need to search on both the old and the new term? (These are good nitty-gritty questions to ask the vendor's search help desk.)
  - With any browsable indexes, do they offer a "paste to search" function, so you don't have to retype the entry in the search interface? (This saves time and the risk of typing errors.)
- Abstracts:
  - Do the records offer abstracts?

- Are they simply replications of the first paragraph of the article, or are they actually evaluative or summarizing? (The former are more likely to have been machine generated, while the latter are most likely to have been written by a person.)
- Are the abstracts generally long and detailed or short?
- Title enhancements:
  - If titles in this subject discipline's literature are frequently "cute" or clever rather than straightforward, is a supplemental title added, to clarify what the article is really about? (And to give you a better chance of retrieving it with a keyword search.)
  - If the database offers materials in different languages, are the article titles offered in translation?
- Full text: If full text is available, is it searchable?[1] Are there better tools for searching full text available, e.g., proximity operators?
- Does the database offer a "find more like this" function?
- Overall, does the database use features and conventions that are similar to other databases?

An additional point that bridges both "searchability" and the next category, user interface, is the idea of search history. This is a user interface functionality that does not have to do with indexing or cataloging practices, but that certainly contributes to a database's searchability. Does the database keep track of your search history: can you reuse previous searches; combine them with other previous searches or with new terms?

User Interface—Usability

This is an area that is open to both objective and subjective evaluation, and can be particularly important in the case of the same database offered by multiple vendors. As you work with the database, besides assessing the content and search function, keep track of your experiences and reactions to the interface—the *way* you access that content and those search functions. In the broadest sense: Does it work? How well? When comparing vendors, searching the same information through a different interface can feel like a totally different experience. Some specific things to be look for are:

- Are different skill levels accommodated—novice, expert?
- Is the interface easily understood?
- Does it make it clear how to use it, both by layout and by the terminology used? For example, are field names clear and understandable to the user?
- If icons are used, are they meaningful?
- Is the interface so bare and simple that it's "naked," or is it cluttered, busy, or mysterious?
- Are there too *many* options (or too many ways to do the same thing)?
- How is color contrast used? Is color used to demarcate functional areas of the screen, or is everything uniform in color?

- Is the interface visually appealing? For instance is the color scheme easy on the eyes? Are the fonts too small, too big, too hard to read, etc.?

- Are search fields well defined?

- Does it provide good navigation links—is it well designed?

- How much control do the navigation links exert: for example, if you use the Back button rather than a "modify search" link, does it wipe out your search? (This is very annoying.)

- Can you initiate a search by just pressing Enter, or is it necessary to always click a "Search" button?

- How many clicks does it take to get to your "goal" (abstract, full-text, etc.), and back?

- How easy is it to adjust or modify your search? Do you have to go back to a main search screen, or is a search interface available on every screen?

- How easy is it to find help? What terminology is used for help?

- Are functions like save, e-mail, and download easy to see and understand?

- If the database has a "time out" function, that is, you get disconnected after a certain period of inactivity, does it provide a warning before disconnecting you? Can the time out period be adjusted?

- If the subscription is based on a limited number of users, what sort of message is displayed if all the "seats" are in use when you try to sign on?

- Is the database browser or platform dependent, that is, it will only work with a specific Web browser, on a specific type of computer (usually Windows rather than Mac, Unix, or Linux)?

- If the database is browser dependent, what sort of warning does it provide if you attempt to use it with an unsupported browser?

- If you encounter nonfunctioning tools (buttons/features that don't work), is it because you are on an unsupported platform? This is another good excuse to phone the vendor's tech support line.

Treatment of Research

This is an important factor for any institution that works with students who are writing papers. Terms frequently used for research articles are "peer reviewed," or "scholarly." Databases such as EBSCO's *MasterFile Select* or ProQuest's *Research Library*, which offer both popular and scholarly articles, provide a limit function for "Peer Reviewed."[2] Provision of such a limit or similar functionality only makes sense when a database includes a wide range of materials, however. Databases that consist almost entirely of scholarly materials, such as the *Science Citation Index* or *EconLit*, do not need this type of filtering functionality. Questions to ask in evaluating a multidisciplinary database are:

- Does the database provide "research" level material?

- How can scholarly materials be identified? By a limit in the search interface?

- Or is there a way to distinguish scholarly materials in search results, even if you haven't used a limit, e.g., by an icon in the record, or by a separate tab in the results display that filters for scholarly articles?

- Is there anything in the product literature to indicate how many journals, or what proportion of the sources, are scholarly?

- One other point to check: scholarly articles almost always have a bibliography of sources at the end. If the database provides full text in HTML rather than PDF format, check to be sure such bibliographies are included.

Sorting/Display/Output Capabilities

Sorting:

- What's the default sort order for displaying results? Can you change it?

- Where is the sort function offered: in the search interface, in the results display, or in both?

- What are the sort options?

- What fields can you sort by?

- If the database allows you to select certain records and create a list of just the selected, or marked, records, can those be sorted?

Displaying:

- How many results are displayed per page? Can you change the number?

- Are the search parameters (words searched, limits used) reiterated on the results list screen?

- What is the default record display—full or brief? Can you change it?

- Are search terms highlighted in the results display?

- Are format options indicated for each record, for example, icons indicating HTML or PDF availability?

Output:

- What formats are offered for output? Plain text, HTML, or PDF?

- Can you e-mail records? What e-mail options are offered, for example, sending the information formatted as plain text, HTML, or as a PDF attachment? How much can you customize the e-mail: can you put your e-mail as the return address, put in your own Subject line, or add a note? Can you choose to include the search history with the e-mailed results?

- When printing records, do you get to choose what gets printed (which fields)? Note especially in databases that provide full text: can you select a group of records, and then print the full records in one continuous stream? Or are you forced to print full text records one by one?

- If you have reason to believe that many of the people who would use this database use software programs such as Reference Manager to keep track of their citations, does the database offer an export function for bibliographic management software programs?

Benchmarking

The first three types of benchmark activities listed below are, obviously, most important when you are trying to choose between two databases, especially if you already subscribe to one and are contemplating whether to change to the other. The next point addresses the fact that in academia, there is always a set of schools with which your school compares itself, and such comparisons are important to administrators. The final point below is perhaps not a realistic goal, but is a significant concept.

Source List Comparisons

In choosing between rival databases, a good first step is to compare their lists of sources, that is, which journals (or other document types) does each one offer? How much overlap is there? How many unique titles are there? Among the unique titles, which list has more titles that are of interest to *your* institution? Among the titles that are in the same in both databases, is the coverage the same: that is, how do the dates of coverage, and the availability of full text (if any), compare? If you can obtain the source lists in Excel format, and merge them into one spreadsheet, it can greatly facilitate this comparison process. This comparison is also almost entirely quantitative and objective, and therefore carries more weight in a request for purchase. And you may not have to do this comparison "by hand" with your own spreadsheets: check the recent library literature, and ask colleagues in Collection Development, Acquisitions, or Cataloging to see what comparison products are available to you.

Search Result Comparisons

Just as it sounds, you will want to run the same searches in the databases you are comparing, and see how the number and nature of the "hits" compares. The number refers to how many results, and the "nature" refers to the quality of the results: if one database yields ten more hits on a search, but of those extra ten, eight are from popular magazines or are only brief articles, are you really getting any significant advantage? Absolutely equal searches are somewhat difficult to achieve, since each database may use differing subject terms, the default fields that get searched may be different, etc., but this is still a very useful exercise to do. Experiment with keyword searches, phrase searches, and field searches. If there are subject terms that are the same in both databases, those are ideal for benchmark searches. Simply spending some time with the two subject lists side-by-side on the screen can be useful too: try to get a sense of the level of detail of subject terms used, and the nature of the language. Even in the realm of "controlled vocabulary," there are some that are more formal, and others that sound more like natural language. Users are more likely to benefit by accident when the subject terms are less formal (e.g., because the terms they type in happen to match the subject vocabulary).

Be sure to keep a record of everything you do while you're "benchmark searching:" exactly what the search was, the number of results, and comments on the results. Don't count on your memory: by the next day the similarities and differences will be a blur. Keeping a good log helps this activity stay in the quantitative, objective realm, rather than the gut instinct, subjective realm.

Finally, be sure to test searching at different times of day, to compare response times. Based on the vendor's location, figure out what represents "peak hours" and test during that time. Significantly slower response times or access refusals are not a good sign.

Technical Support Comparisons

If you are comparing two databases, come up with some questions for the Technical Support staff at both vendors. Compare the time required to get answers, how accurate the answers are, and the general effectiveness of the staff.

Peer Institution Holdings

As mentioned above, administrators at colleges and universities are very aware of, and sensitive to, comparisons with other schools that are recognized as "peers." It has nothing to do with the intrinsic worth of the database at hand, but if you can show that a significant number of your school's peer institutions already subscribe to this database, it may be helpful in persuading your administration to fund the purchase.

Ideal Assessment of Coverage

The "ideal assessment of coverage" is represented by this question: How much (what percentage) of the total literature in the discipline is covered by this database? This is an ideal, because, frankly, I can't imagine how one would go about determining it with any kind of precision, but it is an interesting and thought-provoking point to raise. (If the database is subject-specific, one strategy might be to see if there is a matching subject category in *Ulrichs*, and then compare numbers of titles. This is still bound to be pretty crude, however.) It could be a good question for the database vendor.

Making a Request for Purchase

As mentioned as the beginning of this chapter, one of the reasons you would choose to go through this much work is if you were considering a new database subscription. Now that you've done the work, what can you do to try and make the new subscription a reality? You've done your homework well, but keep in mind that administrators, like the rest of us, have limited time and attention spans. They don't want to read ten pages of detail, they just want to see a succinct argument that shows why database XYZ is necessary, how it will benefit library users, and, quite likely, how you propose to fund the purchase. Most organizations will have a process in place for making such requests, but the following list of points will probably mesh with, or may be used to enhance, the existing process.

What Does This Database Bring to the Institution?

Show what material this database offers that is not available via any other existing service (this is could topic areas, material types, specific publication titles, date ranges, etc.). Use numbers rather than text as much as you can. Relate the database directly to the goals of your organization, e.g., to specific classes, areas of expansion (new programs), etc. If you need to highlight textual elements such as publication titles, provide at most four key titles, and list any additional titles you think are important in an appendix. Once you have demonstrated why this database is unique, it is also important to address the following consideration.

How Does This Database Complement the Existing Collection?

While the database needs to bring something new to your organization (otherwise, why would you be interested in it?), it's also important to demonstrate how the material in this database will complement and extend the existing library collections. For example, if your library has a subscription to the ASI, SRI, and IIS fiche collections, you can make a strong argument for subscribing to the extended version of LexisNexis *Statistical*, as it will provide an electronic index to the fiche collection. If your library doesn't have the fiche, however, it doesn't make much sense to get this version of the database: you'll only be leading users to materials you can't provide locally. Similarly, if you are trying to make a case for a new religion database, but your school doesn't offer any kind of religion degree—you'll certainly be able to say it brings something new to your resources, but what exactly would be the point? There would be little complementary material in the collection, and, unless there were popular courses on religion offered in another department, it would be difficult to identify a strong user base.

If you are proposing to change from an existing database to a rival product, obviously you'll do a lot of comparisons, as mentioned in the first two types of benchmarking, above. You'll want to emphasize differences in the new database that are important to your stated audience for the database. The following section discusses this key point, the potential database users.

Who Will Use the Database?

Who will be interested in the material in this database? How many potential users will it have? If at all possible, try to get some of those potential users involved during the database trial period. Have them "test drive" the database, or at least take a look at the source list. Comments from users ("it helped me with a paper," "I needed this for my thesis research," "it seemed easy to use"), or even better, purchase requests from users ("the library should definitely have this resource"), can be very persuasive. If you found a database review that included a strong comment relating to the audience for the database, which matches your potential audience, include it here.

Marketing the Database

If you get the database, how will you let people know the new resource is available? As always, strive for brevity, but try to outline all the avenues you propose to use to market the database. For example: mass e-mail to department faculty and students (possibly more than once), adding links to appropriate Web pages, posters, flyers, a brown bag (or better: free pizza) information or training sessions, etc. People have a lot vying for their attention, and as vociferously as your users may have said they wanted this new database, you will still need to put out quite a bit of effort to get them to integrate the new tool into their work habits.

In addition, it's a good idea to include how you plan to evaluate database usage after a year. How well did your marketing work? Usage statistics are one obvious measure, but some kind of quick, informal survey (by e-mail, or via a Web page) of your target communities shows a bit more initiative on your part. Besides, such a survey has the added benefit of providing additional marketing as well as assessing!

How Will the Purchase Be Funded?

Usually the "make or break" factor: What is the cost, and where will the money come from? With the cost, indicate whether it includes any discounts, what pricing model was used (say, if you opted for only two simultaneous users rather than five), etc. If you have competing price quotes from multiple vendors, indicate that you've chosen the most economical one (or if you haven't, why). Where the money will come from might be from canceling something else (another database, or several serial titles), or, if your accounting system permits, a permanent transfer of funds from a monographic to a serial budget. If you feel your case is strong enough, there is always the option of simply requesting additional funds to be added to your budget line to pay for the new subscription.

Addenda

If the database has been favorably reviewed, include citation(s) to the review(s) in an appendix. Particularly useful, pertinent quotes might be included in appropriate sections of the main document. If in the course of your review and testing you have discovered features you feel are particularly compelling, mention those now. Indicate that you can provide detailed title comparisons, or search logs, if requested.

Your overall goal is to present a succinct, clear, and quantitative as well as qualitative case. Your first attempt may not be successful, but you will have shown that you can perform a rational and cogent analysis. Your funding agents are more likely to trust you and try to do their best for you when you try again. So take a refusal like a good sport, and just keep gathering data for the next attempt.

Exercises and Points to Consider

1. This list of things to consider in evaluating a database is fairly comprehensive (perhaps daunting?), but no list can ever be absolutely complete. You've been working with databases a lot by now: What other points or issues have *you* encountered that you'd add to this list?

2. A major project: choose a database that is new to you, either from the resources available at your institution, or by requesting a trial from a vendor. Do a thorough evaluation of it, from the point of view of either writing a review of the database for publication, or

writing up a purchase request for your management. (If you aren't currently employed in a library or other type of information center, make one up.) Then either:

Write the review.

OR

Write up the purchase request.

If you choose the review option, write the review as if you were going to submit it for publication. Include the name of the publication to which you would submit the review, and follow its guidelines in terms of formatting, length, etc. (See "Instructions for authors" on the publication's Web site.) After your professor has seen it, he or she may well encourage you to follow through with the submission—this is a realistic goal.

If you choose the purchase request option, include a separate description of your (real or fictional) library or information center, to set the scene. Be sure to describe your user community, and your institution's overall budget situation. Make it as realistic as possible. If you are currently working in a library or information center, choose a database you'd actually like to obtain: you may be able to put your work here to good use on the job.

In either case, do not feel compelled to work through every single point mentioned in this chapter: choose the ones that make sense and are feasible for your chosen project.

Suggested Reading

Sabin-Kildiss, Luisa, Cool, Colleen, and Hong Xie. 2001. Assessing the Functionality of Web-Based Versions of Traditional Search Engines. *Online* 25(2): 18–26. Although we take it for granted now that databases are Web-based, and the names of some of the products mentioned here have changed, the fundamentals of this article are still sound and useful.

Notes

1. This is not as silly a question as it sounds. For example, the *Investext Plus* database consists of nothing but full-text PDF documents, but you cannot search the full-text content. Only the material in the "citation" portion of the records is searchable, and the records are very brief.

2. Tip: if a database includes both popular and scholarly materials, and doesn't provide any functionality for distinguishing between them but does use subject headings, then some subject terms that might help sift out research articles are "methodology," "sampling," "populations," "results," "variables," or "hypotheses."

12
Teaching Other People about Databases

If the thought of getting up in front of other people and speaking makes your blood run cold, and you were hoping that by becoming a librarian you could avoid having to do that kind of activity... *my* hope is that after reading through this chapter, and getting some experience, you will change your mind, and come to understand that teaching and presenting are a vital part of librarianship. Let us consider the importance and ramifications of presenting for a moment, and then we'll get into some more specific nuts and bolts.

The library profession needs spokespeople and champions. The focus of this book has been, of course, databases—but what good are a group of wonderful databases if you can't convey to others that they exist and how to use them? How long do you think funding for these expensive resources will last if you can't defend them? In the larger scheme of things, it's never too early to get used to the idea of justifying your existence: public, school, and state-employed librarians need to be able to talk to their communities, and to local and state legislatures. Academic librarians make points for their libraries in the eyes of the budget controllers by successfully engaging in the academic game: by giving presentations at conferences, and by holding offices in state and national professional organizations. Our profession may not be in crisis, but we certainly are challenged by the Internet as almost no other profession is. The Internet is "free," and libraries are expensive: we are cost centers, not profit centers. It's difficult to quantify the value we give back. If you've chosen to become a librarian, or are already in the profession, presumably you've made that choice because you enjoy and believe in libraries as an institution and librarianship as a vocation. Isn't it worth it to learn to get up in front of people and talk for a short period of time to ensure that your chosen path has a future? And *any* kind of speaking you do: whether it's an Information Literacy session for a freshman writing class, an evening program for adults at a public library, a talk at a conference, 3 minutes of impassioned defense before a state legislature, even a brief discussion in an elevator—makes a difference. It makes a difference both for libraries in general and for your own career, to be able to tell others effectively what we do, why our (expensive) tools are useful, and the benefits they bestow.

Doing this means getting up in front of people and talking. Humans like to communicate (look at the popularity and omnipresence of cell phones), and teaching is just another form of communicating. Still, if public speaking ranks right up there with getting a root canal in your list of favorite things to do, be assured that it can be done. It gets easier, and you might even enjoy it someday. Honest. Maybe you enjoy teaching and presenting already—good for you! If not, the following principles should help make the experience manageable if not totally enjoyable.

Teaching Principles

The second half of this chapter discusses the opportunities to teach people about databases that librarians commonly encounter. Of the four types of teaching or public speaking opportunities considered, I count myself as quite lucky to have experienced them all (with the exception of the public or school library versions of the second point). These experiences have informed my thoughts about what works and what doesn't, and what's important and what isn't, in the process of conveying skills or knowledge from one person to another, or from one person to a group. The process of writing up my thoughts for this chapter included double-checking my instincts against some representative examples from the teaching literature (see the list of Suggested Readings at the end of the chapter), including essays by two professors who have been recipients of the undergraduate teaching award at my university. It was gratifying to find my instincts born out by this review. A particular acknowledgement goes to Celia Applegate, Professor of History at the University of Rochester, whose list of "Rules" both inspired and frequently informed the following list of Principles.

These are guidelines that can be applied to any type of teaching, not just of databases, although there are underlying assumptions (for example, in the emphasis on use of technology) that what is being taught is technical or online in nature. You'll find the list ranges from the more philosophical "Teach to Your Audience" to the very directive and practical "wait for someone to answer when you ask a question." You will be able to use these "principles" as a kind of checklist and support system as you strive for all the hallmarks of an effective teacher. Repeated studies have shown that "concern for students, knowledge of the subject matter, stimulation of interest, availability, encouragement of discussion, ability to explain clearly, enthusiasm, and preparation" are the qualities that students cite most often in describing effective teachers (Feldman, 1976). Those are your goals—and these suggestions will help you achieve them.

Principle 1: Teach to Your Audience

Be very clear who your audience is, and keep them firmly in mind as you prepare the session. Make your teaching objectives, material, and handouts—everything about what you're doing—appropriate to the needs and interests of *that* audience. It's quite easy to decide what you want to tell people, but it takes a good deal more effort to determine how to deliver your message in a way they will really *hear* and perhaps remember. Ten-year-olds, undergraduates, lawyers, or the PTA are all very different groups of people, and your approach needs to be different in each case.

Principle 2: Avoid Lecturing

Avoid pure lecture at every opportunity. As Professor Applegate (1999) puts it: "Never miss an opportunity to keep your mouth shut." You probably thought if you were asked to teach or present, that you should fill every moment—but silence truly can be golden. Do not be afraid of silence (Applegate, 1999). People need time to process what you're saying, which means you need to stop speaking from time to time. Give people time to "think about what they have been told" at regular intervals (Felder and Silverman, 1988). Something as simple as pausing to write a point on the board, and not talking while you do it, can provide a moment of needed silence. We're lucky in our subject matter, too, in that when you're teaching about databases, you have all kinds of ways you can stop lecturing and give your audience time to *use* what they've heard as well as think about it. For example:

- In a hands-on situation, have people start doing their own searching. Try to make that the preponderance of the class rather than the lecture. Talk about one idea, then have them try it, then go on to another idea, and have them try it . . . trade-off between talking and activity.

- In a demonstration (not hands-on) situation, you might present them with a search statement, and then have them work alone, or with the person next to them, to come up with as many synonyms as they can for each of the concepts in the search.

- Use the projector to display, or hand out a paragraph describing a search request, either in the form of discursive text, or a dialogue between a patron and a librarian. Have the class—individually, in groups, or as a whole—figure out one or more search strategies to try. Then have members of the audience come up and type in the chosen searches.

- If you are going over a computer function of some kind (for example, looking materials up in the online catalog), ask the class if anyone has done this before. (*Wait* for an answer.) Then have one or two of the "volunteers" come up and demonstrate how they do it.

- Use questions such as "what are all the uses you can think of for (XYZ)?" to start discussions. To get even the quiet people involved, hand out brightly colored Post-it™ notes to everyone, and have them *write* their ideas, one per note. Stick them up on a wall or a white board, in categories, and start a discussion from there.

In general, look at the list of concepts you wish to get across, and come up with alternatives to straight lecture. Small groups, discussion, writing on the board, Post-its, other hands at the "instructor" keyboard, any kind of physical activity or acting out (you can do some fun things with people acting out Boolean logic)—all of these are lecture alternatives. People learn best when they are developing and putting concepts into practice themselves, so aim for that if possible. You don't have to do this all on your own—brainstorm with a colleague; it will be fun for both of you.

Principle 3: *Wait* for Answers

When you ask questions (which is definitely a good thing to do), first, ask with a purpose: ask a question for which you really want an answer, and second, *wait* for someone to answer. Give your audience a chance to marshal their thoughts and come up with a response. Resist with every fiber of your being the desire to answer your own question. The moment you do, the audience will decide your questioning is all a sham, and won't bother to make any further effort. You will have no chance of getting them to answer any subsequent questions.

Waiting for someone to answer is definitely one of the hardest things to do in a teaching situation. That silence seems to stretch out forever, but try to remember two things. One, the time will seem much longer to you than it does to your audience. Two, the silence will eventually start to bother the people in your audience as well, and they will realize that you really mean it; you *do* want to hear from them. Sooner or later someone will crack and say something. If you really can't stand it, pick someone in the group and push the matter by asking, "what do you think?" in a friendly way.

Of course, the kinds of questions you ask make a difference, too. Questions that ask people to relate things to their own lives or experience are generally more comfortable, and can usually get *someone* to pipe up. Once they do, if you're looking to foster more group discussion, don't immediately respond yourself—look around for someone else who looks on the verge of speaking and give that person an encouraging look, or just ask, "what do you think?" Try not to be the arbiter, the touchstone for every response from the group. It is not necessary to "respond to every response" (Applegate, 1999).

Principle 4: Less is More

Don't overwhelm your audience by trying to do too much. Guided by Principle 1, choose only a limited number of concepts or instructions that you feel will be the most useful information for *that audience*. Take these two—perhaps three—things you think would be most helpful for *that audience* to remember or learn, and build your presentation around those items. One of the biggest pitfalls for new professors—and this extends to anyone new to teaching—is that they tend to over-prepare lectures and try to present too much material too rapidly. Successful teachers, however, present material "paced in a relaxed style so as to provide opportunities for student comprehension and involvement" (Boice, 1992).

This may well sound like an advocation that you set your sights pretty low, and you may feel that it's a disservice to only show a few features of a wonderful database that is loaded with functionality. The problem is, you can't possibly cover as much material in interactive, nonlecture classes; they aren't very efficient in that sense. If you are adhering to Principle 2, sincerely trying to avoid pure lecture (which is the most ineffectual form of instruction anyway), and instead trying to foster discussion and engagement and "active learning," you can't go over every bell and whistle. It will be frustrating at times: "They should know this! They should know that too! And this other thing!" but consider this: if you show them two or three things that get their interest, enough so that they go back on their own, don't you think they might discover some of the other "things they should know" on their own? It's likely they can. Motivated, interested people are pretty smart that way.

Overall, the outcomes of a nonlecture style of teaching can be much more useful and rewarding to your students. If you only cover two or three things in an interesting, "here's how this will benefit you" way, the participants are much more likely to remember at least some of the content. And, if you manage *not* to alienate your audience, and *not* make the session one they can't wait to get out of, they are much more likely to seek you out again for help later, in what is probably the more useful one-on-one situation at the Reference Desk.

Principle 5: "Transparency" in Teaching

Don't be inscrutable (Applegate, 1999): lay out clearly the goals and objectives for the class, the assignment, or the exercise—whatever you are doing. Always keeping in mind Principle 1, relate the goals and objectives to your audience. Do your best to make them feel like it's worth their while to be there. Keep things simple, straightforward, and honest—you are not a god(dess) or keeper of keys to special mysteries, you just happen to have some useful knowledge you'd like to share that will, hopefully, make your audiences' lives better in some way. This is important because of the next Principle.

Principle 6: You Have the Right to be Wrong

It is acceptable to be wrong occasionally, or not to know the answer to every question. Acting inscrutable is often allied with trying to be infallible, and both are terrible ideas. Of course you will have done your best to master your material (Principle 8), but it is still inevitable that someone will ask you a question you don't know the answer to, or that some alert person will point out something you've gotten wrong, pure and simple. Laugh at yourself, thank the person (sincerely) for noticing, make a note to fix it for next time, and get over it. No one is perfect, and most audiences will relate to you more easily if they think that you're human rather than a remote and infallible being. Consider this wonderful quotation:

> Arnold Schoenberg wrote in the introduction to his 1911 text on musical harmony that "...the teacher must have the courage to be wrong." The teacher's task, he continued, "is not to prove infallible, knowing everything and never going wrong, but rather inexhaustible, ever seeking and perhaps sometimes finding." The more we can involve the students with us in this task, "ever seeking and...sometimes finding," the better...(Applegate, 1999)

Ever seeking and perhaps sometimes finding—what a perfect expression for librarianship. So don't get upset if you make a mistake, you are in excellent company.

Principle 7: Teaching with Technology

If working with technology of any kind, there are two things to keep in mind: (1) slow down, and (2) anticipate technology failure.

When you are working with "technology," that is, either a projected computer screen, or a hands-on computer classroom, you need to build more time into presentation plans. Especially in a hands-on situation in which people are looking back and forth from your (projected) screen to their own (and maybe back to yours yet again), *slow down*. This takes much more time, but it's essential: you know where you're going, but your audience doesn't. This is all uncharted territory for them. You must give the people trying to follow you time to process. Even if they are not trying to replicate what you are doing on their own computers, and are just watching the screen, take your speed down one or even several notches. Don't scroll rapidly up and down, and practice mousing from point A to point B without a lot of whizzing around on the screen. These may sound like tiny things, but again, your audience is madly trying to follow you (and may be trying to take notes); this is new territory, and their minds will be doing a lot more processing than yours. Excessive scrolling and mousing in that situation is distracting, if not downright annoying, so work on keeping that to a minimum.

The other thing about technology: be ready for things to go wrong. Plan for how you will handle it if the projector bulb goes, or you can't get on the Net, or the computer crashes. For example, if you're leading a hands-on session and the projector malfunctions, simply designate one or two of the people in the class as your "hands," and have them follow your directions while the other students gather around those computers. Invite all the students to help as backseat drivers. They'll probably all have more fun and get more out of it than if things had gone according to plan! If you're presenting in a non-hands-on situation and are left projection-less, start a discussion instead. Ask the group something about what you have just been trying to cover. As noted above, questions that relate the material to their own experience ("what do you folks usually do when you need to find XYZ?") are good for getting the ball rolling.

If you're presenting somewhere else and intend to show something live on the Internet, take a PowerPoint file (with screen snaps of what you intended to show live) along as backup. It's a fair amount of extra work (depending on the length of your presentation), and you may not need it, but oh, if you do need it, you will be intensely thankful that you took the time. So take the time. It also gives you a way to rehearse (if you take a laptop with you) on the plane or in the hotel room the night before.

If you're in your "home" situation and something goes wrong: first, call tech support (if you have it); second, restart the computer; third, start some kind of discussion.[1] With students, ask them about their assignment (or whatever has brought them to you today), what they've done so far with it, their familiarity with the library and its systems. In a nonacademic situation, ask them what brought them to the session, what they hope to get out of it, etc.

Above all in a technology failure situation, do not betray your anxiety. Don't wring your hands and whimper helplessly. Groaning is permitted, as long as you also laugh. Maintain your aplomb. This is much easier to do if you've rehearsed in your mind what you'll do if the technology lets you down. Because it will: not every time, but at least sometimes. Dave Barry says your household plumbing makes plans in the middle of the night for how it will go wrong and disrupt your big party. These devices—computers, projectors, servers, etc.—undoubtedly do the same thing. And speaking of rehearsal...

Principle 8: Practice

There is an old gag that asks, "How do you get to Carnegie Hall?" Answer: "Practice, practice, practice." Practice is essential. If you are not used to presenting, or are uncomfortable with it, I cannot emphasize enough the importance of rehearsal. Practice is crucial for a number of reasons. First and foremost, the time you have available will always be limited, and a live run through is the only way to find out how long the session you have planned actually lasts. Practicing also will help you get more comfortable, and will help identify "bugs" in your presentation, saving embarrassment later. Let's look at the "limited time" issue in more detail.

No matter what sort of group teaching or presentation situation it is (Information Literacy, staff development, etc.) you will always be working within a specified time limit. Until you have run through what you plan to say—actually spoken the words *out loud* (to the wall, feeling like an idiot)—you won't know how long your presentation really takes. Unless you have a lot of experience, you cannot mentally run through a talk at a slow enough pace to mimic a verbalized version reliably. Especially when a presentation or sample class is part of a job interview, practice it and be sure it fits within the time allotted. If you practice and find that your presentation is too long, the only option is reducing the amount of information you attempt to convey. When in doubt, cut it out. Talking faster is *not* an option, nor is running over. Both things will irritate your audience. If you simply keep talking and have to be cut off before you're finished, you will look not well prepared. Practice by yourself (but aloud!), or, better still, round up some classmates, friends, or family, and give your talk to them. Especially if you are trying to simulate a class situation, with questions and back-and-forth, practicing with friends is extremely helpful in determining your timing and pacing. They can also help identify any *non sequiturs* or outright errors in your talk. In a job interview situation, if you teach only one thing but do it well, appear relaxed, interact with your audience, and stay within your time limit, they will feel as if you've taught them much more, and generally have far more positive feelings about you than if you try to cram in every last nuance, are forced to rush, and lecture the entire time. Unless you are really unusually gifted in this area, your audience will almost always be able to tell if you have practiced or not.

At the same time, being well rehearsed doesn't mean rattling off your "script" like—well, like a memorized script. Rather, it means full mastery of your material, so that you are talking about your topic naturally and easily, you are able to field questions or take small side trips (or encounter technical difficulties) without getting flustered or derailed from your main intent, and your enthusiasm and enjoyment of your topic come through. If you are suffering, your audience will suffer as well. So take some lessons from Hollywood: rehearse, know your lines, and deliver them with sincerity and enthusiasm. Act like you're enjoying it, even if you aren't. Your audience will enjoy it a great deal more (and you may too). Remember to smile occasionally: write yourself a note if necessary. And breathe. You can't panic when you're breathing deeply and slowly. So practice, then breathe, smile, open your mouth, and share the wonderful information you have with your audience. You'll be great!

Database Teaching Opportunities

Let's take a look at the kinds of opportunities for teaching or presenting information about databases you are likely to encounter as a librarian.

In order of frequency of occurrence (from most to least), these can be summarized as:

- One-on-one with a patron over a question at the reference desk.
- One-off, one-time sessions, known as Information Literacy classes (or sometimes: "bibliographic instruction" or BI) in college and university settings. Presenting such a class is a common part of an academic job interview. The public library equivalent might be an evening or noontime continuing education session. In a school library, these are usually referred to simply as classes, and tend to be quite brief: 15 to 20 minutes.
- A database introduction or review, such as one would present at a staff meeting or staff development session.
- A sustained, semester-long class.

These are all quite different sorts of encounters, yet you'll find many of the Principles apply to them all. Here are some thoughts about applying the Principles in each case to make your database instruction more effective.

Teaching at the Reference Desk

This is probably the type of "teaching encounter" that people generally find most comfortable: it's intimate, one-on-one, you only have to deal with one personality and can focus entirely on him or her. It's also reactive, rather than proactive: the person has *chosen* to approach you, and you can focus on his or her "topic of the moment," and then the encounter is over. True, you can't prepare (Principle 8), exactly, but that can be a plus: you won't be over-prepared. You have your life knowledge, your library science education, and your professional experience, and you simply apply these in various ways to meet each person's individual information needs.

Introducing a patron to a database at the reference desk provides an opportunity for a "teaching moment"—but if you take advantage of that, keep it to a moment. Don't overwhelm (Principle 4, less is more). Pick one or two things to try and actually "teach" the patron (such as, "this is how you get to the list of databases on (subject X)" and "see this drop-down? If you change it to Subject, the articles you get should be right on target."). *Suggest* the power of the database, but don't try to impart all your knowledge. Go through the process with the patron, asking questions about the topic, etc., and explaining in a general way what you're doing, but not necessarily going into all the details. That is, try to be "transparent" (Principle 5) without being overwhelming or lecturing (Principle 2, avoid lecturing). For example: "let's try this database—it's got psychology articles" rather than "well, first you should go to the list of psychology databases, and then read the descriptions to decide which one to use..." Attempt to gently engage the patron, as well as being quiet from time to time. A good time to be quiet is when you're looking at a list of results together, so that the patron can study the screen and process. It's much better to hold back a bit, and have the patron ask "how did you do that?" than to overwhelm him/her with information. Let's face it, not everyone will be that interested, or *need* to do this kind of research again (Principle 1, Teach to Your Audience). Dropping a limited number of "teaching seeds" is more likely to result in further questioning and ultimate "skill flowering" than 10 minutes of unmitigated, and probably unappreciated, lecture.

Teaching an Information Literacy Session

The classroom situation a librarian is most likely to encounter is really quite the hardest: the one-off, limited time (usually only around an hour) class, whose purpose may range from the typical Information Literacy, or "library," session for freshman English students, to how to search the Internet in an evening class for adults at the public library. Now you as an instructor are facing a roomful of people who may or may not wish to be there, and with whom you will probably only get one class session. You are supposed to have some idea of what makes them tick, make contact with them, communicate, and impart two or three bits of useful knowledge about a fairly sophisticated topic (database or Web searching) in the limited time allotted. Certainly it is a challenge, but by keeping the Principles in mind you can meet that challenge.

Even in this situation, you can still teach to your audience: you will have advance notice that the session is coming, which gives you time to find out something about who your audience is going to be. In any kind of school situation, the instructor should be willing to tell you the reason he or she has requested an instruction session in the library, and something about the class, e.g., personalities, skill levels, etc. In a community education situation, talk to other librarians who have taught such classes before: who tends to show up? What are they usually most interested in? How are their skills? If you feel you need more information, do some reading: there has been plenty of research done on teaching adults (and every other age group). Here's your chance to go to ERIC and get "a few good articles."

We'll assume that, based on your research, some demonstration or hands-on training with a database will be part of your session. Or possibly two databases, or a database and the library's online catalog—but that is probably pushing the limits of Principle 4, Less is More. It depends on the point you are trying to make with each resource. For example, for a first freshman introduction to the library, you might decide that a multidisciplinary database that offers mostly full-text is the resource most attuned with their needs and interests, and that you will show them the pertinent features of that database. For an upper level course, you might opt to demonstrate a subject-specific, abstracts-only database (or one of the *Web of Science* Citation Indexes), along with the library OPAC, with an explanation of how the two can be used in concert. One thing you can almost be sure of, no matter who will be in your class, is that they won't know about databases, but they will know about Google (or whatever search engine is hot at the moment). Use this to your advantage: you know one thing that represents familiar ground to them, so work it in: compare and contrast the search engine with the properties of databases to introduce what databases are. (What is frustrating is that having to explain that there are such things as databases always uses up one of the few, precious two-to-three learning objectives!)

Here is a step-by-step scenario that might be used in an introductory session:

- Explain that the students' instructor has told you about their assignment, and you want to familiarize them with (Database X), a resource that will help with the research for that assignment: make it go faster, be more efficient, and provide better quality information, so they can write better papers. (Transparency, and some motivation.)

- Ask if any of them have used Database X before. (Wait for an answer.) If anyone has, pursue briefly—when and for what?

- Demonstrate a search that uses just a couple of features, e.g., use of a Subject field AND another field, or a field search and a Date, or Peer-reviewed (or Full-text) Limit. Bring up the results, and mark several that look particularly "good." Keep your eye on the class: if they don't look like they're verging into a glazed-over state, show a full record for one of the results. If their attention is slipping, though, skip it: they can look at full records for themselves. (Less is more)

- In another window, do the same search on Google. The idea is to demonstrate why the database has some advantages over the Web search. (Rehearsal is good here to make sure the results are consistent with the message you want to get across.) Ask the group if they have a favorite search engine—take a quick poll, try to get them all to answer.

- If you are in a computer lab, have the students now set up another search with you, and look at the results. (Remember not to move too fast.) It can actually be just as effective if the students are paired up on the computers—they can help each other. Tell them to mark some records and figure out how to send the records to their e-mail account. (Avoid lecturing; encourage "active learning.")

- Then turn it over to them entirely: have them work alone or in pairs, and work on searching for material on their particular topics. Encourage them to try comparison searching on their favorite search engine. Work your way around the group to answer questions and provide individual help.

Here are two additional variations on this theme, this time dealing with a common teaching objective.

One of the most difficult things to convey to undergraduates seems to be how to identify and obtain scholarly articles, especially when the full text has to be tracked down from physical copies of journals in the library. You might decide that all you want to be sure the students come away with is (1) the idea that special purpose databases exist, and (2) databases provide an efficient means to identify articles on a topic. If you are at an institution that subscribes to many databases that offer full text, or that has implemented a link resolver system such as SFX, you might limit your goals to just those two basic ideas, and tell the students to ask at the Reference Desk when they need help accessing the physical journals. Then structure the session along the lines just described above.

Alternatively, you could start at the idea that (1) special purpose databases provide an efficient means of identifying articles. Then you might demonstrate a sample search (without trying to explain Boolean concepts, or the importance of synonyms or other searching concepts), whose results include a "perfect" article not available in full text online. Ask the students what they would do at this point. (Remember to *wait* for somebody to say something. Anything.) Then go for your point (2): how to get from a citation to a physical bound journal on a shelf. If it's possible to have the class all look up the journal, get its call number, and head out into the stacks in-search-of, all the better. Give hints, but don't lead. Let them work together—perhaps divide the class into two or more teams and turn it into a competition. If all that isn't possible, bring the appropriate volume into class with you, and at least give it to one of the students to find the actual article within the bound volume. Encourage him to get help from a friend if he wants, and discuss something else while they work on that. Basically, don't try to do too much, and if possible, try to make what you *do* do interactive, collegial, and physical. If you should be lucky enough to have someone ask a question (and don't forget, of course, to solicit questions), great, explain, but otherwise, remember the thought in Principle 2: never miss an opportunity to keep your mouth shut. Resist the urge to "data dump" to your audience.

These examples are heavily oriented to Undergraduates, since that is the group with which I am most familiar, but you should be able to turn the basic ideas, the Principles, to your advantage for whatever group you are teaching. For example, a class of adults from the community will, of course, have quite different learning objectives: rather than finding articles to support research papers, you may be trying to show them how to find reputable health information on the Web, or how to assess the validity or quality of any Web resource. You might decide your goals are to introduce the idea of Advanced Search, and how to use it to limit a Web search to .gov or .edu sites. If you are introducing article databases, it's probably for different purposes, e.g., current events, genealogy, business, or investment research. No matter what the subject matter, the Principles still apply: try to determine what information will be most pertinent to *that* audience, don't just lecture, definitely ask questions (an adult group may actually answer, and it can be easier to get an interesting discussion going), don't try to do too much, and be extra careful to take it slow in a hands-on session. An adult group also may be more likely to point out a mistake, or ask you a new question, and that's great: you'll learn something, and they'll secretly enjoy the idea that they stumped the teacher. It's a win-win situation.

In general, although the brief, one-off session[2] can be challenging, it is challenging in a good way. True, you don't get to establish much rapport with the group, you don't have the opportunity to see their growth or progress, and you don't get another chance next week to repair any blunders in this week's class. On the other hand, you are forced to be really rigorous in developing your one class (draw up your list of learning objectives ... and then cross most of them out), so that what your attendees receive is a carefully honed, very targeted product. The quality will be just as high, if not higher, than many of their regular classes, and the session is likely to be more interactive and memorable as well. If nothing else, the class will come away knowing that (1) you exist (2) something other than Google exists, and (3) you were trying to show them something that would enhance some aspect of their life. Just as we discussed in the Reference Interview chapter, if you can leave them with a positive impression, it will be more likely that the students as individuals will later seek you out at the Reference Desk, or via e-mail, chat, etc.

Presenting a class as part of a job interview has been mentioned a few times already, but let me add some specific notes about it here. First, the time will probably be shorter (20–30 minutes) than in any real class situation. This will tend to make it more of a lecture situation, which your audience is expecting, but try to surprise them: try to work in at least one of the interactive, nonlecture approaches suggested under Principle 2. Second, something that may sound obvious: do your homework. The library where you will be interviewed most likely has a Web site. If the library is part of an institution of higher education or a corporation, the organization probably has a Web site. Study these, and use them to inform your presentation: make the class you create look as if you already work there. Base your presentation on a database available at that library, and make your audience a group at that institution (a particular class, with a real class number and professor's name, or a real group within the company or organization). For a public library, study the schedule of classes already on offer, and try to come up with a session that would augment or complement an existing class. If you decide you want to demonstrate a database that is only available at your target library, and not wherever you currently are, call up the vendor and get a trial so you can learn it, and use the library's link when you are on site. (Create a PowerPoint as backup just in case.) Create one or more appropriate handouts to go with your presentation, and again, don't be shy about copying the library or organization's logo off their Web site to "brand" your handouts. In as many ways as possible, act like you're already on board. And hopefully soon you will be!

A Staff Presentation

Teaching your colleagues about a database is quite different from all of the other situations described here. For one thing, knowing your audience shouldn't be an issue: even if you are a new hire right out of library school, you should have a pretty good sense of what librarians are interested in and will want to know. Since they are your peers and colleagues (which may make the whole thing both more and less comfortable), it should be much easier to plan and deliver your message. Note, though, if your group includes members from throughout the library and not just reference librarians, it changes the playing field a good deal. Staff from departments outside of Reference, including computer support, may have little or no idea that databases exist or how they are used, and teaching in this situation is much more akin to teaching a group of adults from the community. But teaching a group of reference librarians about a database turns many of the Principles on their ear.

- Principle 2—Avoid Lecturing. You might be able to get away with more lecture than in any other situation. It will still be appreciated if you try to break things up, however, and give your audience time to absorb what you're saying from time to time. I think you'll find, though, that a lecture naturally devolves into a more participatory session, for the reason noted in the next point.

- Principle 3—Wait for Answers. You probably won't have to wait for answers or need to work at fostering discussion—your colleagues will likely be very forthcoming with comments and questions. This is a group that is truly interested in what you are talking about, and eager to explore it with you. (They are glad that you've done the work to master this database, so that they can ask *you* questions.)

- Principle 4—Less is More. You can set higher goals for the amount of information you plan to impart: again, this audience is *interested* and does want the details. They are already knowledgeable, and will be more interested in salient differences from what they know, rather than the basics. You can start at a much higher level of discussion. However, take some guidance from Principle 4, and don't overwhelm. A rule of thumb might be: master as much of the database as you can, plan to present 50–60 percent of that (all of which is "beyond the basics"), and let questions bring out whatever else people want to know.

The other Principles do not change much. Principle 5, Transparency, still applies. These librarians are likely to have chosen to attend your session, so they are willing participants, but it's still a good idea to outline clearly the goals and objectives of your talk, i.e., give them good reasons to stay and listen. You will very likely get a good workout of Principle 6, You Have a Right to be Wrong. You are talking to a very knowledgeable audience—who will undoubtedly catch something or know something you don't. Don't worry about it! It's a benefit, not a contest. The two Technology points of Principle 7, go slower, and be ready for it to fail, both apply as in any other situation. Just because they are librarians doesn't mean they can look from their screen to your projected screen (or from your projected screen to their notes) any faster than anyone else. In fact, it may take longer, because they are studying all the details more closely. So give everyone plenty of time. If the technology fails, you will probably find you have a whole roomful of people ready to jump in and help, so it's not all up to you. Still, you will want to show that you can stay calm, and have a plan in mind for what you'll do if the technology lets you down. And, of course, Principle 8 applies to every situation: *practice* your database demonstration, in as realistic a situation as possible (e.g., out loud, in front of people if possible), before heading off to your staff development meeting.

If an Information Literacy session presents the most challenging *format* for teaching, a session for your colleagues undoubtedly presents the most challenging *audience* for your teaching. But again, let it be a good challenge. Learn the database, and practice, but don't kill yourself preparing. You'll never remember it all anyway, and you'll just make yourself nervous and uptight. If one of your "students" knows something you don't, let him or her teach you. If someone asks a question that you don't know the answer to, and neither does anyone else in the room, make it an opportunity to explore and find out together. It's really much more interesting that way.

The Full Semester Class

Here at last we have a chance to aspire to what is "truly important" in teaching, that is: "connection, communication, and the stimulation of critical thinking" (Brown, 1999). Instead of one session, you'll get to see this class over and over, get to know your students, and get beyond a few nuts and bolts "how to's" of only one database to broader, philosophical considerations of databases and information seeking. These opportunities are, sadly, quite rare for librarians, so we will not spend a great deal of time on this topic. However, I would like to say enough to indicate that this is a *feasible* project. Should you ever get offered the chance to develop and provide such a class, think seriously about taking it on.

A full semester class, obviously, requires considerable planning, and there are entire books devoted to teaching and curriculum planning (the Suggested Readings include two titles, and a search of WorldCat or

Amazon.com would reveal many, many more). However, it is not an insurmountable effort. Consider these six steps that are recommended in planning a course (Davidson and Ambrose, 1994):

- Assessing the backgrounds and interests of your students.
- Choosing the course objectives (note that these are often set by the department, and you just need to determine how to achieve them).
- Developing the learning experiences within the course.
- Planning feedback and evaluation of student learning.
- Preparing a syllabus for the course.

You are already familiar with the concept in the first point: know your audience. With a full semester to work with, you can now choose overall course objectives, as well as objectives for each session. In both cases, though, you still need to be careful not to overwhelm. In each individual class meeting you shouldn't try to deliver too much, and the sum total of all the sessions will ultimately determine the amount of material you can get through in a semester. You may find it useful to approach a semester-long course as an organizational activity: to work from large, overarching ideas, to the components of those ideas, and finally to the steps needed to teach those components. As you work out the steps, you can plan the best learning experiences to support them. As you determine the components, you can then plan ways to assess mastery of them. And when all of that is done—you will have enough material to write up a syllabus.

A discouraging aspect of a whole semester's course for many people is that it seems like they would have to come up with *so much material*. But, at least in the area of databases and research techniques, the large ideas—the overall objectives—can be broken down into many component parts. If you start analyzing, breaking down the knowledge or skills that you take for granted into a series of intellectually manageable chunks, you'll be surprised at the amount of material this represents. (And students like clearly defined "chunks" of information.) As you present the course, those component ideas will build on each other, as you head toward those overall course objectives. Along the way you are presenting learning experiences to convey those ideas, assessing to see if the ideas have been conveyed, and giving feedback. It's an organic, iterative, growing process. Go for it.

Exercises and Points to Consider

1. Think back over all your schooling. Which teachers do you remember most vividly (both good and bad)? See if you can come up with a list of reasons why those instructors either "worked" or didn't for you. Use this information to form your own list of "Teaching Principles."

2. A major effort: decide what type of library you would be most likely to apply for a job in, then develop a 20-minute mock teaching session that could be used in your interview. This could be an academic, school, public, corporate, law, or medical library.

In real life, outreach is an increasingly important aspect in the services of all of these types of libraries (their very survival may depend on proving their value to the overall organization), so even if such a session is not listed as part of your interview schedule, be proactive: offer a session as an added extra to your interview.

Suggested Readings

Applegate, Celia. "Teaching: Taming the Terror." Chapter 2 in *How I Teach: Essays on Teaching by Winners of the Robert and Pamela Goergen Award for Distinguished Achievement and Artistry in Undergraduate Teaching.* Rochester, NY: University of Rochester, 1999.

Brown, Theodore. "Connection, Communication, and Critical Thinking." Chapter 1 in *How I Teach: Essays on Teaching by Winners of the Robert and Pamela Goergen Award for Distinguished Achievement and Artistry in Undergraduate Teaching.* Rochester, NY: University of Rochester, 1999.

Lippincott, Joan K. "Net Generation Students and Libraries." In *Educating the Net Generation.* Diana G. Oblinger and James L. Oblinger (Eds.). EDUCAUSE, 2005. Available at http://www.educause.edu/educatingthenetgen/. An excellent source for learning more about and achieving a better understanding of this "audience."

McKeachie, Wilbert J. *Teaching Tips: Strategies, Research, and Theory for College and University Teachers.* 9th ed. Lexington, MA: D.C. Heath and Company, 1994. A totally practical, down-to-earth guidebook, covering every aspect of teaching. Although oriented toward the creation and delivery of a semester-long class, Chapters 4 and 5, on Organizing Effective Discussions, and Lecturing; Chapter 13, on Peer Learning, Collaborative Learning, Cooperative Learning; and Chapter 19, Teaching in the Age of Electronic Information, are all universally applicable.

Reis, Richard M. "Insights on Teaching and Learning." Chapter 11 in *Tomorrow's Professor: Preparing for Academic Careers in Science and Engineering.* Piscataway, NJ: IEEE Press, 1997. In the world of databases and technology, we are operating closer to (computer) science and engineering than to the humanities, which is why I deliberately chose this particular guidebook. However, most of the guidance provided could apply to any teaching situation, not just science or engineering.

Notes

1. Tech support people may hate me for presenting these actions in this order, but if you restart the computer and that *doesn't* solve the problem, you've lost a lot of precious time before initiating contact with tech support, who will inevitably take some time to respond.

2. Actually, you might find you get invited back to give a library session every time the professor teaches the class, so definitely hang on to your notes and whatever materials (e.g., PowerPoint) you use.

References

Preface

Tennant, Roy. 2003. *Endeavoring to Do Our Best: Library Systems as if Users Matter*. Endeavor General Session. Welcome and Keynote Speech, Endeavor User Group Meeting, April 25, 2003. Available at http://escholarship.cdlib.org/rtennant/presentations/2003end/enduserRT.ppt (Accessed March 28, 2005).

Chapter 1

Computer History Museum. 2004. *Timeline—Networks*. Available at http://www.computerhistory.org/timeline/timeline.php?timeline_category=net (Accessed January 29, 2005).

Dialog (a Thomson business). 2005. *Company Background—Dialog History Movie Transcript*. Available at http://www.dialog.com/about/history/transcript.shtml (Accessed February 3, 2005).

Encyclopædia Britannica. 2005. s.v. "digital computer." Available at Encyclopædia Britannica Online, http://search.eb.com/eb/article-1825 (Accessed August 1, 2005).

Lexikon's History of Computing. 2002. *Master Chronology of Events*. Available at http://www.computermuseum.li/Testpage/01HISTORYCD-Chrono1.htm (Accessed August 1, 2005).

Chapter 2

Walker, Geraldene and Joseph Janes. 1999. *Online Retrieval: A Dialogue of Theory and Practice*, 2nd ed. Englewood, CO: Libraries Unlimited, p. 63.

Chapter 4

Institute of Education Sciences, U.S. Department of Education. 2005. *ERIC News—New Content Added to the ERIC Database*. Available at http://www. eric.ed.gov/ERICWebPortal/resources/html/news/eric_news_25.html (Accessed July 2, 2005).

"OCLC Adds to, Enhances the Content on FirstSearch." 1998. *Information Today* 15 (October): 19, 75.

Ovid Technologies, Inc. 2005. *Ovid Technologies Field Guide PsycINFO® (PSYC)*. Available at http://gateway.ut.ovid.com.gate.lib.buffalo.edu/gw2dsc/psycdb.htm (Accessed June 6, 2005).

Tenopir, Carol. 2003. "Databases for Information Professionals." *Library Journal* 128 (October): 32.

Tenopir, Carol. 2004. "Eric's Extreme Makeover." *Library Journal* 129 (September): 36.

Viadero, Debra. 2004. "ERIC Clearinghouses Close; New System in Works." *Education Week* 23 (January): 20–21.

Chapter 5

NCBI *PubMed*. 2005. *PubMed Help*. Available at http://www.ncbi.nlm.nih.gov/ entrez/query/static/help/pmhelp.html#PubMedSearching (Accessed April 23, 2005).

Tenopir, Carol. 2001. The Power of Citation Searching. *Library Journal* 126 (November): 39–40.

Thomson Scientific. 2005. The Index With All the Answers. *2005 A Year of Celebration*. Available at http://scientific.thomson.com/promo/celebration/sci (Accessed May 6, 2005).

U.S. National Library of Medicine. 2005. *Medical Subject Heading (MeSH®) Fact Sheet*. Available at http://www.nlm.nih.gov/pubs/factsheets/mesh.html (Accessed May 6, 2005).

U.S. National Library of Medicine. 2005. *MEDLINE® Fact Sheet*. Available at http://www.nlm.nih.gov/pubs/factsheets/medline.html (Accessed May 6, 2005).

U.S. National Library of Medicine. 2005. *What's the Difference between MEDLINE® and PubMed®? Fact Sheet*. Available at http://www.nlm.nih.gov/pubs/ factsheets/dif_med_pub.html (Accessed June 7, 2005). Fact Sheet includes additional added materials, and a list of other *PubMed* services.

Chapter 6

Helfer, Doris Small. 2002. OCLC's March into the 21st Century. *Searcher: The Magazine for Database Professionals* 10 (February): 66–69.

Hogan, Tom. 1991. OCLC Looks to End-User Market with FirstSearch. *Information Today*. 8 (November): 1, 4.

Jordan, Jay. 2003. Cooperating during Difficult Times. *The Journal of Academic Librarianship* 29 (6): 343–345.

OCLC. 2005. *WorldCat homepage*. OCLC Online Computer Library Center. Available at http://www.oclc.org/worldcat/ (Accessed June 18, 2005).

Chapter 7

MLA. 2004. *Descriptors and Indexing*. Modern Language Association. Available at http://www.mla.org/publications/bibliography/bib_descriptors (Accessed August 2, 2005).

MLA. 2005. *Frequently Asked Questions*. Modern Language Association. Available at http://www.mla.org/publications/bibliography/bib_faq (Accessed August 2, 2005).

ProQuest Information and Learning Company. 2005. *Information Centre: About MLA International Bibliography*. *Chadwyck-Healey Literature Collections*. Available at http://collections.chadwyck.co.uk/marketing/products/about_ilc.jsp?collection=mla (Accessed June 14, 2005).

Speck, Vicky H. 2002. *America: History and Life on the Web*. *Product Information Sheet*. ABC-CLIO. Available at http://www.abc-clio.com/visitortools/productSheet/preview.aspx?productid=109711 (Accessed June 16, 2005).

Chapter 8

Bates, Mary Ellen. 1998. Statistical Universe. *Database* 21 (October/November): 96.

Gauthier, Jason G. 2002. *Measuring America: The Decennial Censuses From 1790–2000*. (U.S. Bureau of the Census/Dept of Commerce), Washington, DC: U.S. Government Printing Office. Appendix A, p. A-1. Quoted in Joe Beine, The Cost of the US Census. Available at http://www.genealogybranches.com/censuscosts.html (Accessed June 21, 2005). Cost per person figures calculated and added by Mr. Beine.

Golderman, Gail and Bruce Connolly. 2005. Numbers Beyond Borders. *Netconnect* (Spring): 28–35.

Jacsó, Péter. 2000. Peter's Picks & Pans. *Econtent* 23 (August/September) (Accessed online via WilsonWeb).

Kmetz, Tom. 2003. Statistical Universe (Base Edition). *The Charleston Advisor* 4 (January). Available at http://www.charlestonco.com/review.cfm?id=137 (Accessed June 22, 2005).

Chapter 9

Abels, Eileen, Lily Griner, and Maggie Turqman. 2004. If You Build It Will They Come? *Information Outlook* 8 (October): 13–17.

ALA. 2004. *Guidelines for Behavioral Performance of Reference and Information Service Providers*. American Library Association. Available at http://www.ala.org/ala/rusa/rusaprotools/referenceguide/guidelinesbehavioral.htm (Accessed April 16, 2005).

Bates, Mary Ellen. 1998. Finding the Question behind the Question. *Information Outlook* 2 (July): 19–21.

Booth, Sally. 2004. Getting It Off the 'Net: Use of the World Wide Web in a Firm of Solicitors. *Legal Information Management* 4 (Summer): 97–104.

Carter, David S. 2002/2003. Hurry Up and Wait: Observations and Tips about the Practice of Chat Reference. *The Reference Librarian* 79/80: 113–120.

Cogdill, Keith W. 2003. Information Needs and Information-Seeking In Primary Care: A Study of Nurse Practitioners. *Journal of the Medical Library Association* 91 (April): 203–215.

Cramer, Dina C. 1998. How to Speak Patron. *Public Libraries* 37 (November/December): 349.

Curtis, Karen L., Ann C. Weller, and Julie M. Hurd. 1997. Information-Seeking Behavior of Health Sciences Faculty: The Impact of New Information Technologies. *Bulletin of the Medical Library Association* 85 (October): 402–410.

Dewdney, Patricia and Gillian Michell. 1996. Oranges and Peaches: Understanding Communication Accidents in the Reference Interview. *RQ* 35 (Summer): 520–535.

Dewdney, Patricia and Gillian Michell. 1997. Asking Why Questions in the Reference Interview: A Theoretical Justification. *Library Quarterly* 67(1): 50–71. Quoted in Marshall Eidson, 2000.

Duff, Wendy M. and Catherine A. Johnson. 2003. Where Is the List with All the Names? Information-Seeking Behavior of Genealogists. *The American Archivist* 66 (Spring/Summer): 79–95.

Eidson, Marshall. 2000. Using Emotional Intelligence in the Reference Interview. *Colorado Libraries* 26 (Summer): 8–10.

Eisenberg, Michael B. 2005. Stage 2—Information Seeking Strategies (Big6 Special Section). *Library Media Connection* 23 (March): 34–37.

Ellis, David. 1993. Modeling the Information-Seeking Patterns of Academic Researchers: A Grounded Theory Approach. *The Library Quarterly* 63 (October): 469–486.

Fagan, Jody Condit and Christina M. Desai. 2002/2003. Communication Strategies for Instant Messaging and Chat Reference Services. *The Reference Librarian* 79/80: 121–155.

Fister, Barbara. 2002. Fear of Reference. *Chronicle of Higher Education* 48 (14 June): B20.

Green, Samuel Swett. 1876. Personal Relations between Librarians and Readers. *Library Journal* (October): 74–81. Quoted in David Tyckoson, 2003.

Hallmark, Julie. 1995. The Effects of Technology on the Information-Seeking Behavior of Scientists. In: *Changing Gateways: The Impact of Technology on Geoscience Information Exchange: Proceedings of the Twenty-Ninth Meeting of the Geoscience Information Society*, October 24–27, 1994, Seattle, WA (n.p.): Geoscience Information Society.

Harter, Stephen P. 1986. *Online Information Retrieval: Concepts, Principles, and Techniques*. Orlando, FL: Academic Press.

Jankowska, Maria Anna. 2004. Identifying University Professors' Information Needs in the Challenging Environment of Information and Communication Technologies. *The Journal of Academic Librarianship* 30 (January): 51–66.

Kern, Kathleen. 2003. Communication, Patron Satisfaction, and the Reference Interview. *Reference & User Services Quarterly* 43 (Fall): 47–49.

Kuhlthau, Carol C. 1991. Inside the Search Process: Information-Seeking from the User's Perspective. *Journal of the American Society for Information Science* 42 (5): 361–371. Quoted in Johannes G. Nel, 2001.

Loertscher, David V. and Blanche Woolls. 2002. Teenage Users of Libraries: A Brief Overview of the Research. *Knowledge Quest* 30 (May/June): 31–36.

Lorenzen, Michael. 2001. The Land of Confusion? High School Students and Their Use of the World Wide Web for Research. *Research Strategies* 18 (2): 151–163.

Marcum, Deanna B. and Gerald George. 2003. Who Uses What? Report On a National Survey of Information Users in College and Universities. *D-Lib Magazine* 9 (October). Available at http://www.dlib.org/dlib/october03/george/10george.html (Accessed April 17, 2005).

Massey-Burzio, Virginia. 1998. From the Other Side of the Reference Desk: A Focus Group Study. *The Journal of Academic Librarianship* 24 (May): 208–215.

Minkel, Walter. 2004. They Can't Always Find What They Want. *School Library Journal* 50 (August): 29.

Murphy, Janet. 2003. Information-Seeking Habits of Environmental Scientists: A Study of Interdisciplinary Scientists at the Environmental Protection Agency in Research Triangle Park, North Carolina. *Issues in Science & Technology Librarianship* 38 (Summer). Available at http://www.istl.org/03-summer/refereed.html (Accessed June 11, 2005).

Nel, Johannes G. 2001. The Information-Seeking Process: Is There a Sixth Sense? *Mousaion* 19 (2): 23–32.

Njoku, Ifeanyichukwu Faith. 2004. The Information Needs and Information-Seeking Behaviour of Fishermen in Lagos State, Nigeria. *International Information & Library Review* 36 (December): 297–307.

Novotny, Eric. 2004. I Don't Think I Click: A Protocol Analysis Study of Use of a Library Online Catalog in the Internet Age. *College & Research Libraries* 65 (November): 525–537.

Oblinger, Diana G. and James L. Oblinger, Eds. 2005. Is it Age or IT: First Steps toward Understanding the Net Generation. In: *Educating the Net Generation*. EDUCAUSE. Available at http://www.educause.edu/ir/library/pdf/pub7101b.pdf (Accessed June 12, 2005).

Owen, David J. and Min-Lin E. Fang. 2003. Information-Seeking Behavior in Complementary and Alternative Medicine (CAM): An Online Survey of Faculty at a Health Sciences Campus. *Journal of the Medical Library Association* 91 (July): 311–321.

Pelzer, Nancy L., William H. Weise, and Joan M. Leysen. 1998. Library Use and Information-Seeking Behavior of Veterinary Medical Students Revisited in the Electronic Environment. *Bulletin of the Medical Library Association* 86 (July): 346–355.

Peterson, Lisa C. 1997. Effective Question Negotiation in the Reference Interview. *Current Studies in Librarianship* 21 (Spring/Fall): 22–34.

Prince, Monique. 2003. *Changes in the Information Use Patterns of College Freshmen*. MSLS thesis, University of North Carolina at Chapel Hill.

Radford, Marie L. 1999. *The Reference Encounter: Interpersonal Communication in the Academic Library*. Chicago: Association of College and Research Libraries. Quoted in Catherine Sheldrick Ross, 2003.

Reneker, Maxine H. 1993. A Qualitative Study of Information Seeking among Members of an Academic Community: Methodological Issues and Problems. *The Library Quarterly* 63 (October): 487–507.

Riedling, Ann Marlow. 2000. Great Ideas for Improving Reference Interviews. *Book Report* 19 (November/December): 28–29.

Ronan, Jana. 2003. The Reference Interview Online. *Reference & User Services Quarterly* 43 (Fall): 43–47.

Ross, Catherine Sheldrick. 2003. The Reference Interview: Why It Needs to be Used in Every (Well, Almost Every) Reference Transaction. *Reference & User Services Quarterly* 43 (Fall): 38–42.

Ross, Catherine Sheldrick and Patricia Dewdney. 1998. Negative Closure: Strategies and Counter-Strategies in the Reference Transaction. *Reference & User Services Quarterly* 38 (2): 151–163.

Scott, Sean Cunnison. 2004. Process, Practice, and Psychic Stress at the Reference Desk. *OLA Quarterly* 10 (Fall): 19–23.

Shenton, Andrew K. and Pat Dixon. 2004. The Nature of Information Needs and Strategies for their Investigation in Youngsters. *Library & Information Science Research* 26: 296–310.

Shenton, Andrew K. and Pat Dixon. 2003. Youngsters' Use of Other People As An Information-Seeking Method. *Journal of Librarianship and Information Science* 35 (December): 219–233.

Somerville, Arleen N. 1982. The Pre-Search Reference Interview—A Step by Step Guide. *Database* 5 (February): 32–38.

Spink, Amanda and Charles Cole, Eds. 2004. Special Topic Issue: Part I: Information-Seeking Research. *Journal of the American Society for Information Science and Technology* 55 (June): 657–766.

Spink, Amanda and Charles Cole, Eds. 2004. Special Topic Issue: Part II: Information-Seeking Research. *Journal of the American Society for Information Science and Technology* 55 (July): 767–842.

Taylor, Robert S. 1968. Question-Negotiation and Information Seeking in Libraries. *College & Research Libraries* 29 (3): 178–194.

Todd, Ross J. 2003. Adolescents of the Information Age: Patterns of Information-Seeking and Use, and Implications for Information Professionals. *School Libraries Worldwide* 9 (2): 27–46.

Tyckoson, David. 2003. Reference at Its Core: The Reference Interview. *Reference & User Services Quarterly* 43 (Fall): 49–51.

Valentine, Barbara. 1993. Undergraduate Research Behavior: Using Focus Groups to Generate Theory. *The Journal of Academic Librarianship* 19 (November): 300–304.

Vesey, Ken. 2005. Eliminate Wobbly Research with the Information Resource Tripod. *Teacher Librarian* 32 (February): 35–37.

Whitmire, Ethelene. 2003. Epistemological Beliefs and the Information-Seeking Behavior of Undergraduates. *Library & Information Science Research* 25: 127–142.

Young, Nancy J. and Marilyn Von Seggern. 2001. General Information-Seeking in Changing Times: A Focus Group Study. *Reference & User Services Quarterly* 41 (Winter): 159–169.

Zach, Lisl. 2005. When Is Enough Enough? Modeling the Information-Seeking and Stopping Behavior of Senior Arts Administrators. *Journal of the American Society for Information Science and Technology* 56 (January): 23–35.

Chapter 12

Applegate, Celia. 1999. Teaching: Taming the Terror. In: *How I Teach: Essays on Teaching by Winners of the Robert and Pamela Goergen Award for Distinguished Achievement and Artistry in Undergraduate Teaching.* Rochester, NY: University of Rochester, pp. 23–36.

Boice, R. 1992. *The New Faculty Member: Supporting and Fostering Professional Development.* San Francisco, CA: Jossey-Bass. Quoted in Richard M. Reis,

Tomorrow's Professor: Preparing for Academic Careers in Science and Engineering. New York: IEEE Press, 1997, p. 276.

Brown, Theodore M. 1999. Connection, Communication, and Critical Thinking. In: *How I Teach: Essays on Teaching by Winners of the Robert and Pamela Goergen Award for Distinguished Achievement and Artistry in Undergraduate Teaching.* Rochester, NY: University of Rochester, pp. 9–20.

Davidson, C. I. and S. A. Ambrose. 1994. *The New Professor's Handbook: A Guide to Teaching and Research in Engineering and Science.* Bolton, MA: Anker Publishing. Quoted in Richard M. Reis, *Tomorrow's Professor: Preparing for Academic Careers in Science and Engineering.* New York: IEEE Press, 1997, p. 277.

Felder, R. M. and L. K. Silverman. 1988. Learning and Teaching Styles in Engineering Education. *Journal of Engineering Education* 77 (2). Quoted in Richard M. Reis, *Tomorrow's Professor: Preparing for Academic Careers in Science and Engineering.* New York: IEEE Press, 1997, p. 265.

Feldman, K. 1976. The Superior College Teacher from the Students' View. *Research in Higher Education* 5 (3): 243–288. Quoted in Richard M. Reis, *Tomorrow's Professor: Preparing for Academic Careers in Science and Engineering.* New York: IEEE Press, 1997, p. 261.

Index

(Page numbers in italics represent figures.)

About the Author

SUZANNE S. BELL is Economics/Data Librarian in the Rush Rhees Library Reference Department at the University of Rochester, and an adjunct faculty member with the Department of Library & Information Studies, SUNY Buffalo.